CREDIT, DEBIT & CHEQUE CARDS
Law and Practice

Graham Stephenson
LLM, Solicitor
Principal Lecturer in Law, University of Central Lancashire

CENTRAL LAW PUBLISHING
A Division of Central Law Training Ltd

© *Graham Stephenson 1993*

Published by
Central Law Publishing
A division of Central Law Training Ltd
Centre City Tower
7 Hill Street
Birmingham B5 4UA

ISBN 1 85811 018 1

Typeset by York House Typographic Ltd
Printed in Great Britain by BPCC Wheatons Ltd, Exeter

CREDIT, DEBIT & CHEQUE CARDS

LAW AND PRACTICE

Contents

v

References

References by name in the text to the following authors are to the published works indicated:

Diamond   Diamond, A.L., *Commercial and Consumer Credit — An Introduction* (Butterworths, 1982)

Goode   Goode, R. [ed.], *Consumer Credit Legislation* (Butterworths, looseleaf)

Jones   Jones, S.A., *The Law Relating to Credit Cards* (BSP Professional Books, 1989)

Preface

The origins of this book lie in the belief of the author that the plastic revolution and the so-called cashless society are here to stay. The use of credit, debit and cash cards is plainly on the increase and there is therefore a need to be aware of the statutory and extra-statutory controls on the agreements underlying the supply of such cards to the public. The book aims to meet this need by focusing on the regulation of credit card agreements under that important statute, the Consumer Credit Act 1974, and the regulation of other types of agreement by the common law and the Banking Code of Practice. The groundwork for the book was carried out in conjunction with the successful delivery of an in-house course for solicitors by the author on behalf of Central Law Training Ltd. Thanks are also owed to Central Law Publishing, in particular to Peter Turtle for the efficient way in which the material has been transformed into the finished product.

The book is dedicated to my parents, Marion and Ronald Stephenson.

Graham Stephenson

Table of Statutes

Table of Statutory Instruments

Table of Cases

CHAPTER 1

Credit, Debit and Cheque Cards — The Categories

1.01 Introduction — the plastic revolution

The use of a piece of plastic to pay for goods or services does not have a lengthy history in the United Kingdom. Nonetheless, for a significant proportion of the UK population, the use of a credit or debit card to pay for goods and services has become commonplace, a fact of life, as has the use of cash cards to obtain cash from machines outside bank and building society premises. This so-called 'plastic revolution', which for many people includes paying not just for the weekly shopping, petrol and consumer goods but also for the provision of services such as dental treatment and legal advice, could hardly have been envisaged in 1971 when the Crowther Committee carried out its monumental review of consumer credit (Cmnd. 4596). The result of this review was the Consumer Credit Act 1974, a massive piece of legislation which took a full eleven years to become fully operational. As we shall see, the Act does have many provisions which deal quite specifically with some types of card which form the subject of this book. However, it will become evident that Parliament could not have anticipated the enormous growth in the use of credit cards, the development of the debit and cash cards and the radical progress in technology over the last twenty years or so, enabling in particular the electronic transfer of funds (known as EFTPOS — electronic funds transfer at the point of sale). The Crowther Report itself devoted no more than a couple of pages to the subject of credit cards, commenting that this would be a growth area in the future. That this was an understatement is dramatically underlined by recent estimates that some 80 million plastic cards are issued every year by the two main providers, banks and building societies, the latter now able to offer a wider range of services than ever before as a result of the Building Societies Act 1986. These developments, according to the Association for Payment Clearing Services, lend themselves to fraud on a grand scale, as it is also estimated by the same body that some 2 million plastic cards

1

are lost or stolen every year, an average of 5,500 per day (*Guardian*, 4th March 1992).

Liability for the misuse of credit, debit and cash cards is a highly controversial issue, one which crops up regularly in the annual reports of both the Bank and Building Society Ombudsmen. Whilst there are provisions in the Consumer Credit Act 1974 which seek to regulate the position, they are limited to credit cards only and, furthermore, their precise scope is far from certain. Normally, a so-called debit card or cash card is outside the Act, but the potential for fraud and consequent hardship for the customer are just as great. As we shall see in Chapters 7 (Misuse of Credit-Tokens) and 13 (Debit and Cheque Guarantee Cards), the Banking Ombudsman has been called upon to give his view on the meaning of the statutory provisions. In addition, the government has felt the need, following the recommendation of the Jack Committee (*Banking Services: Law and Practice* (1989), Cmnd. 622) to cajole the banks into agreeing a non-statutory Code of Practice, in particular covering the issue of liability for misuse of cards other than credit cards. After consultation, the final version of this code was published in December 1991, and came into force in March 1992. There will be more of this later.

In addition to the topical controversy surrounding the misuse of the various types of card mentioned above, there is one other area that has raised a significant number of problems over the last fourteen years or so. Credit card issuers have become extremely concerned about the impact of s.75 of the Consumer Credit Act 1974. This section imposes joint and several liability on a creditor/card issuer and a supplier of goods and services in appropriate instances for the supplier's misrepresentation or breach of contract. Precisely how this operates is explored in considerable depth in Chapter 9, but suffice it to say at this stage that the section is highly unpopular with the credit card issuers if their attempts to avoid or minimise its effect are anything to go by.

1.02   Reasons for increase in use

The reason for this large increase in the use of credit, debit and cash cards would seem to lie in their all-round convenience for the parties to any particular transaction. The customer with a credit or debit card does not need to carry large quantities of cash, nor does he or she have to suffer embarrassment at a temporary shortage of cash. It also saves the need to carry a cheque book and, in addition, the processing time for a transaction by credit or debit card in the store must compare favourably with that for a payment by cheque. Credit, debit or cash cards enable customers to obtain cash from machines at times when the bank or building society is either busy or closed. Armed with a card the customer should never be without cash, provided he or she has access to an appropriate machine. Payment by card is convenient for the retailer, in that it is unnecessary to carry large amounts of cash in the till, thus reducing the chances of theft or robbery. It encourages impulse buying by consumers, increasing sales and turnover and presumably profits. It is also capable of speeding up mail order transactions, which can be easily completed over the telephone, once the details of the customer's credit, or more often recently, debit card have been obtained. There is no need to wait for the cheque and then for it to be cleared. Goods can effectively be posted on the same day as the order is received.

Naturally, credit card issuers benefit by charging retailers who agree to accept their cards a discount which they deduct from the payment they make, or by charging interest to the customer who does not pay off the monthly account in one lump sum. The issuer of a debit card will make a similar charge on the retailer where the card is used to pay for goods or services.

There is naturally a downside to all this in that it has been suggested in some quarters that credit card spending, easy and flexible as it is, contributes to the debt-laden nature of modern society, encouraging cardholders to live well beyond their means. It is perceived as less of a stigma to run up debts by use of a piece of plastic than by the more traditional hire-purchase.

1.03 Varieties of card

We have already seen that there are millions of plastic cards in circulation in the UK. These cards take a bewildering variety of forms. This is readily understandable, given the competitive state of the financial services market, in particular the intense rivalry between the banks and building societies. It is important in practice to be able to differentiate between the various types of card, as this will often have important consequences depending on the way the card or a particular transaction is regulated by the law or the Code of Practice mentioned above.

The problem has been exacerbated somewhat by the introduction by banks and building societies of the 'multi-function' card. As the name suggests, this card has more than one function: for example, it may be a credit card, debit card and cheque guarantee card all rolled into one; or, more commonly, a debit, cash and cheque guarantee card combined. A current illustration of the latter is the Cashline card promoted by the Royal Bank of Scotland. What is more, there is no statutory definition of any of the types of card discussed below, although there is annexed to the Code of Banking Practice a useful, if brief, glossary of terms containing references to the various cards. As the Code emphasises, these are not to be treated as precise legal or technical definitions but, nonetheless, they do provide a useful starting point.

1.04   Credit cards

This is a card which permits a customer to obtain goods or services on credit by producing it at a retail outlet which has agreed to accept payments by means of the card. The customer may also obtain cash advances either over the counter at a bank or, if issued with a personal identification number (PIN), from an automatic telling machine (ATM). The customer will be bound by the contract between himself or herself and the card issuer, on receipt usually of a monthly statement, to repay the balance in full, or in part subject normally to a certain minimum payment. This arrangement is commonly called a three-party credit card to differentiate it from the two-party credit card. The latter is sometimes also called a store card. As this variant of the name suggests, this is a card which allows the holder to purchase goods or services in a particular store or chain of stores. In fact, the card issuer and the department store proprietor are one and the same. This type of card, although far simpler in its operation than the three-party card, is nonetheless likely to be a credit-token within s.14 of the Consumer Credit Act 1974 and regulated by the Act generally. Much of the discussion in Chapters 2 to 12 and elsewhere applies equally to such cards. There is another variant known as a budget card, which requires customers to pay an agreed fixed amount into their card account each month, usually direct from a bank account by standing order or direct debit. Apart from this requirement, such cards are in other respects similar to credit cards.

Returning to the so-called three-party credit cards, this name itself can be misleading in that there are often four parties involved in any particular transaction. The fourth party, known as a 'merchant acquirer', arranges to receive the credit card slips from the retailer and makes the appropriate payments to the retailer less a handling discount. Normally, it is a merchant acquirer which recruits retailers into its card scheme, be it Visa or Access/Mastercard. Not all card issuers are merchant acquirers and, as a consequence, where one of the non-merchant acquirer cards is used in payment, four parties will be involved. This point does not normally affect the regulatory issues under the Consumer Credit Act 1974. However, in Chapter 9 (Joint and Several Liability) we shall have cause to discuss this matter again, as it has been argued by one of the leading card issuers that the point affects the scope of s.75 of the Act.

Further discussion of this important and controversial issue is postponed till then.

Cards belonging to the Access/Mastercard and Visa schemes are good illustrations of the type of card falling under the designation of three-party credit cards. Occasionally, a card may be considered a three-party card in respect of the purchase of goods or services, but be only a two-party card when it comes to obtaining cash, as the cardholder might be restricted to cash outlets controlled by the card issuer. This arrangement is rare these days, as there are agreements between banks that allow customers to use ATMs at banks where they do not have their account.

A typical example of the store card would be the Marks and Spencer card, inappropriately called a 'chargecard', in the sense attributed to this expression below. All these types of credit card, whether two- or three-party, are likely to be credit-token agreements and regulated by the 1974 Act (see Chapters 2 and 3).

1.05   Chargecards

The expression 'chargecard' is frequently used to denote a particular type of card such as American Express or Diner's Club and certain versions of Visa and Mastercard known as 'Gold' cards. Because of the types of outlet at which they may be used, they are often referred to as 't and e' (travel and entertainment) cards. Whilst such cards enable the holder to obtain goods or services on credit in the same way as the cards discussed previously, they are fundamentally different on one score: unlike the normal Visa or Mastercard agreements, on receipt of the monthly statement the holder must pay the balance in full. As we shall see in the next chapter, this factor takes this type of card outside the scope of the vast majority of the provisions of the Consumer Credit Act 1974, despite the fact that they involve the grant of credit. They are clearly short-term credit only, as depending on the time of the particular transaction and the time of the monthly accounting period, the maximum length of the deferment of payment is usually calculated at fifty-six days only.

Some would argue that these cards are not credit cards in the sense used above, as they are exempt from some of the more onerous requirements of the Consumer Credit Act 1974 (Chapter 2). The issuer of such a card is not required to have a licence under the Act, nor is there any requirement to comply with the advertising regulation imposed by the Act. Nonetheless, such a card may be a credit-token, although the precise implications of such a finding are in some doubt. We shall have cause to return to this issue in subsequent chapters.

1.06   Debit cards

In essence this is a card which operates as a substitute for a cheque. It can be used to pay for goods or services at the point of sale, or to obtain cash either at the point of sale or, if the holder has a PIN, from an ATM. In this latter capacity it is being used as a cash card. Some cards issued by banks and building societies have only this latter function. Normally, unless the bank or society has agreed an overdraft with the customer, the use of a debit or cash card in whatever way does not involve the provision of any credit. The customer's current account is automatically debited, without any deferment of payment. The supplier is paid more or less immediately by the corresponding crediting of his account. Completion of the transaction is sometimes slightly delayed in circumstances where the debit card transactions for the day are stored on magnetic tape. At the close of business the debits and corresponding credits are then made in bulk. As the debit or cash card is not a credit agreement, it is normally outside the scope of the 1974 Act. In practice, however, many debit or cash cards may form part of a current account agreement whereby the customer has been granted agreed overdraft facilities. In such a case, particularly where there has been alleged misuse of the card, it is necessary to be alert to the possibility that the misuse provisions in the Act may apply (Chapter 7), thus minimising the customer/debtor's liability for the misuse. It has also been suggested that this would be the case even if the bank had not agreed an overdraft facility and the customer either deliberately or inadvertently drew on the account causing a debit balance. This is on the basis that the card issuer is under an obligation to pay the supplier. In these circumstances it is argued that the card is a credit-token, although the agreement underlying it is not a credit-token agreement. Whilst the latter part of this suggestion is unobjectionable, the first proposition is of doubtful validity. However, we shall see that there are specific provisions in the Code of Banking Practice concerning the misuse of debit and cash cards, in many respects similar to those laid down in the statute minimising the customer's liability in the event of misuse. Thus, in future there may be little difference in the way the misuse of the cards is treated by the creditor.

The most common debit cards at present in the UK are Switch and Visa Delta. The latter can be used anywhere in the world, but Switch is at present restricted to the UK. It has been reported that this will change in 1993, when a new Mastercard/Eurocard payment system becomes operative (*Which?*, June 1992, p.328). The most disadvantageous aspect of the debit card, from the cardholder's point of view, is that the monies are taken immediately from his or her current account. There is no period of credit at all, not even the short period during which the monthly account accumulates as in a credit card or chargecard agreement. Effectively, this means that the cardholder is using money he or she currently has, rather than spending next month's salary before it is received. This may be the major factor inhibiting the growth of such cards. On the other hand, they do enable cardholders to remain in better control of their finances. Debit cards and cash cards will be discussed in more detail in Chapter 13, but there will be references to them throughout the work, wherever it is necessary to draw comparison with the credit card.

1.07   Cheque guarantee cards

This is totally different from all the cards discussed previously, although it must be remembered that some cards are multi-functional and one card may be a credit, debit, cash and cheque guarantee card all in one. Whether this is the case or not, however, when used as a cheque guarantee card it is altogether different. Such a card is issued by a bank or building society to be used in conjunction with a cheque book. If used in accordance with the the conditions of use, it guarantees the payment of a cheque up to the amount specified in the card itself. The amount is generally fixed at £50, although some multi-functional cards do cover cheques drawn for up to £100. Whilst it is in practice possible for a customer to obtain some short-term credit by using the card in a particular way, it is not a credit agreement and is consequently outside the bulk of the provisions of the 1974 Act. It will be discussed in more depth in Chapter 13.

1.08   Forms of regulation

The regulation of the various categories of plastic cards highlighted above is a curious mixture of common law, the terms of the contract itself, statute and self-regulation in the shape of the Code of Banking Practice, backed by the private sector Ombudsmen schemes. There is no doubt that the law and practice relating to the use of plastic cards of the kind covered in this book come from a complex combination of sources. Not only is it necessary to be fully conversant with the relevant provisions of the Consumer Credit Act 1974, at times complex and obscure in themselves, but an adviser must have a good knowledge of the Code of Banking Practice and, just as important, be aware of the views and decisions of the two Ombudsmen operating in this sector. When we look at joint and several liability issues in Chapter 9, it will be evident that the adviser in this field must also be an expert on consumer protection law in general, including the implied terms in the Sale of Goods Act 1979 and the Supply of Goods and Services Act 1982, Part 1 of the Consumer Protection Act, misrepresentation at common law and under the Misrepresentation Act 1967, and the difficult rules on exemption clauses in the Unfair Contract Terms Act 1977.

It is proposed in the first instance to consider those card agreements which are caught as credit-token agreements by the 1974 Act. Chapter 2 looks initially at the way in which an agreement may be analysed at common law under the general law of contract. Second, the chapter will go on to consider how a credit card agreement is brought within the scope of the Act, as a regulated agreement. We shall look at the exemption for certain kinds of credit card agreement and the partial exemption for agreements known as small agreements. Following to the categorisation adopted above, we shall be concerned principally with credit cards such as those in the Visa or Access schemes. In Chapter 3 the classification of agreements under the 1974 Act will be continued. There, we shall see what is meant by a credit-token agreement, restricted and unrestricted-use credit agreements, debtor–creditor–supplier and debtor–creditor agreements, linked transactions and multiple agreements. Apart from the first of these, this classification is the general one adopted by the Act in respect of the wide variety of forms of credit granting. However, they are all important aspects in the regulation of credit card agreements. The regulatory provisions of the Act will often depend on the classification system as to how they intervene in the relationship between the card issuer and the cardholder. Much of the discussion in Chapters 4 to 12 is predicated on a good understanding of the various categories of agreement.

CHAPTER 2

Credit Card Agreements: Regulation

2.01 Introduction

In this chapter a number of important and central issues are to be considered in relation to credit card agreements. First, it is proposed to analyse the various relationships between the parties involved in the typical two- and three-party credit card agreement under the general law of contract. Secondly, we shall (somewhat briefly) consider the licensing provisions of the Consumer Credit Act 1974, concentrating in particular on the consequences of unlicensed trading in credit. Thirdly, the categorisation of credit under the Act and the concept of a regulated agreement will become the focus of attention. This will necessarily involve a discussion of exempt and part exempt agreements, namely, in the case of the latter, what the Act calls the 'small agreement'. In Chapter 3 we shall take the classification even further and elaborate on the statutory meaning of the 'credit-token', a term of vital significance in the working of the Act's provisions dealing specifically with credit cards and the like. Next, but just as importantly for an understanding of the operation of some of the Act's crucial sections, we must concentrate on the complex terminology of the contrasting debtor–creditor–supplier and debtor–creditor agreements including the important sub-classification of restricted- and unrestricted-use credit, together with the closely allied concept known as the linked transaction. Lastly in Chapter 3, the classification will be completed with a consideration of the nature of the multiple agreement under the 1974 Act. All these must be grasped at the outset if the later chapters are to be fully understood.

2.02 Credit cards at common law

For the most part the Act is silent on the issues about to be discussed. However, where the agreement is considered to be regulated by the Act,

9

then, in appropriate situations, its provisions will override any contractual terms and conditions.

2.03   Two-party cards

This is the simpler of the two types of credit card. The card is issued by
the supplier or an associate company. It can be used only on the issuer's
premises and the issuer is the supplier of both the goods or services on the
one hand and the credit on the other. If there is a problem with the
quality of the goods, or with, for example, delivery, then as this is a form
of credit sale agreement, the Sale of Goods Act 1979 will regulate the
contract. If the supply is a mixture of goods and services, or the provision
of a pure service, the implied terms of the Supply of Goods and Services
Act 1982 will come into play, if there is a dispute about quality. As we
shall see, although the agreement is a debtor–creditor–supplier agreement (see Chapter 3), there is no need to resort to the joint and several
liability provisions in s.75 of the 1974 Act (Chapter 9). This is because the
creditor (i.e. the card issuer), as pointed out above, is also the supplier of
the goods and/or service and is therefore directly responsible under the
sale or supply contract for the quality of what is purchased. The issues as
to quality will also be discussed in Chapter 9 in the context of the joint
and several liability debate.

One issue which might arise is whether the supplier can refuse to
accept the card in payment. It is important to differentiate between any
potential criminal liability which might follow such refusal and any civil
law consequences. Refusing to take the card in circumstances where its
logo is clearly displayed and intended to be taken as an indication of the
supplier's willingness to accept it may constitute an offence under s.14 of
the Trade Descriptions Act 1968. If a retailer refused to supply goods or
services at the advertised or displayed price on the basis that that was the
cash price and there was a higher price when a customer wished to pay by
credit card, it would constitute a prima facie offence under s.20 of the
Consumer Protection Act 1987. The offence would be one of supplying
goods or services to which a misleading price indication had been given.
This was certainly held to be an offence under s.11 of the Trade
Descriptions Act 1968, the provision replaced by s.20 of the 1987 Act
(see *Read Bros Cycles Ltd* v. *Waltham Forest LBC* [1978] RTR 397).
However, suppliers are now entitled to discriminate between cash and
credit card purchasers if they so wish. Until recently, it was invariably a
term of the agreement between the supplier and the card issuer that the
supplier would not discriminate in such a way. This practice has now
been declared unlawful, following a report of the Monopolies and

Mergers Commission, by the Credit Cards (Price Discrimination) Order 1990, SI 1990 No.2159, despite a legal challenge to the report by Visa (*R v. The Monopolies and Mergers Commission, ex parte Visa International Service Association* (1991) 10 Trad LR 97). However, the supplier must make it clear to potential customers that different prices operate depending on whether payment is in cash or by credit card, otherwise a misleading price offence will be committed. Matters concerning these two pieces of legislation are discussed in Chapter 4.

So far as civil consequences are concerned, normally suppliers would be within their rights today (following the change in the law mentioned above) to refuse to accept the card as a means of payment. However, where the supplier is also the creditor under a two-party store card, for example, it might be held bound to accept the credit card as payment. This is on the assumption that there was no irregularity in the use of the card. The customer might well be able to argue that there was an implied obligation to accept the card, at least where there was no obvious, prominently displayed indication that it would no longer be an acceptable method of payment. Even such a notice might not be sufficient. Another possibility is that there might be a 'shop' or 'floor' limit in operation. If the transaction exceeded this limit, the supplier would be entitled to refuse payment by the card without some further verification at least as to the identity of the customer. In those circumstances, it is suggested that there would be an implied term that the use of the card was subject to such a limit.

2.04   Three-party cards

Naturally, these are rather more complex. At first sight there appear to be three separate sets of relationships between the three parties, assuming that the creditor is also a merchant acquirer as discussed in the preceding chapter. The credit agreement is between the creditor and the debtor/customer; there is a contract of sale, for example where the debtor acquires goods, between the supplier and the debtor; and, finally, there is an agreement between the creditor and the supplier. These need to be considered in a little more detail at this stage.

2.05   Creditor and debtor

The relationship between these two will in the first instance be regulated by the express terms of the contract. However, a major part of this book is concerned with the way the Consumer Credit Act 1974 intervenes in this particular relationship and, where appropriate, overrides any express terms. It should not be forgotten, however, that the essence of the relationship is primarily contractual. The debtor's fundamental obligation is to repay to the creditor, with interest in suitable cases, the amounts incurred by the use of the credit card. Of course, in situations where the credit card is not regulated by the Act, and it does not fall within the definition of a credit-token, the bulk of the Act's provisions will not apply. Such an agreement is regulated by the common law of contract. In addition, in some instances the Code of Banking Practice and/or one or other of the Ombudsmen may exercise some control over the relationship (see Chapter 13).

2.06 Debtor and supplier

It was assumed above that where the debtor agrees to buy goods from the supplier and produces the credit card by way of payment, the transaction was a sale of goods within the meaning of the Sale of Goods Act 1979. This is far from settled, however, for as Diamond points out (p.329) s.2(1) of the 1979 Act requires the buyer to pay a money consideration. Payment by credit card would seem to fall outside this, at least technically. Diamond rightly goes on to suggest that the consequence of such an analysis, namely, that the supplier is not under the implied obligations as to quality, description and title, is too difficult to accept. The better view seems to be that the contract is one of sale, but that the creditor is liable for the price. The debtor, it is suggested, is not personally liable for the price as is normal under the Sale of Goods Act. It was held by the High Court in *Re Charge Card Services Ltd* [1987] Ch 150 (affirmed by the Court of Appeal [1988] 3 All ER 702) that the discharge of the payment by the acceptance of the credit card is prima facie absolute. Therefore, the debtor cannot be sued for the price if the creditor becomes insolvent or refuses to pay for some other reason. It might be possible for the supplier to indicate by means of a prominent notice that payment by credit card was conditional, but it is unlikely that creditors would agree to this in their contracts with the suppliers. In this situation the risk of the creditor becoming insolvent would appear to remain firmly with the supplier.

We considered in para.2.03 above, whether the supplier is obliged to accept the card in payment. The same point might be answered differently in relation to the three-party card, at least so far as the civil law is concerned, although in practice the supplier may have little room for manoeuvre, as it is likely to be a term of its contract with the creditor that it will not refuse payment by card unless the circumstances are such that the floor limit is exceeded or there is some irregularity in relation to the card.

If the supplier is in breach of the supply contract with the debtor, it seems that the debtor can sue for the breach even though he or she may not at this stage have paid the creditor. Jones suggests (p.265) that there might be some difficulty in making a restitutionary claim, i.e. for a refund of the purchase money on a major breach, but nonetheless concludes, on the strength of *Re Charge Card Services Ltd*, that the debtor would be entitled to make such a claim. After all, that case decided that the contracts between the various parties are independent of one another. It is up to the creditor to enforce its rights separately under its contract with the debtor.

An additional problem arises where the cardholder requests the issue of another card for use by an authorised user who is not a joint account-holder: for example, a married woman is the cardholder under the account with the creditor and an additional card is supplied for use by her husband. He then buys an item, using the card. It seems likely that the husband will not be regarded at common law as the agent of the cardholder wife. Therefore, the appropriate analysis is that the husband would be contracting as principal with the supplier and has the normal rights against the supplier in the event of a breach. The wife would be liable to the creditor under her agreement with the latter, who has no recourse against the husband should the wife fail to pay. The additional card problem also arises in the context of the joint and several liability discussion in Chapter 9.

2.07 Supplier and creditor

Likewise, this is normally a contractual relationship whereby the creditor agrees to discharge the amount due under the contract between the supplier and the debtor, subject to the deduction of an agreed discount. The creditor is bound to discharge the obligation to pay the supplier whether or not it receives payment from the debtor. As Goode observes (I[2275]), 'each of the three contracts generated by use of the credit card is in principle autonomous and does not depend for its enforceability on performance of either of the others'. As we shall see later (Chapter 9), s.75 makes a substantial dent in this position by the creation of joint and several liability between the supplier and the creditor.

No doubt, the agreement between the creditor and the supplier will be in standard form. One would expect it to deal with such matters as the discount to be deducted from the payments by the creditor, the issue of invalid vouchers, the question of indemnity of the creditor by the supplier, floor limits (if any) and telephone sales. The indemnity is likely to be wider than that contained in s.75(2) of the 1974 Act, which relates solely to liability incurred by the creditor under the joint and several liability provisions in s.75. In the three-party card situation, it is unlikely that the supplier will be regarded as the agent of the creditor at common law. However, s.56 of the Act alters the position in certain circumstances and creates a deemed agency (see Chapter 10).

2.08   Regulation under the Consumer Credit Act 1974

So far we have attempted to analyse credit card agreements in terms of basic contract law. Attention must now be firmly focused on the way in which the legislation intervenes in the relationships between the parties discussed above.

2.09   Licensing

It would seem useful at this stage to enter into some discussion about the licensing requirements under the 1974 Act, as the consequences of a failure to have a suitable licence may have a dramatic effect on the rights and obligations of the parties. The Act requires a person carrying on a consumer credit business to obtain a licence. Section 189(1) defines such a business as 'any business so far as it comprises or relates to the provision of credit under regulated consumer credit agreements'. What amounts to a 'regulated consumer credit agreement' is considered shortly, but suffice it to say at this juncture that the issue of credit cards to private individuals by banks and building societies constitutes carrying on a consumer credit business requiring a licence. It can also be stated at this point that a consumer credit licence is not required by those organisations which issue the so-called 'chargecards' or 't and e' cards for, as we shall see, they are not regulated consumer credit agreements. Nor are issuers of purely debit or cash cards required to obtain a licence in respect of that activity alone.

2.10   Types and classes of licence

There are broadly two types of licence: standard and group licences under s.22(1). The latter may be granted by the Director General of Fair Trading on application or on his own motion. However, the standard licence is more appropriate in the case of the credit card issuer. This is issued by the Director on the application of the creditor. Until recently, licences lasted fifteen years, but from 1st June 1991 the period has been reduced to five years (Consumer Credit (Period of Standard Licence) (Amendment) Regulations 1991, SI 1991 No. 817). There are six administrative categories of licence: consumer credit business, consumer hire business, credit brokerage, debt-adjusting and debt counselling, debt collecting and credit reference agency. One would normally expect a credit card issuer to be interested in the first of these only.

2.11 Right to a licence

A person is entitled to a licence provided the Director General is satisfied on two matters specified in s.25(1) of the 1974 Act. These are, first, the fitness of the applicant to engage in the activities covered by the licence and, secondly, that the name or names under which the application is made, and in which the licence is to be granted, is or are not misleading or otherwise undesirable. To some extent there may be an inherent contradiction between the 'right' of the applicant and the 'satisfying' of the Director on these two important points. Goode comments (I[704]) that the 'right', bearing in mind the subjective nature of the Director's task, 'is in reality much more akin to an administrative discretion'. That, however, is not to say that the discretion is an absolute one, as he can refuse a licence only on one of the two grounds itemised above. Goode rightly suggests that it is not open to the Director to deny the applicant a licence on the ground that there are too many consumer credit businesses in a particular area.

2.12 Refusal to grant a licence

The Director has the right to refuse to grant a licence where the two conditions are not satisfied. However, the Act does not appear to preclude him from granting a licence even where he is not so satisfied. The better view seems to be that a court would interpret the wording so as to make it clear that a licence could be granted if, and only if, the two conditions are fulfilled.

2.13 Fitness of the applicant

The first and, arguably, more important of the two conditions concerns the fitness of the applicant. One would imagine that most credit card issuers (being banks, building societies and leading department stores) would normally have little difficulty satisfying the Director on this point. However, it is worth bearing in mind that the licence holder's behaviour is monitored continually to ensure that he, she or it remains a fit person to undertake the activities specified in the licence. It is useful, therefore, to be aware of the types of offensive behaviour that might lead to a refusal to renew a licence. Section 25(2) lays down the criteria to be considered by the Director in deciding this issue:

> 'In determining whether an applicant for a standard licence is a fit person to engage in any activities, the Director shall have regard to any circumstances appearing to him to be relevant, and in particular any evidence tending to show that the applicant, or any of the applicant's employees, agents or associates (whether past or present) or where the applicant is a body corporate, any person appearing to the Director to be a controller of the body corporate or an associate of any such person, has
> (*a*) committed any offence involving fraud or other dishonesty, or violence,
> (*b*) contravened any provision made by or under this Act, or by or under any other enactment regulating the provision of credit to individuals or other transactions with individuals,
> (*c*) practised discrimination on ground of sex, colour, race or national or ethnic origins in, or in connection with, the carrying on of any business, or
> (*d*) engaged in business practices appearing to the Director to be deceitful or oppressive, or otherwise unfair or improper (whether unlawful or not).'

This significantly wide approach is fortified by s.170(2), which provides that when exercising his functions under the Act, the Director 'may take account of any matter appearing to him to constitute a breach of a requirement made by or under this Act, whether or not any sanction for that breach is provided by or under this Act and, if it is so provided, whether or not proceedings have been brought in respect of the breach'.

What seems clear from the wording of both these provisions is that the Director is given an extensive remit in considering the applicant's suitability. The list in s.25(2) is not to be regarded as exhaustive. In addition, the conduct of third parties may be scrutinised, whether these are business or family ties, whether past or present. The activity under scrutiny need not be unlawful, as long as it can be classified as 'oppressive, or otherwise unfair or improper'. This might include high-pressure selling techniques or persistently selling credit to those unable to afford it. What is more, the misconduct need not be connected with activity in the credit market. The word 'associate' is widely defined in s.184 to include relatives and some forms of business associates. For the purposes of s.25, subs.(3) extends the meaning of 'associate' to include 'business associates' not specifically covered in s.184. The term 'business associate' is not itself defined, but according to Goode (I[720]), it 'presumably covers any person in collaboration with whom any kind of business is transacted'. He goes on to give two examples. Uncontroversially, he cites the situation between a creditor and a dealer who is regarded as a credit-broker under the Act (effecting introductions to the creditor). More interestingly, and less obviously, he suggests that a credit card issuer and the various suppliers who have agreed to accept the card are associates for the purpose of s.25. Thus, a card issuer may be tainted by the unlawful or improper behaviour of retailers. There would seem to be an ever-present need to be vigilant as to the way in which retailers carry out their activity, to avoid any problem of revocation or refusal to renew a licence.

2.14 Meaning of 'associate'

Section 184 of the Consumer Credit Act 1974 reads:

'(1) A person is an associate of an individual if that person is the individual's husband or wife, or is a relative, or the husband or wife of a relative, of the individual or of the individual's husband or wife.

(2) A person is an associate of any person with whom he is in partnership, and of the husband or wife or a relative of the individual with whom he is in partnership.

(3) A body corporate is an associate of another body corporate —

(a) if the same person is a controller of both, or a person is the controller of one and persons who are his associates, or he and persons who are his associates, are controllers of the other; or

(b) if a group of two or more persons is a controller of each company, and the groups either consist of the same persons or could be regarded as consisting of the same persons by treating (in one or more cases) a member of either group as replaced by a person of whom he is an associate.

(4) A body corporate is an associate of another if that person is a controller of it or if that person and persons who are his associates together are controllers of it.

(5)   In this section 'relative' means brother, sister, uncle, aunt, nephew, niece, lineal ancestor or lineal descendant, and references to a husband or wife include a former husband or wife and a reputed husband or wife; and for the purpose of this subsection a relationship shall be established as if any illegitimate child, step-child or adopted child of a person had been a child born to him in wedlock.'

The net is indeed cast wide to catch almost anybody connected in a business or domestic way with the applicant. The Director is on record as saying that he is concerned primarily with criminal convictions. However, just as important, he has issued 'minded to refuse' and 'minded to revoke' notices where the applicant/licensee has been guilty of sending unsolicited credit-tokens under s.51 of the 1974 Act (see Chapter 4), has failed to make the annual percentage rate of charge clear to customers or has raised the interest rate above the level permitted in the contract. Many other grounds are used by the Director but these seem the ones most likely to relate to credit card issuers. It is unlikely, however, that an isolated occurrence will bring the full weight of the Director's wrath on a card issuer. In any event, the Director cannot refuse or restrict a licence in the first instance. Under s.27(1), unless he decides to issue the licence in accordance with the application, the Director must give notice to the applicant that he proposes either to refuse or to restrict a licence, inviting the applicant to submit representations in support of the application. There is always an opportunity to set the record straight. However, prevention is always better, so it is essential that a credit card issuer should be ever alert to the behaviour of employees and that of 'associates'.

2.15   Name of the business

The Director must be satisfied that the name of the proposed licensee is not misleading or otherwise undesirable. He will be unwilling to grant a licence, for example, where the name is too much like an existing name, suggests links with the Crown or a government department, is misleading about the nature of the organisation, the cost or ease of borrowing or the scope of the activities of the organisation. Section 24 provides that the licensee may carry on the business under the name or names detailed in the licence, but not under any other name. A licence is not normally transferable in any way at all (s.22(2)). Usually, a card issuer will be granted an unrestricted standard licence, which will cover the activities of employees or other agents. However, the card issuer should check whether those who might introduce customers to it themselves have the appropriate licence as a credit-broker. There might indeed be serious consequences if a licence has not been obtained, as we shall see below.

2.16 Regulation after issue of a licence

It should be evident from what has already been said about the licensing system that the regulatory powers of the Director continue after the issue of a licence. A licence may be varied, suspended or revoked in appropriate circumstances (see ss.31 to 33 and regulations made thereunder) and there are provisions dealing with the termination of licences (s.37). It should be noted, however, that corporate licensees are outside the scope of the statutory termination provisions.

2.17 Consequences of unlicensed trading

Unlicensed trading is an offence under ss.39 or 147 of the 1974 Act. Just as important, however, there are severe consequences at civil law for the unlicensed trader. A regulated agreement made when the creditor is unlicensed is unenforceable against the debtor, unless the Director is prepared to make a validating order under s.40 of the Act. What is more, a regulated agreement entered into by a debtor following an introduction to the creditor by an unlicensed credit-broker is likewise enforceable only on a validating order under the similar provision in s.149(1). Whilst a creditor, such as a card issuer, may be satisfied that its own activities are covered under an appropriate standard licence, its contracts with its customers may be tainted by the failure of a third party to obtain a licence. For example, if a card issuer enters into an arrangement with a department store in a special promotion of the card issuer's cards, whereby the store effects introductions to the creditor (see s.145(2)), it is essential that the creditor checks to satisfy itself that the store is licensed. This can of course be done by asking to see the licence itself or by checking the public register (see s.35).

If the agreement is unenforceable, the creditor is unable to pursue the debtor for repayment of the money used to effect the purchase at the store. Naturally, the creditor might have recourse to the Director under either s.40 or s.149(1). In deciding whether to make a validating order, the Director must consider any prejudice suffered by a debtor during the unlicensed period, whether he would have been willing to grant a licence for the period in question, and the creditor's degree of culpability in failing to obtain a licence. On the creditor's application, if he is thinking of refusing it in whole or in part, the Director must serve a 'minded to refuse' notice inviting representations from the creditor. The Director, in his discretion, may make any order limited to specified agreements, or agreements of a specified description or made at a specified time, as well as making the order conditional on the creditor doing specified acts. The refusal to make an order would severely penalise a creditor, but it is unlikely to happen often provided the failure was trivial or technical in nature. According to Goode (I[817]), there has been a tightening up by the Office of Fair Trading in relation to orders under s.40. He states that current practice is against granting a total dispensation in favour of the creditor; rather, the Director will make an order limited to specified agreements. It is, of course, preferable not to be dependent on the Director's discretion in the first place.

There are one or two other consequences of unlicensed trading which might prove to be thorny problems in practice. One of these is raised by Hill-Smith (*Consumer Credit: Law and Practice*, 1985, p.267): can the debtor sue the creditor for the return of any money paid under an unenforceable agreement before the debtor was aware of the unenforce- ability? In a credit card context, a debtor may well have elected to pay off his indebtedness in full on receipt of the monthly account. Hill-Smith's view is that the payment would be recoverable on the basis that the 1974 Act is a 'class-protecting statute' to protect the interests of debtors, citing *Kiriri Cotton Co* v. *Dewani* [1960] AC 192. As he points out, the exact legal position is not clear and this particular interpretation is in some doubt.

Another problem in this context is the enforceability of the agreement by the debtor against the creditor. For example, should the goods purchased by the debtor turn out to be defective, can the debtor sue the creditor? The answer is that this is no doubt possible where, for example, the agreement is a hire-purchase agreement (see Hill-Smith, ibid., p.269). The position is not so straightforward, however, where the debtor has paid for the item using a regulated credit card agreement. The contract between the supplier and the debtor is obviously not affected by the creditor's lack of a licence. The debtor will have the usual rights under the Sale of Goods Act 1979. Can he or she, however, enforce those rights against the creditor using s.75 of the 1974 Act? The Act says that an agreement is enforceable as against the debtor only by order of the Director, so it would seem that there is no obstacle to the enforcement of the agreement in this way. It might be argued that using s.75 does not amount to enforcement of the credit agreement in any event.

2.18 Regulated agreements under the 1974 Act

So far, we have based the analysis of the normal credit card agreement and the licensing requirements on the assumption that the agreement is regulated. We must now turn our attention to the issue of what constitutes an agreement regulated under the Act. According to Goode (p.84), the regulated agreement 'is the key to an understanding of the Act'. The licensing requirements discussed above are tied in with the concept of the regulated agreement, but its importance is much more pervasive than that. Nearly all of the provisions of the Act are concerned with regulated agreements. If a credit card agreement is regulated, the consequences for the creditor and the debtor are much affected by the general provisions of the Act as well as those specifically directed at credit-token agreements.

Section 189(1) defines a regulated agreement as 'a consumer credit agreement, or consumer hire agreement, other than an exempt agreement'. Naturally, the type of agreement we are concerned with is the consumer credit agreement. Section 8(1) defines a personal credit agreement as one between an individual (the debtor) and any other person (the creditor) by which credit of any amount is given. This is further refined by s.8(2), which defines a consumer credit agreement as a personal credit agreement under which the creditor provides the debtor with credit not exceeding £15,000. A regulated agreement is then stated by s.8(3) to be a consumer credit agreement which is not an exempt agreement. Assuming for the moment that the credit card agreement is not exempt (this is discussed below), it is necessary to consider the credit limit and the status of the debtor to decide whether it is regulated.

2.19 Credit limit

The current credit limit is £15,000. A credit card agreement clearly entails the provision of credit, whether the card is used to purchase goods or services or to obtain cash, so we need not dwell on that point. Also, there cannot be many cards in issue allowing the cardholder more than £15,000 worth of credit. Nonetheless, it is useful to discuss precisely how the credit limit is calculated.

The Act distinguishes between fixed-sum credit and what it calls running-account credit. Fixed-sum credit, as its name suggests, is where the amount borrowed is a fixed figure, for example a personal loan of £5,000. Hire-purchase or conditional sale agreements are other examples. A credit card agreement is, however, an illustration of running-account credit, or revolving credit, a phrase which is perhaps a more apt description. Here, the debtor is allowed to use an account up to an agreed credit limit. The actual amount of credit at any one time will vary, depending on the use the debtor makes of the facility. The debtor will normally be required to discharge, or at least reduce, his indebtedness on a regular basis, thus increasing the amount of actual credit available for use the next time. By contrast with fixed-sum credit, where the amount of the credit is set from the beginning, the precise amount of credit is known only when the debtor draws on the account: in the case of a credit card, when it is used to obtain goods or services, or cash.

In order to ascertain whether an agreement for running-account credit is within the financial ceiling of the Act, s.10 contains special rules designed to clarify the position. Section 10(2) states that the credit limit for any period is the maximum credit balance which, under the credit agreement, is allowed to stand on the account during that period, disregarding any term of the agreement allowing a temporary excess over the maximum. All that this means is that if the credit limit is fixed by the agreement to be normally £15,000, but there is a proviso in the agreement for the figure to be exceeded temporarily, this will not take the agreement outside the regulatory framework of the Act for that reason alone. The alternative, and more likely, situation is that where the debtor makes a temporary drawing over and above the agreed credit limit and there is no clause in the agreement covering this possibility. Under banking law, this constitutes a new agreement, varying the original agreement with the agreed credit limit. Section 82(2) provides that the new agreement revokes the original contract, combining the provisions of the old and the new agreements into one single agreement. Section 18(5) states that in the case of an agreement for running-account credit, a term of the agreement allowing the credit limit to be exceeded merely temporarily shall not be treated as a separate agreement or as providing fixed-sum credit in respect of the excess. This seeks only to reinforce the point in s.10(2), confirming that the new agreement is still within the Act. It should be noted that, by s.82(4), the new agreement is not subject to the formalities of agreement in Part V of the Act, except for s.56, which will still apply (see Chapters 5 and 10).

Section 10(3) makes a significant contribution to the way in which the credit limit is to be calculated, Section 10(3)(*a*) states that if the credit limit does not exceed £15,000, the agreement may be regulated. That is merely restating the rule in relation to fixed-sum credit. However, there may be situations where the agreement specifies a figure beyond £15,000. To counter the possibility of the creditor avoiding the statutory regulation by setting an artificially high credit limit, s.10(3)(*b*) specifies three types of situation where there is no credit limit, or where there is one but it exceeds £15,000.

(1)   If at any one time the debtor cannot draw more than £15,000, the agreement will be caught by the Act, no matter how high the limit.

(2)   Where the agreement provides that if the debit balance rises above a given amount (not exceeding £15,000), the rate of the total charge for credit increases or any other condition favouring the creditor or its associate comes into operation, the credit will be deemed not to go beyond £15,000. For example, if the agreement provides for the interest rate to increase as soon as the £15,000 figure is reached, it would still be regulated. However, if the increase were postponed merely until the figure of £15,001, the agreement would not attract the regulatory provisions.

(3)   Where, at the time the agreement is made, it is probable, bearing in mind the terms of the agreement and other relevant considerations, that the debit balance will not at any time exceed the £15,000 limit, the agreement will be regulated. It should be noted that the agreement will remain regulated, notwithstanding the fact that the actual amount eventually borrowed goes beyond the £15,000 figure. The probability has to be assessed at the time of the making of the agreement. According to Goode (I[490]), the onus is on the debtor to show that the probability is in his or her favour. Any credit card agreement which specifies a limit in excess of £15,000 would nonetheless normally fall foul of this anti-avoidance provision.

Quite apart from these special rules designed to aid the calculation of the credit limit, there are other ways in which running-account credit is treated differently by the 1974 Act. Brief mention only will be made here as these matters will be explored later. The criteria for exemption from the provisions of the Act under s.16 and regulations made thereunder vary according to whether the agreement is for fixed-sum or running-account credit. Several of the provisions requiring the giving of information to the debtor depend on the distinction, for example statements of account, information to be included in advertisements, quotations and agreements.

2.20   Total charge for credit

When calculating the figure for the purposes of the credit limit, it is important to remember that the amount in question is the credit advanced as opposed to the cash price, or the total amount the debtor might have to pay. Certain other items are excluded when working out the amount of the credit advanced by the creditor. These items, referred to as the total charge for credit, are essentially items for which the debtor would not have had to pay had the transaction been for cash. Naturally, interest charges fall within this (s.20 and the Consumer Credit (Total Charge for Credit) Regulations 1980, SI 1980 No.51), but so do many other matters, in particular insurance premiums which the debtor is required to pay under the terms of the agreement and which are often included in the total charge for credit. In the normal run of things, card issuers rarely seem to insist on anything of this nature and recourse to the Regulations is therefore unnecessary.

2.21 Analysis of running-account credit agreements

It would seem useful to comment here about the nature of a running-account credit agreement such as a credit card agreement, although all that is said applies equally to other forms of revolving credit facility. Goode (I[370]) neatly describes an 'agreement' for revolving credit as 'in effect an umbrella for future credit transactions'. The fact that the parties have agreed terms, may even both have signed a document setting out those terms, is not necessarily indicative of a binding contractual relationship at that stage. A credit card arrangement in these circumstances is a facility provided by the creditor and at this early point the debtor is under no obligation to avail himself or herself of any credit. It is seen as a species of unilateral contract, a continuing offer by the creditor which does not mature into a binding contract until the credit facility is first used by the debtor. Each time it is used creates a separate acceptance of the creditor's offer, thus constituting a distinct contract. Either party is free to create future obligations, or not as the case may be.

The above is a rather neat and tidy analysis of the common law position with regard in particular to the credit card agreement. It is, however, of some practical significance in the context of the Consumer Credit Act 1974, particularly where it is essential for the working of certain provisions in the Act to decide when an agreement comes into being. This may be of considerable importance in relation to the prescribed precontractual steps required under the Act in certain situations (Chapter 4), as well as having a possible bearing on some of the issues of joint and several liability and agency (see Chapters 9 and 10 respectively).

Whilst the credit card arrangement has been described above as one of a unilateral nature, as Goode observes (I[370]), there may be a bilateral aspect to the arrangement; for example, a credit card agreement will require a debtor to keep the card safe. Until the card is used, the agreement will not be fully operative, but it is highly likely that it would be in force at least to the extent of the sakekeeping obligation (see the further discussion on this in Goode, I[472]–[475]).

2.22 Status of the debtor

To be regulated under the Act, not only must an agreement be within the financial ceiling discussed above but the debtor must also be an 'individual'. This term is defined in s.189(1) as including a partnership or other unincorporated body of persons not consisting entirely of bodies corporate. In the context of a credit card agreement, this issue is hardly likely to arise, but as a general point of interest the Act gives a very wide meaning to 'consumer' in its title, something which may be changed in the near future under government proposals.

2.30 Exempt agreements

Another hurdle for the credit card agreement in its pursuit of regulation is that it must not be one made exempt by virtue of s.16 of the Act or the regulations made thereunder. The concept of the exempt agreement is a fundamental one for many creditors, in particular building societies, banks and first mortgage lenders. As far as creditors as card issuers are concerned, the only exemption category which is of any real interest is that which grants exemption by reference to the number of payments made. This assumes that creditors are charging a normal commercial rate of interest and are consequently precluded from taking advantage of the low-cost credit exemption in art.4 of the Consumer Credit (Exempt Agreements) Order 1989, SI 1989 No.869.

Article 3(*a*)(ii) provides exemption for running-account debtor–creditor–supplier agreements which prescribe the making of payments by the debtor in relation to specified periods and require that the number of payments made by the debtor in repayment of the whole amount of the credit provided in each period shall not be more than one. So far we have not discussed in any depth the debtor–creditor–supplier (DCS) agreement; it is covered in the next chapter. Suffice it to say at this stage that a credit card agreement is a DCS agreement in so far as the debtor can and does use the card to acquire goods and/or services from the retailer. Thus Access/Visa-type cards and American Express and Diner's Club cards are included. As we have already established they all provide running-account credit and they would all seem also to satisfy the third limb in art.3(*a*)(ii), namely, they require the debtor to repay the credit in relation to specified periods, usually monthly in respect of those cards mentioned. The final requirement is that the repayment must be by one single sum in respect of the credit extended in the period in question. Thus, as American Express and Diner's Club cardholders are required by their agreements to repay the credit in one single amount they are exempt agreements. By way of contrast, Access/Visa cards typically allow the cardholder to pay by instalments if he or she so wishes. This prevents the agreement from having exempt status quite irrespective of whether the cardholder as a matter of habit pays by a single sum or not.

It bears repetition that the extortionate credit bargain provisions still apply to agreements such as American Express or Diner's Club, notwithstanding their exempt status as described above (see Chapter 11). A pure debit or cash card, not being a credit card in any event, does not need the exempt status to be found in art.3. One final point concerns the use of an unregulated credit card such as those discussed above to obtain cash from an ATM. Used in this way a card is not a DCS agreement and the exempt status under art.3(*a*)(ii) would be denied it in that particular capacity. The agreement would be partly regulated, partly exempt and be a multiple agreement under s.18 (see below).

2.24   Small and non-commercial agreements

Some agreements are granted partial exemption from the Act. A small agreement falls into this category. Whilst few, if any, credit card agreements will fall into this class, a brief mention is necessary. A small agreement is defined in s.17 of the Act as a regulated consumer credit agreement where the credit does not exceed £50. It does not include hire-purchase or conditional sale agreements, or secured transactions other than by guarantee or indemnity. Also, the Act cannot be evaded by dividing a transaction involving credit beyond £50 into two or more small agreements. The major advantage granted the small agreement is that it is exempt from the formality provisions in Part V of the Act, except ss.55 and 56 in certain circumstances. A credit card agreement might conceivably fall into this category, but it is more likely to apply to check trading agreements where the values of the checks tend to be on the low side.

A brief mention of non-commercial agreements is also necessary. Such agreements are outside the scope of the majority of the provisions of the Act, which is concerned primarily with the professional grantor of credit. It is assumed that those issuing credit cards of the type discussed in this book consider themselves as in the business of providing credit.

2.25 Conclusion

In this chapter we have considered some of the important classifications applicable to credit card agreements. The concept of the regulated agreement is fundamental to the working of the Consumer Credit Act 1974 in general, but in particular it has significant consequences for any credit card agreement brought within its scope. In the next chapter we shall consider some further vital classifications of credit card agreements which may have a crucial and practical impact on the obligations of both the creditor and the debtor.

CHAPTER 3

Credit Card Agreements: Further Classification

3.01 Introduction

In this chapter we shall encounter some of the most difficult concepts introduced by the Consumer Credit Act 1974. In particular, the distinction between debtor–creditor–supplier and debtor–creditor agreements is difficult to grasp, as are the concept of the linked transaction and the nature of the multiple agreement. However, to start with we shall consider what is meant by a credit-token within the Act. If a card can be regarded as a credit-token, this will trigger off certain provisions which are specific to credit-tokens. These provisions may nonetheless be operative even if the credit-token does not form part of a regulated agreement. The Act also has provisions which relate especially to credit-token agreements, namely, regulated agreements. It is important to keep in mind the distinction between the credit-token itself and the agreement which underlies it, if any.

3.02 Definition of credit-token

The first point to note is that a credit-token is widely defined in s.14(1) of the Act to include a card, check, voucher, coupon, stamp, booklet, form or other document or thing given to an individual by a person carrying on a consumer credit business, who undertakes:

'(a) that on production of it (whether or not some other action is also required) he will supply cash, goods and services (or any of them) on credit, or

(b) that where, on the production of it to a third party (whether or not any further action is also required), the third party supplies cash, goods and services (or any of them), he will pay the third party for them (whether or not deducting any discount or commission), in return for payment to him by the individual.'

Despite the roundabout language, there is nothing too complicated in this definition in relation to the two standard situations it seeks to cover. Goode's comment (I[549.1]) that 'in essence a credit-token is a piece of paper or plastic which unlocks the door to credit' is apposite. Paragraph (a) relates to the two-party credit card where the creditor and supplier are one and the same person, namely, the in-house store or budget card. By way of contrast, paragraph (b) is concerned, in the context of credit cards, with the three-party situation we identified in Chapter 1, with the creditor, debtor, and the supplier of goods and services. Access, Visa, American Express and Diner's Club cards are all examples of this category. It matters not that the latter two types of agreement are exempt as discussed previously.

Section 14(4) makes it clear that a card used to obtain cash from an ATM may be a credit-token within s.14(1)(*a*) or (*b*). It is thought that a cheque guarantee card is not a credit-token. Indeed, the draftsman wished to make this clear, and did so in example 21 in Sch.2 to the Act. The bank which issues the cheque guarantee card is merely honouring its promise to guarantee payment of the cheque. However, Diamond (p.325) suggests, against the general trend, that such a card might be a credit-token where it is used at other branches of the issuing bank than that at which the customer has his or her account, provided there is an agreed overdraft facility. This is not an entirely convincing argument as the function of the card in this instance is no different, namely, it is merely a guarantee that a cheque will be met. We shall return to this discussion in Chapter 13.

3.03   Debit and cash cards

There is some debate as to whether a debit card or a cash card might be regarded as a credit-token under s.14(1)(*b*). This would involve a strained interpretation of the wording and, as Goode points out forcibly (I[549.3]), there is no rational policy for regulating tokens such as this which have nothing to do with the granting of credit in the normal way of things. It has been suggested that the use of a cash card to obtain cash from an ATM of banks other than the one which issued the card makes it a credit-token. Similar arguments can be made against this suggestion also. This kind of arrangement has normally nothing to do with credit provision. Reliance is sometimes placed on the wording of s.14(3) to support the argument that debit and cash cards are credit-tokens. This states: 'Without prejudice to the generality of section 9(1), the person who gives an individual an undertaking within subsection (1)(*b*) shall be taken to provide him with credit drawn on whenever a third party supplies him with cash, goods or services.' Goode's view is that this does not enlarge the scope of s.14(1)(*b*), but merely seeks to delineate the act which constitutes the provision of credit, given that credit is being provided. This argument is strengthened by the fact that debit cards and cash cards are a more recent development than the Consumer Credit Act 1974. The draftsman could hardly have had them in contemplation.

As we shall see in Chapters 7 and 13, the debit card may constitute a credit-token, as may the cash card, if it is used in conjunction with an agreed overdraft facility. This particular issue has been brought to the attention of the Banking Ombudsman over the last few years in relation to the question of liability for misuse of credit, debit and cash cards. As we shall see, with the advent of the Code of Banking Practice, some of the sting may have been removed from the problem in circumstances where the Code applies, as there has been an attempt to assimilate the rules on misuse of debit and cash cards with those on misuse of credit-tokens.

Still on the subject of cash cards and the use of ATMs, it is accepted, or so it seems, that where a customer is given a cash card with an overdraft facility by his bank and he uses it at the ATMs of other banks, these latter banks are acting as agents for the customer's bank. Consequently, the card is a credit-token, if at all, under s.14(1)(*a*) rather than (1)(*b*).

3.04 Meaning of 'undertakes'

The final point on credit-tokens for the present concerns the meaning of the word 'undertakes' in s.14. It has been held that the word does not necessarily imply that there must be a contractual relationship in force before a card will be considered a credit-token. In *Elliot* v. *Director General of Fair Trading* [1980] 1 WLR 977 a company sent out to the public envelopes containing advertising material and other documents including one similar to a credit card which was stated to be for immediate use, although this was not in fact the case. It was held by the Divisional Court to be a credit-token, even though there was at this stage no binding contract.

3.05 Restricted- and unrestricted-use credit agreements

Without doubt the Consumer Credit Act was a revolutionary measure designed to bring all types and flavours of agreement within its compass. The difficulty faced by the draftsman was to cater for hire-purchase, credit sale, conditional sale, credit cards, check trading, and moneylending by individuals and a whole host of differing institutions. He sought to achieve this, at least partly, by creating the classification of restricted-

and unrestricted-use credit. The distinction is important for a number of reasons which will become clear later.

Section 11(1) of the Act defines a restricted-use agreement as a regulated consumer credit agreement:

'(a) to finance a transaction between the debtor and the creditor, whether forming part of that agreement or not, or

(b) to finance a transaction between a debtor and a person (the 'supplier') other than the creditor, or

(c) to refinance any existing indebtedness of the debtor's, whether to the creditor or another person.'

From these provisions alone it is not possible to decide what is restricted-use credit. Rather unhelpfully, s.11(2) provides that any regulated agreement not falling within s.11(1) is one for unrestricted-use credit. It is s.11(3) that supplies the key to distinguishing restricted- and unrestricted-use credit. It states that an agreement is not for restricted-use credit if the credit is given in such a way as to leave the debtor free to use it as he chooses, even though he may be bound by contract to use it in a particular manner. What this comes down to is whether the debtor has access to the money or whether the creditor undertakes the responsibility for ensuring that the credit is applied for its proper purpose, for example by paying the supplier directly. It should be noted that, by s.11(4), an agreement may nonetheless fall within s.11(1)(*b*), even though the identity of the supplier is not known at the time the agreement is made. This may often be the case in respect of credit card agreements as we shall see. We shall now look at the situations which fall within s.11(1)(*a*) and (*b*) respectively, as credit card agreements may fall into either category.

3.06 Creditor/supplier

Section 11(1)(*a*) governs the situation where the creditor and the supplier are the same person. Several types of credit agreement fall into this class, including hire-purchase agreements. For our purposes, the two-party credit card agreement (store or budget cards) will fall into this category of restricted-use credit agreement. In this type of case the credit takes the form of a deferment of the purchase price for goods and/or services.

3.07 Third-party supplier

Section 11(1)(*b*) covers the position where the supplier is a third party and the creditor pays the credit directly to the supplier or gives the debtor a credit-token to be used with designated suppliers. In either case the debtor has no power to misdirect the credit. Clearly, Access/Visa-type credit cards, where used to pay for goods or services in the now familiar way, are restricted-use agreements falling within this category.

3.08   Unrestricted-use credit

If the control of the credit is given to the debtor, then it is unrestricted-use, irrespective of whether the debtor is bound by the agreement to use the money for a specific purpose. Credit card agreements which permit a debtor to obtain cash advances, either over the counter at a bank or building society or by use of an ATM, are in this instance unrestricted-use agreements. Access/Visa cards may fall into the restricted- or unres-tricted-use categories depending on how they are used in particular situations. They are examples of what the Act calls 'multiple' agreements, considered shortly.

3.09   Importance of the distinction

The distinction between restricted- and unrestricted-use credit is important for many reasons under the Consumer Credit Act 1974. Many of these are not relevant in the context of credit card agreements. However, the classification is highly relevant to the next significant classificatory labels employed by the draftsman, namely, debtor–creditor–supplier and debtor–creditor agreements.

3.10   Debtor–creditor–supplier (DCS) and debtor–creditor (DC) agreements

The most difficult and, arguably, the most important classification introduced by the 1974 Act concerns DCS and DC agreements. Goode's view (I[538]) is that the difficulty is 'visual rather than conceptual'. The DCS terminology is the draftsman's attempt to express the Crowther Committee's 'connected loan' concept where there is a business connection of some sort between the creditor and the supplier (Cmnd.4596, para.6.2.24). This 'business connection' idea is central to the concept of the DCS agreement and becomes the focal point of the justification of joint and several liability under s.75 of the Act (see Chapter 9).

3.11   Debtor–creditor–supplier credit

The DCS agreement may take one of three disparate forms as set out in s.12 of the Act:

'A debtor–creditor–supplier agreement is a regulated consumer credit agreement being —

(*a*)   a restricted-use credit agreement which falls within section 11(1)(*a*), or

(*b*)   a restricted-use credit agreement which falls within section 11(1)(*b*) and is made by the creditor under pre-existing arrangements, or in contemplation of future arrangements, between himself and the supplier, or

(*c*)   an unrestricted-use credit agreement which is made by the creditor under pre-existing arrangements between himself and a person (the 'supplier') other than the debtor in the knowledge that the credit is to be used to finance a transaction between the debtor and the supplier.'

3.12   Creditor and supplier the same person

These definitions are closely tied in with the preceding discussion on restricted- and unrestricted-use credit. Indeed, para.(*a*) coincides entirely with s.11(1)(*a*). This is the situation where the creditor and the supplier of the goods or services are one and the same person. Included, therefore, in this category of DCS agreement will be the in-house store or budget card. It may seem odd to call such an agreement a DCS agreement, which implies that three parties are involved in the relationship. In a sense, however, there are three parties, in that the creditor has two parts to play in the relationship: supplying both the credit and the goods or services to the debtor on production of the credit-token.

3.13   Creditor and supplier different persons

The more widely used three-party credit cards will fall into the s.12(*b*) category of DCS agreements. As we have already seen, a credit card agreement is one for restricted-use credit where, on its production, a third-party supplier provides the debtor with goods and services. It is restricted-use because the creditor pays the supplier directly for the goods and services on receiving the signed slips or vouchers from the supplier. When a credit card is used to obtain cash either over the counter or from an ATM this is unrestricted-use credit as discussed above. Clearly, it cannot be a DCS agreement within either s.12(*a*) or (*b*). Nor does it seem possible to argue that it falls within s.12(*c*), because at the time the agreement is made the creditor does not have the necessary knowledge of how the cash is to be used. The creditor may know how the credit might be used but this does not create a sufficient business connection between himself and the supplier to satisfy s.12(*c*). To summarise: it seems that a credit card agreement may be a DCS agreement for restricted-use credit within s.12(*a*) or (*b*), depending on whether it is a two-party or three-party type of card. If the credit is unrestricted-use, the agreement cannot be a DCS agreement at all, and is therefore relegated to the DC category within s.13.

3.14   Meaning of 'arrangements'

We have assumed so far that the business connection between the creditor and the supplier has been satisfied, thus constituting the credit card agreement a DCS within s.12(*b*). 'Arrangements' are defined in s.187 of the Act as follows:

'(1)   A consumer credit agreement shall be treated as entered into under pre-existing arrangements between a creditor and a supplier if it is entered into in accordance with, or in furtherance of, arrangements previously made between persons mentioned in subsection 4(*a*), (*b*) or (*c*).

(2)   A consumer credit agreement shall be treated as entered into in contemplation of future arrangements between a creditor and a supplier if it is entered into in the expectation that arrangements will subsequently be made between persons mentioned in subsection 4(*a*), (*b*) or (*c*) for the supply of cash, goods and services (or any of them) to be financed by the consumer credit agreement.'

Subs.(4) provides that the persons referred to in subs.(1) and (2) are the creditor and the supplier, one of them and an associate of the other, an associate of one and an associate of the other. The meaning of 'associate' was discussed in the previous chapter. Subsection (5) further provides that where the creditor is an associate of the supplier, there is a rebuttable presumption that the consumer credit agreement was entered into under pre-existing arrangements between the creditor and the supplier.

In the context of the credit card agreement, it would seem that the pre-existing arrangement criterion is easily satisfied where the supplier and the creditor have agreed beforehand that the former will supply goods and/or services to the debtor on the basis that the account will be settled by the creditor on receipt of the credit slip from the supplier. Whilst this is likely to be a contractual relationship in its own right, as discussed in

Chapter 2, 'arrangements' does not necessarily entail such a relationship. Something falling short of a contractual nexus may well suffice. On the other hand, where the creditor enters into arrangements with a new supplier after the making of the credit card agreement, something which obviously happens all the time, the situation would appear to fall within subs.(2) as being 'in contemplation of future arrangements'. It is, therefore, not open to the creditor to argue that a particular transaction does not fall into the DCS category on the basis that the supplier in question was not within the particular credit card network at the relevant time and has been subsequently recruited.

3.15   Cheque guarantee and debit cards

Both these types of card may be used in conjunction with the supply of goods and services: the one in support of a cheque payment, the other as a substitute for payment by cheque. At first sight, it might appear that both are potential DCS agreements, as in both cases it would be possible to argue that there are pre-existing arrangements. Such an interpretation would miss the point that neither card is normally concerned with the provision of credit. As only regulated consumer credit agreements are capable of being DCS agreements, neither of these lookalikes is in the DCS fold.

In some instances, however, it is conceivable that both may give rise to the debtor obtaining credit. This is certainly more likely in the case of the debit card. As far as the cheque guarantee card is concerned, s.187(3) provides that it is not to be considered a DCS agreement. Similarly, s.187(3A) (Banking Act 1987, s.89) provides that arrangements for the electronic transfer of funds (known as 'EFTPOS') from a current account at a bank within the meaning of that word in the Bankers' Books Evidence Act 1879 shall be excluded from s.187(1) and (2). This means that the debit card, whether it enables the debtor to receive credit or not, is not capable of being a DCS agreement. One of the important implications of this is that the issuer of a debit card cannot be held jointly and severally liable with the supplier for breach of contract or misrepresentation by the latter under s.75 of the Act. (For discussion of such liability, see Chapter 9.)

3.16   Debtor–creditor credit

There is no need to be too elaborate on what is meant by debtor–creditor agreements. Section 13 goes into some detail when it would perhaps have been easier to say simply that any regulated consumer credit agreement not falling into one of the three DCS categories in s.12 is a DC agreement. The essence of such an agreement is, to use the Crowther Committee terminology, an 'unconnected loan'. In the context of credit cards, the use of a credit-token to obtain cash over the counter or from an ATM is DC credit. This, it seems, would include the use of a debit card and/or a cash card where the debtor's account was subject to an agreed overdraft and had a debit balance at the time of the particular transaction (see the discussion earlier in this chapter on credit-tokens and also Chapters 7 and 13).

3.17   Importance of the distinction

In several respects the debtor under a DCS agreement is afforded better quality protection than under a DC agreement. The most significant of these is, of course, the joint and several liability provision in s.75, mentioned briefly in the previous section. In addition, there are enhanced rights for DCS agreements among the cancellation and linked transaction provisions. Also, the distinction affects the criteria for exemption, as we have already seen, and, further, it affects the canvassing and disclosure rules (Chapter 4).

3.18   Linked transactions

Another important label is the linked transaction. This was introduced to bring within the Act's control transactions which are not necessarily credit agreements themselves, but which are so closely associated with credit agreements that it is difficult or unrealistic to divorce them from the credit agreement. In a sense the fates of both the credit agreement and the connected transaction are considered to be bound up together.

Section 19(1) defines the linked transaction as:

'A transaction entered into by the debtor or hirer, or a relative of his, with any other person (the 'other party'), except one for the provision of security, is a linked transaction in relation to an actual or prospective regulated agreement of which it does not form part (the 'principal agreement') if —
(*a*)   the transaction is entered into in compliance with a term of the principal agreement; or
(*b*)   the principal agreement is a debtor–creditor–supplier agreement and the transaction is financed, or to be financed, by the principal agreement; or
(*c*)   the other party is a person mentioned in subsection (2), and a person so mentioned initiated the transaction by

suggesting it to the debtor or hirer, or his relative, who enters into it —

   (i)   to induce the creditor or owner to enter into the principal agreement, or

  (ii)   for another purpose related to the principal agreement, or

 (iii)   where the principal agreement is a restricted-use agreement, for a purpose related to a transaction financed, or to be financed, by the principal agreement.'

Subsection (2) includes the creditor or owner, or his associate, as well as a person who, in the negotiation of the transaction, is represented by a credit-broker who is also a negotiator in antecedent negotiations for the principal agreement, and a person who, at the time the transaction is initiated, knows that the principal agreement has been made or contemplates that it might be made.

The word 'transaction', it seems, is to be given a very wide meaning and is not to be restricted to binding agreements. Section 19(1) talks about the provision of security as being exempt from the linked transaction provisions. As security is not normally required on entry into a credit card agreement, we need not consider this further. For the linked transactions provisions to operate, the principal agreement must be either an actual or prospective regulated agreement. A further point to note is that the transaction may be between persons who are not parties to the principal agreement itself, provided there is the necessary link between the parties in s.19(1) and (2). Indeed, the situation might easily arise whereby the other party to the linked transaction may be totally unaware that his transaction is linked in any way to a credit transaction. One final general point is that the linked transaction must not form part of the credit agreement itself.

3.19 Credit card agreements and linked transactions

If, unusually, a term of a regulated credit card agreement required the debtor to enter into a transaction, this would be a linked transaction in accordance with s.19(1)(*a*). It would not matter if the requirement was that a relative of the debtor should enter into such a transaction.

The most likely category of linked transaction to a credit card agreement is one falling within s.19(1)(*b*), namely, where the credit agreement finances or is to finance the transaction. We have already established that a regulated credit card agreement is a DCS agreement within s.12(*b*) when used to pay for goods or services from the supplier. As the agreement finances the purchase transaction, the latter is clearly a linked transaction within s.19(1)(*b*).

The final category of linked transaction divides into three. In each instance the other party to the transaction must be a person within s.19(2) who initiates the transaction by suggesting it to the debtor. The first subdivision, (*c*)(i), is unlikely to be applicable in a credit card context. The requirement is that the debtor is persuaded to enter into the transaction as an inducement to the creditor to make the credit agreement. The credit card agreement is more likely to be already in force before the suggestion is made by the person in s.19(2). Category (*c*)(ii) looks more promising. Goode (I[2512]) suggests that if a person enters into an agreement with a tour operator for a holiday on credit and at the operator's suggestion takes out a policy covering death or disability while travelling, this would be a transaction 'for another purpose linked to the principal agreement'. The question to ask here is whether the position would be the same if the credit was being provided under a regulated credit card agreement, rather then by the giving of credit by the tour operator itself? The answer would seem to be that this would more likely fall within s.19(1)(*c*)(iii), as the purpose of the transaction is related to the holiday and not the credit agreement itself. In this instance, the holiday transaction would itself be linked under s.19(1)(*b*). Needless to say, these provisions in s.19(1)(*c*) seem obscure, although the draftsman's purpose may not be.

3.20   Importance of the linked transaction

There are many areas in the Act where the linked transaction is important. Principal among these are the cancellation and withdrawal provisions (see Chapter 6) and the extortionate credit bargain provisions (see Chapter 11).

3.21   Multiple agreements

Mention has already been made of the fact that a credit-token agreement may be an example of a multiple agreement as defined in s.18 of the Act, which provides:

'(1)   This section applies to an agreement (a "multiple agreement") if its terms are such as —

(*a*)   to place a part of it within one category of agreement mentioned in this Act, and another part of it within a

different category of agreement so mentioned, or
within a category of agreement not so mentioned, or

(*b*) to place it, or part of it, within two or more categories
of agreement so mentioned.

(2) Where part of an agreement falls within subsection (1), that
part shall be treated for the purposes of this Act as a
separate agreement.

(3) Where an agreement falls within subsection (1)(*b*), it shall
be treated as an agreement in each of the categories in
question, and this Act shall apply to it accordingly.

(4) Where under subsection (2) a part of a multiple agreement
is to be treated as a separate agreement, the multiple
agreement shall (with any necessary modifications) be
construed accordingly; and any sum payable under the
multiple agreement, if not apportioned by the parties, shall
for the purposes of proceedings in any court relating to the
multiple agreement be apportioned by the court as may be
requisite.'

A significant degree of controversy surrounds the precise meaning of
these provisions, which on the face of it seek merely to state the obvious.
They are aimed at making it clear that the impact of the Act is not
avoided by combining essentially different contracts into a single agreement, whereas if treated separately, one or even both would be within
the ceiling of £15,000. In addition, where an agreement falls into two or
more categories within the Act, the Act seeks to make it clear that the
agreement must comply with the relevant rules relating to each category.
So, for example, the credit-token agreement which can be a DCS under
s.12(*b*), when used to buy goods or services, or is an unrestricted-use DC
agreement under s.13 when used to obtain cash, is such an agreement.
This is described by Goode (I[564]) as a 'unitary' agreement, namely, an
indivisible agreement stretching beyond the boundary of more than one
category in the Act. The danger that might face a creditor here is that if
s.18(2) were to be applied literally to such an agreement, it would have to
be treated as two (or more) separate agreements. One consequence
(there are others but this is most likely to affect a credit-token agreement) would seem to be that the financial particulars for each separate
agreement would have to be kept apart, an extremely onerous burden on
the creditor. This would result in significant artificiality, in that the credit-
token agreement is seen as an integrated package, rather than two or
more distinct packages. The better view would appear to be that a court

would not be willing to come to a conclusion which blatantly defies business sense (see Goode, I[579–582]).

3.22 Conclusion

The type of credit card agreement such as Access/Visa is clearly a credit-token agreement, the card itself being a credit-token within s.14 of the 1974 Act. It may be for restricted- or unrestricted-use credit depending on the circumstances of its use and, consequently, a DCS or DC agreement respectively. Where it is used to obtain goods or services from a supplier it is a DCS agreement and the supply contract is a linked transaction. Finally, the agreement is a multiple agreement, probably unitary in nature. As the discussion proceeds in the following chapters it will become readily apparent just how these various classifications play their part in the regulation of the credit card agreement. In the next chapter we shall consider the controls at common law, under other statutes, and in particular under the Consumer Credit Act 1974, which exist to protect the debtor prior to the making of the credit agreement.

CHAPTER 4

Precontractual Regulation of Credit Card Agreements

4.01 Introduction

This chapter is concerned with the regulation of the steps leading up to the making of the credit card agreement. The chapter is essentially in two parts. In the first part, the focus will be on the general controls on the activities of those seeking business in the credit card field, both at common law and by statute. The second part is concerned with the way in which the Consumer Credit Act itself regulates the precontractual statements and activities of the prospective creditor. The focal point of attention is the credit card agreement made or to be made between the creditor and the debtor, but the relationships between the supplier and the debtor on the one hand and the supplier and the creditor on the other will be discussed as appropriate.

Much of what follows relates only to those agreements which can be classified as credit-token agreements. We saw at the end of the previous chapter that the Access/Visa-type credit card agreement clearly falls into this category and, therefore, the discussion will centre primarily on such agreements. However, we shall be looking at the general contractual, criminal and self-regulatory controls on advertising in particular, as well as the specific regulation of advertising, canvassing and quotations contained in the Consumer Credit Act itself. Those seeking business in the credit card and allied fields are as much subject to this general control as any other trade or business and must be wary of breaking the civil and criminal law as well as failing to comply with relevant codes of practice, as this might affect the credit card issuer's ability to retain its licence.

The discussion starts with the potential liability of the creditor and supplier at common law, contractual and tortious, for statements made in the precontractual negotiations with the debtor. Secondly, we consider the impact of the criminal and other public law controls on the statements of the creditor and supplier under legislation other than the Consumer Credit Act. Thirdly, consideration will be given to the self-regulatory aspect of the codes of practice. Finally, the provisions of the Act itself and the way they seek to control the precontractual negotiations will be discussed.

4.02   Common law regulation

As mentioned in para.4.01, we are concerned primarily with the regulation of negotiations leading up to the making of the credit card agreement, the contract between the creditor and the debtor. This is an intensively regulated relationship. In this section, we consider the way in which statements made by the creditor, prior to the making of the contract, are dealt with by the civil law and the consequences for the agreement (if any) eventually entered into by the parties. The discussion quite naturally centres on the creditor's words and behaviour, rather than those of the debtor, because the law intervenes on behalf of the weaker party in the relationship, the party with the inferior bargaining power.

The creditor's liability to the debtor for precontractual statements by the supplier is covered for the most part in Chapters 9 and 10, but the supplier's own personal responsibility for such statements will be covered in this chapter.

4.03   Liability of the creditor to the debtor

The creditor is likely to make statements to the debtor during the precontractual negotiations culminating eventually in a credit card agreement between them. These may appear in publicity information, including advertisements, mail-shot literature, or in direct correspondence with the debtor who may be an existing customer of a bank or building society for other services. They may relate to various matters such as the interest rate for the credit (APR), or the availability of free gifts on entering into the agreement. These statements, wherever they appear and to whatever they relate, may well induce the debtor to enter into the credit agreement with the creditor. If the statements turn out to be inaccurate, the debtor may wish to take action; any such action will depend on whether he or she can show a breach of the general law of contract or an actionable misrepresentation of some kind by the creditor. Where the eventual agreement is not a regulated credit-token agreement, these may be the only types of action open to the debtor, although an approach to the Banking or one of the Building Society Ombudsmen may not be out of the question (Chapter 13). If liability is established for either a breach of contract or misrepresentation on the basis of inaccurate precontractual statements, it may well affect the validity of the contract, depending on the remedies available to and chosen by the debtor. There is a distinct possibility that a regulated agreement might be brought to a premature end under the common law rules, irrespective of any provisions of the 1974 Act. This will depend on the nature of the breach of contract or misrepresentation.

4.04   Categories of precontractual statement

A statement may take a number of forms in the eye of the law:
(1)   a commendatory expression, too vague or imprecise to have any legal significance — the sort of statement nobody would take seriously;
(2)   a representation — a statement which is outside the contract but which does have legal significance and induces the representee to enter into the contract;
(3)   a collateral contract — one which is ancillary to the main contract and is based on the statement by one party which induces the other to enter into the main contract with a third party;
(4)   a term of the contract — a statement which the law regards as being part of the contractual promise.
Leaving aside those within (1) above, statements by the creditor may fall into categories (2) and (4). Statements falling within (3) are more likely to be those made by a supplier which induce the debtor to contract with the creditor, and are discussed later.

The legal test for differentiating between precontractual statements which are representations and those which are treated in law as terms of the contract is the intention of the parties. Frequently, this is not at all evident from what they say and the courts must resort to looking at the circumstances in which the statement was made to ascertain intention. Factors such as the relative expertise of the parties, whether the statement is or is not omitted from any documentary evidence of the contract, the precise stage at which the statement was made in the precontractual negotiations, are considered. None is usually conclusive of itself.

Negotiations leading to credit card agreements are conducted by means of advertisements, publicity material, e.g. brochures and leaflets, mail shots in some instances and direct correspondence between the parties. Generally, statements made in the advertising and publicity material will be regarded as mere representations rather than express terms of the contract, unless they are repeated in the contract documents. For example, statements about the annual percentage rate (APR) contained in the publicity material will be included in the contract document; those about the provision of free gifts offered as an inducement will probably not be.

4.05   Statement as a term

If the statement is regarded as a term of the contract and it turns out to be untrue or, if promissory, the promise is unfulfilled, the debtor has an action for breach of contract. The remedy available will depend on the nature of the breach in accordance with general contractual principles: repudiation and/or damages for breach of a major term, a condition; damages only for breach of a minor term, a warranty. Of course, there is scope for adopting the innominate term approach, i.e. 'wait and see' whether the breach is serious enough to justify repudiation. For example, the creditor might break the contract by charging a much higher APR than was mentioned in the precontractual negotiations and the contract document itself. The APR is the price of credit and, as such, is an important item for the debtor. The court might, using the innominate term approach, decide that where the APR charged was significantly higher than was indicated, the debtor was entitled to treat himself as discharged from the contract. On the other hand, a slight increase in the APR would be treated as only a minor breach and the debtor would be denied the opportunity to repudiate the contract, being restricted to a claim in damages only.

4.06   Statement a mere representation

If the statement can at best be regarded as only a representation, then in the event that it is false the debtor's remedy will depend on the rules of actionable misrepresentation. To succeed a debtor would have to show that the statement was one of existing or past fact which was false and that it induced the debtor to contract with the creditor. The action might be in deceit if the misrepresentation was fraudulent, i.e. made knowing it to be false, or recklessly, careless whether it is true or false. A successful plea of fraud, difficult to establish at the best of times, may permit the debtor to rescind the contract with the creditor and sue for damages in the tort of deceit, on the basis that the creditor is liable for all the direct consequences of its intentional act, irrespective of foreseeability. The right to rescind may be lost where, e.g., the debtor affirms the contract, i.e. knowing the facts he or she elects to carry on with the contract, or where restitution is not possible for the parties.

If fraud cannot be established, the debtor may argue that the untrue statement was negligently made. Under the Misrepresentation Act 1967, s.2(1), the creditor would have to establish that it had reasonable grounds to believe and did believe up to the time that the contract was made that the statement was true. The Act places the burden of proof firmly on the representor, and the creditor, being in the superior position as to knowledge and expertise, may find it difficult to discharge such a burden. The remedy for the debtor is damages, recently decided by the Court of Appeal as being based on the deceit principle enunciated above (*Royscott Ltd* v. *Rogerson* [1991] 3 All ER 294). The debtor may also be able to rescind, but it should be remembered that this right may be lost in certain circumstances. In addition, under s.2(2), the court has a discretion to award damages in lieu of rescission. This is likely to be done where the misrepresentation is considered to be of a trivial nature. If the debtor is able to establish only a totally innocent misrepresentation, the sole remedy is rescission, subject to the s.2(2) discretion.

The debtor may be able to bring an alternative action in tort, for negligent misstatement, under the principle in *Hedley Byrne* v. *Heller* [1964] AC 465. It is now well established that this principle can apply in the two-party situation, as long as the necessary 'special relationship' can be made out. The disadvantage of this common law action, as compared with that under s.2(1) of the 1967 Act, is that the burden of proving negligence lies with the plaintiff, namely, the debtor. One advantage, however, is that the principle extends beyond statements of existing or past fact to take in statements of opinion or advice. The special relationship arises where the advice or information is given in a business context and the representor knows that reliance by an identified person, or a person from a readily identifiable group of persons, is highly likely. It has been held that a bank does not owe a duty of care to ensure that the customer is capable of repaying the credit (*Williams and Glyn's Bank* v. *Barnes* [1980] Com LR 205). One other limitation of the principle is that it gives the right to claim for damages only; thus in many cases the claim will be better based on the Misrepresentation Act with its reversed burden of proof.

4.07   Liability of the supplier to the debtor

In practice, in the credit card context, it will rarely happen that a supplier will introduce a debtor to a credit card issuer. In the event that this does happen, it is necessary to consider the personal liability of the supplier to the debtor. At common law the liability of the creditor for the statements of the supplier is likely to be non-existent, as it is difficult to establish that the supplier is the agent of the creditor. However, the liability of the creditor for such statements is dramatically increased in the case of regulated agreements, as the discussion in Chapters 9 and 10 will show.

If the supplier makes a false statement to the debtor which induces the latter to enter into the credit card agreement with the creditor, it may be possible for the debtor to use the collateral contract argument (category (3) in para.404) in an action against the supplier. In addition, in the event that the debtor can prove fraud against the supplier, an action in the tort of deceit is a possibility, as also, if carelessness can be established, is an action based on the *Hedley Byrne* principle for negligent misstatement at common law. These actions would be for damages only and not rescission of the contract as this is entered into with a third party, namely, the creditor. For the same reason, the Misrepresentation Act will not provide a remedy at all, as there must be privity of contract for the Act to apply. If the supplier's statement was made prior to the making of a two-party credit card arrangement, it would be possible to use s.2(1) of the 1967 Act and rescission would also be available.

The above is a brief summary of the relevant contractual and misrepresentation principles which might assist a debtor in an action against the creditor/supplier who induces a contract by means of a false statement. It should be emphasised that the initiative for action would lie with the debtor to bring individual proceedings at civil law against the creditor or supplier. By way of contrast — where action is taken by public officials — we shall now consider the public law controls on precontractual statements.

4.08   Criminal controls

Parliament has long recognized that misleading and false statements made to consumers require strict regulation in the public interest. The Trade Descriptions Act 1968 and Part III of the Consumer Protection Act 1987 (misleading price indications) are currently the main pieces of legislation affecting such statements. The 1968 Act, in particular, is seen as the main weapon for trading standards officers in the fight against misdescription in general. It is clearly a piece of legislation which can be used against creditors in relation to precontractual statements, just as it can against any provider of a service.

4.09   The Trade Descriptions Act and misdescription by creditors

Section 14 of the Trade Descriptions Act 1968 creates criminal offences for misdescription of services, accommodation or facilities in the course of a trade or business. The section requires proof of *mens rea* to secure a conviction, by providing that a person commits an offence if, in the course of a trade or business, he makes a statement in respect of a number of listed matters, which he knows to be false, or he recklessly makes a statement which is false. The provision of credit is no doubt a 'facility' within s.14(1) and credit card issuers can hardly deny they are involved in a trade or business. The listed matters include the provision of facilities, the nature of any facilities, the time at which, manner in which or persons by whom any facilities are provided, and the examination, approval or evaluation by any person of any facilities. The word 'provision' is to be interpreted narrowly to mean the fact of provision and not the terms on which it is made. For example, a company falsely indicating that it is prepared to supply credit by means of giving a credit card to a customer would be caught by this. However, a misrepresentation as to the terms on which credit was to be provided by the creditor would not be caught, unless it fell within 'nature', 'time', or 'manner'. Any statement must also be false to a material degree (s.14(4)).

It should be noted that s.14 does not apply to statements about the future (*Becket* v. *Cohen* [1973] 1 All ER 120), unless there is implicit in it a statement of existing or past fact (*British Airways Board* v. *Taylor* [1976] 1 All ER 65). It does not apply to the price of a facility (*Newell* v. *Hicks* (1984) 148 JP 307), but this loophole has since been closed by Part III of the Consumer Protection Act 1987, discussed below.

The *mens rea* requirement has not proved as formidable a problem as might have been expected. The recklessness requirement in s.14(1)(*b*) has been held not to involve proving dishonesty and looks very much as if it will be satisfied by proof of carelessness. In *M.F.I.* v. *Nattrass* [1973] 1 All ER 307 there was a failure to consider the potentially misleading nature of an advertisement by the defendant company, which was held liable on that basis. In the leading case on s.14, *Wings* v. *Ellis* [1985] AC 272, the House of Lords upheld the conviction of the defendant company, even though it was not aware that its brochure still contained a false statement. The company had realised the statement was inaccurate and had attempted to remove it, but this had not happened in every case. One of the charges in the case was brought under s.14(1)(*a*), i.e. knowing the statement to be false. The House took the view that every time the inaccurate information in the brochure was read, an offence was committed, subject to the due diligence defence in s.24 of the 1968 Act. Liability under the Act does not affect the civil law position (s.35), consequently any agreement entered into following an offence under the Act remains valid, although in the light of the previous discussion its validity may depend on whether the debtor has an independent action at civil law and whether he or she chooses to pursue it.

What should be gathered from all this is that it is essential to peruse all publicity material thoroughly to avoid ambiguities and false statements reaching the public. A credit card company ought to operate a 'due diligence system' to qualify for the statutory defence in s.24, whether based on BS 5750 or its equivalent.

4.10   The Trade Descriptions Act and suppliers

The supplier of goods and services who displays the logo of a credit card issuer in a prominent place on his or her premises, but who has no arrangement, or no longer any arrangement, with the the credit card issuer, may well commit an offence under the provisions of s.14 as discussed above. In addition, he or she may misdescribe the goods or services provided. The discussion in para.4.09 applies equally to any misdescription of a service. For a misdescription of goods, s.1 of the Trade Descriptions Act is appropriate. This creates three strict liability offences: applying a false trade description to goods, supplying or offering to supply goods to which a false trade description is applied, provided the statements of description are made in the course of a trade or business. Section 2 of the Act specifies a long list of matters which are to be taken as trade descriptions. The Act covers indications, whether direct or indirect, and by whatever means given, as to any of the listed matters, as follows:

(1)   quantity, size or gauge;
(2)   method of manufacture, production, processing or reconditioning;
(3)   composition;
(4)   fitness for purpose, strength, performance, behaviour or accuracy;
(5)   any physical characteristics not included in the previous paragraphs;
(6)   testing by any person and the results thereof;
(7)   approval by any person or conformity with a type approved by any person;
(8)   place or date of manufacture, production, processing or reconditioning;
(9)   person by whom manufactured, produced, processed or reconditioned;
(10) other history, including previous ownership or use.

Advertisements are covered (s.5), as are oral statements (s.4(3)), and whilst statements must be false to a material degree (s.3(1)), misleading statements are covered (s.3(2)) as well as statements of opinion (s.3(3)). A trade description may be applied in a wide variety of ways (s.4). A supplier may be charged under s.1(1)(*b*) with supplying where the misdescription is applied by someone else (e.g the manufacturer) and with offering to supply where the goods are on display or even in the storeroom or the warehouse (s.6).

The supplier may be able to take advantage of the statutory due diligence defence in s.24, namely, that he took all reasonable precautions and exercised all due diligence to avoid the commission of the offence, and provided he can show that the offence was due to mistake, act or default of another person, reliance on information from another, or an accident or some other cause beyond his control. The burden of proof is on the supplier on the balance of probabilities. The leading case of *Tesco* v. *Nattrass* [1972] AC 153 established that the act or default of another person included the branch manager of a large retailing concern. There is provision for a senior officer of a company to be prosecuted where his 'neglect, consent or connivance' contributed to the offence by the company (s.20), and the prosecution can use the by-pass provision in s.23 to prosecute direct the third party whose act or default caused the supplier to commit the offence. The statutory defence is normally called the 'due diligence' defence and is a common feature of most consumer protection measures which impose strict liability.

A supplier may also be able to employ the so-called 'disclaimer' defence, arguing that the trade description is not false because it has been made clear to the average consumer that it is not to be relied upon. This defence arose primarily in the context of false odometer readings in motor vehicles and it will succeed only where the disclaimer is as 'bold, precise and compelling' as the trade description itself and serves to neutralise what would otherwise be a false message (*Norman* v. *Bennett* [1974] 3 All ER 351).

4.11   Misleading price indications and the creditor

Where the creditor quotes a fee for the issue of a credit-token or quotes the APR for the prospective credit-token agreement, he needs to be aware of the misleading price provisions in s.20(1) of the Consumer Protection Act 1987. These provide that it is an offence if, in the course of a business of his, a person gives, by any means whatever, to any consumers an indication which is misleading as to the price at which goods, services, accommodation or facilities are available (whether generally or from particular persons). Subsection (2) provides for the situation where the price indication becomes misleading after being given and it is reasonable to expect reliance by some or all consumers. In such circumstances, an offence will be committed unless the giver of the indication takes all such steps as are reasonable to prevent those consumers from relying on the indication. By subs.(3) it does not matter whether the person giving the indication is or was acting on his own behalf or on behalf of another, or whether he or she is the person from whom the goods, services, accommodation or facilities are available. 'Consumer' is confined to those who acquire the goods etc. for private use or consumption or otherwise than for a business of the consumer.

The meaning of 'misleading' is spelt out in some depth in s.21 to include, e.g., a price quoted being less than it actually is, and also an indication that the applicability of the price does not depend on certain factors when it does. Section 22(1) makes it clear that 'services or facilities' include the provision of credit or of banking or insurance and the provision of facilities incidental to the provision of such services.

Section 25 empowers the Secretary of State to issue a code of practice following consultation, and this has been done. The Code is designed to provide by way of clarification examples of misleading and non-misleading indications. It should be noted that non-compliance is not conclusive in criminal or civil proceedings, although compliance may be a defence (s.25(2)).

There is, of course, the usual form of statutory defence of due diligence, in s.39 of the 1987 Act, but there are also more specific defences in s.24, e.g. for innocent publishers of a misleading price indication.

It has been held recently by the House of Lords in *R* v. *Warwickshire County Council, ex parte Johnson* [1992] 2 WLR 1 that an employee of a large retail company cannot be liable under s.20 of the Act because it only applies to owners or those with a controlling interest in a business. The case also established that an indication may in appropriate circumstances be a continuing one and that a single failure by the retailer to comply with the terms of the offer renders the indication misleading.

It seems that this is another piece of legislation with which the credit card issuer must be familiar. Again, the need to have some adequate system of 'due diligence' is paramount so as to be able to rely on the statutory defence should an offence be committed. With regard to pricing offences, the system must be specifically geared towards eliminating them if it is to succeed. As with the Trade Descriptions Act, a breach of the pricing provisions does not of itself give rise to any civil action or consequences.

4.12 Misleading price indications and the supplier

The same points can be made about the supplier and his pricing policy as in relation to the creditor. Perhaps more emphasis needs to be placed on the need for a suitable 'due diligence' system. The supplier may be guilty of mispricing offences under s.20(1) in respect of the goods and services he sells or supplies, particularly where he becomes involved in comparative pricing, i.e. reductions from a previous price, or comparisons with another trader's prices. The Code of Practice must be consulted and publicity material brought into line with its provisions. A supplier who misquoted, e.g., the APR under a prospective agreement with a credit card issuer could be caught under s.20, for, as we have seen, the offence extends to indications of prices at which goods or services are supplied by others.

4.13 Other public controls

There are numerous other statutes which create criminal offences in respect of misleading statements, for example the Food Safety Act 1990 and the Medicines Act 1968. Suppliers in the food or medicines fields are liable to conviction if they misdescribe food or drugs. Obviously, creditors will not fall foul of these provisions if they merely continue to trade in credit, but they may have links with suppliers in these areas. It should not be forgotten that these suppliers may be considered 'business associates' of the creditor, a point probably not lost on the Director General of Fair Trading when licences come up for renewal.

The other major area of public control stems from an EC Directive on Misleading Advertising (No.84/450/EEC, OJ L250, 19th September 1984, p.17). The Control of Misleading Advertisements Regulations 1988 (SI 1988 No.915) made under s.2(2) of the European Communities Act 1972 empower the Director General of Fair Trading to seek an injunction to prevent the publication of advertisements which are thought misleading. An advertisement may be misleading if, e.g., it deceives or is likely to deceive persons to whom it is addressed or whom it reaches and is likely to affect their economic behaviour. The Regulations are meant to be a last resort, in that the Director must be satisfied that the complainant has explored and exhausted all other methods of redress. An injunction may be sought against anyone seemingly concerned with the advertisement, and may be granted on such terms as are or appear appropriate to the case. It may extend to advertisements other than the one about which there is a complaint, to include one in similar terms or one which is likely to convey a similar impression. It is immaterial whether the advertisement has caused loss to anyone, or that there was no intention by the publisher to mislead.

4.14 Self-regulation

Advertising is controlled not just by the criminal and other public law measures discussed above, but is subject also to a considerable amount of self-regulation. Independent television and radio advertising was governed by the Code of Advertising Standards and Practice formerly published by the Independent Broadcasting Authority. The functions of this body have now been taken over by the Independent Television Commission and the Radio Authority under the Broadcasting Act 1990. There were specific rules in respect of financial advertising. It is likely that the new rules will be largely based on the old. However, there will no longer be the power to pre-vet advertising copy. For other media, the Advertising Association established long ago the Advertising Standards Authority, operating a Code of Advertising Practice. There is no prior vetting and for the most part the scheme is concerned with complaints after the event. In general, advertisements must be 'legal, decent, honest and truthful'.

In addition, Part I of the Code of Banking Practice (which deals with banking services in general) contains general guidance on the marketing of credit. Paragraph 9.1 states that banks and building societies in their advertising and promotional material will tell customers and potential customers that all lending will be subject to appraisal of their financial standing. Paragraph 9.2 provides that institutions will act responsibly and prudently in marketing, complying with the advertising codes mentioned above. They are to ensure that literature is fair and reasonable, not misleading, and that it complies with all relevant legislation.

4.15 Licensing and the fitness of the holder

It should be recalled that the Director General of Fair Trading has to consider the fitness of an applicant for a licence and also has power to revoke or suspend a licence. This issue will again arise on renewal. The credit card issuer must ensure that it, its employees and its business associates not only steer clear of infringing the criminal law provisions discussed above, but are also vigilant in ensuring compliance with civil obligations. It should also be remembered that the Director can take into account behaviour which may fall short of infringement. Failure to comply with non-statutory codes of practice such as the advertising and banking codes may be relevant.

4.16   Advertising control and the Consumer Credit Act

The majority of the advertising control discussed above is aimed primarily at preventing the consumer from being misled. The Consumer Credit Act does have controls on false or misleading advertising of credit, but it is also concerned with the provision of information to consumers to enable them to make informed and educated choices.

4.17   Scope of control

Section 43(1) of the Consumer Credit Act provides that Part IV applies to any advertisement published for the purposes of a business carried on by the advertiser indicating that he is willing to provide credit. By s.43(2) the business must be one of three types; the relevant one for our purposes is that the advertiser must carry on a consumer credit business. Section 43(3) states that a credit advertisement will not be caught if it indicates that the credit must exceed £15,000 and that no security is required, or the security is to consist of property other than land, nor does s.43(1) apply to credit available only to a body corporate. On the face of it, the controls appear to apply to agreements not otherwise regulated by the Act. However, s.43(5) empowers the Secretary of State to exempt advertisements other than those mentioned above. The current order is the Consumer Credit (Exempt Advertisements) Order 1985 (SI 1985 No.621). It is dangerous to assume that advertisements referring to credit under exempt agreements are themselves automatically exempt from advertising control under the Act. For our purposes, however, the advertising controls do not apply to the type of exempt agreement discussed in para.2.23, namely, the chargecards such as American Express and Diner's Club. Conversely, they will apply to the two- and three-party credit cards we have so far been discussing for the most part.

For those whose advertisements are subject to the controls, there are a number of useful points to consider. First, the word 'advertisement' is given a very wide meaning. By s.189(1), it includes every possible form of publicity: television, radio, notices on display, signs, labels, showcards or goods; distribution of samples, circulars, catalogues, price lists or other material; exhibiting pictures, models or films; or any other method. Goode (I[870]) suggests that not all statements are advertisements, and distinguishes between communications designed merely to inform and those designed to promote business. This distinction may be difficult to draw in some cases. A court would have to consider whether the intention behind the communication was to attract further business or not. It is suggested that a letter written to a credit cardholder giving details of the revised interest rate is not an advertisement, but Jones (pp.38–39) goes further in suggesting that a letter to an existing cardholder inviting him or her to take out a personal loan or an additional card would not be an advertisement as it would not be published. This would seem a doubtful proposition.

Secondly, s.189(1) defines an advertiser as 'any person indicated by the advertisement as willing to enter into transactions to which the advertisement relates'. This suggests plainly that a person may be an 'advertiser' who has neither placed nor published the advertisement. Indeed, a person may be considered such even if no prior approval had been sought or given to the inclusion of the person's name in the advertisement. In such an event, should there be an infringement of the Act, that person would be able to use the statutory defence in s.168. It seems that a person can be considered an advertiser only if he or she is either named explicitly or by implication in the advertisement.

Thirdly, whilst the advertisement must be for the purposes of a business carried on by the advertiser, it need not be the main business as long as it falls within s.43(1) and is not exempted from the advertising controls.

Fourthly, the phrase 'indicating that he is willing' in s.43(1) has troubled the Divisional Court. In *Jenkins* v. *Lombard North Central plc* [1984] 1 All ER 828 a dealer displayed some price display stickers provided by the creditor bearing the latter's name and logo in connection with the sale of his, the dealer's, cars. The court upheld the magistrates' decision that this amounted to no more than corporate advertising and did not indicate a willingness to provide credit, despite the creditor's national reputation as a provider of credit. The display of a credit card logo by a supplier would, therefore, seem to fall into line with this decision and the creditor would not be liable under the section.

4.18   Form and content of advertisements

Section 44 of the Consumer Credit Act gives the Secretary of State the power to make regulations governing what may appear in a credit advertisement, and how. The regulations are to contain such provisions as appear to him to be appropriate to ensure that, having regard to its subject matter and its detail, the advertisement 'conveys a fair and reasonably comprehensive indication' of the nature of the credit and its cost. The regulations may contain requirements that specific information be included in the prescribed manner in advertisements, and other specific matters be excluded. In addition, they may contain requirements to ensure that specific information is clearly brought to the attention of the persons to whom the advertisements are addressed, and that one part of an advertisement is not given insufficient or excessive prominence in relation to any other (s.44(2)).

4.19 The Regulations

The current regulations made by the Secretary of State are the Consumer Credit (Advertisements) Regulations 1989 (SI 1989 No.1125, in force 1st February 1990). They are designed to ensure that the potential debtor is not misled, by prohibiting certain words or phrases which are considered to have this effect. Section 46(1) of the Act, in addition, does this in general terms. The Regulations are also designed to provide the reader of the advertisement with a fair picture of the terms of the credit, in particular its cost. They also ensure that the reader is aware of the ways in which the availability of the credit might be affected by his or her personal characteristics such as age, occupation and residence.

4.20 Scope of the Regulations

The Regulations, it should be recalled, apply not only to advertisements leading to what would be regulated agreements but also to those leading to agreements where the £15,000 figure is exceeded, unless one of the exemptions discussed above applies. Advertisements limited solely to the provision of credit or hire for business purposes are expressly excluded (reg.9). To come within this exclusion, the creditor must ensure that the advertisement is not framed in such a way as to indicate that credit is available to a private debtor. The overall effect of the Regulations is to prescribe four classes of advertisement: simple, intermediate, and two types of full advertisement, one aimed at a potential debtor and the other at existing debtors designed to persuade them to agree to a variation of their existing agreements. Regulation 2 provides that the person who causes an advertisement to be published must ensure that it falls within one of these four categories.

A simple advertisement is designed merely to give a basic impression of the creditor's willingness to provide credit. Only certain items may be mentioned. If any additional matters are included, the advertisement falls into the intermediate range and must include the minimum information prescribed for that type of advertisement. Similarly, where the advertiser goes beyond the prescribed and, in some cases, optional items for an intermediate advertisement, he or she must satisfy the rules covering full advertisements. There is no limit as to what additional information may normally be included in a full advertisement. Goode accurately summarises the position by commenting that 'for simple advertisements there is a maximum information requirement but no minimum; for intermediate advertisements there is both a maximum and a minimum; and for full advertisements there is a minimum but no maximum' (I[918]).

4.21 General points

Regulation 3(1) allows an advertiser to give what is called 'representative information' in appropriate situations. This enables the advertiser to give typical examples in advertisements, such as typical repayment terms and other examples of variable information depending on the personal characteristics of the potential debtor. Such information must be accompanied by a statement that it is representative. This is a particularly useful provision in relation to credit card advertising, as it will allow advertisers to show, for example, preferential terms for certain classes of debtor.

Regulation 2(6) provides that much of the information provided by the advertiser must be clear and easily legible and shown together as a whole, although variable information, such as cost or terms of repayment, may be contained in a separate leaflet or brochure.

In intermediate and full advertisements, the APR must be given greater prominence than any other rate of charge and at least equal prominence with any other financial information (reg.8).

4.22 Simple credit advertisements

The rules for simple credit advertisements state merely what may be included in such an advertisement, leaving the choice entirely to the advertiser (reg.2(1)(*a*). The permitted statements are:
(1)   the name of the advertiser;
(2)   his logo or that of his associate or trade association;
(3)   his postal address;
(4)   his telephone number (but not a Freefone number);
(5)   his occupation or an indication of the general nature of his occupation;
(6)   any other information, other than:
      (a)   information that a person is willing to provide credit; or
      (b)   the cash price, or other price, of any goods, services, land or other things.

4.23   Intermediate credit advertisements

The effect of the Regulations on intermediate credit advertisements is complex. Such an advertisement must contain the information laid out in paras.1 to 9 of Sch.1, Part II. The advertisement may contain further information indicating a willingness to provide credit, as permitted by para.10 (reg.2(1)(*b*)). It must also conform with the APR, clarity and legibility requirements of the Regulations and must not include any prohibited expressions.

4.24   Full credit advertisements

Full advertisements must contain the information set out in Sch.1, Part III, and may contain such other information as the advertiser desires, provided he or she does not use prohibited expressions and complies with the APR, clarity and legibility provisions (reg.2(1)(*c*)). A full credit variation advertisement must give details of the variations of any of the information prescribed, at the same time making it clear that in other respects the information remains the same (reg.2(1)(*d*)). It should be noted that this type of advertisement is only concerned with the situation where the advertiser is inviting an existing cardholder to agree to a variation of the agreement. Most agreements are likely to contain a unilateral power for the creditor to alter the rate of the charge for the credit. The exercise of this power would not fall within the meaning of a full credit variation advertisement.

4.25   Availability of cash terms

Section 45 of the Consumer Credit Act provides that where an advertisement caught by Part IV indicates that the advertiser is willing to provide credit under a restricted-use agreement relating to goods or services supplied by any person, but at the time when the advertisement is published that person is not holding himself out as prepared to sell the goods or supply the services (as the case may be) for cash, the advertiser commits an offence. The rationale of this provision is to ban the use of advertisements which convey the impression that the advertiser is charging nothing or very little at all for the credit. The supplier must not just be willing to supply but must hold himself out as so willing. This can be done in the advertisement itself, or established by past behaviour in actually supplying the goods or services for cash. A false holding out is not an offence under s.45, but may well infringe s.46 (see below). In the credit card context, it is unlikely that this situation would arise where the agreement involved a separate creditor and supplier, but might be something to watch for when advertising two-party cards where the supplier and the creditor are the same person.

4.26   False or misleading advertisements

We have already referred to the provision in s.46 which creates a general offence: where an advertisement conveys information which is in a material respect false. The section is not limited to statements about the credit but could include indications which may be in the advertisement about the goods or services provided. There is considerable overlap here with the Trade Descriptions Act provisions discussed above. Section 46(2) provides that information stating or implying an intention on the part of advertiser which he does not have is false.

4.27   Infringement

A breach of the 1989 Regulations or of ss.45 and 46 will give rise to a criminal offence. Section 47 provides that where an advertiser commits such a breach, or would do so but for the statutory defence in s.168 of the Act, a like offence is committed by:
(1)   the publisher of the advertisement; and
(2)   any person who, in the course of a business carried on by him, devised the advertisement, or part of it relevant to an offence under the Regulations; and
(3)   where the advertiser did not procure the advertisement, the person who did procure it.
Section 47(2) of the Act contains the 'innocent publisher' defence: the publisher must prove that the advertisement was published in the course of a business carried on by him, that he received it in the course of that business, and did not know and had no reason to suspect that its publication would be an offence under the provisions discussed above.

Infringement of these various provisions does not of itself give rise to any issues as to the validity of any subsequent agreement. Any rights to rescind the agreement, claim damages or otherwise will depend on the common law as detailed earlier in this chapter.

4.28   Canvassing

Sections 48 to 51 are designed to deal with some of the more undesirable aspects of the practice of canvassing credit. The provisions are very specific in what they prohibit, namely, canvassing debtor–creditor agreements off trade premises, sending circulars to minors and giving unsolicited credit-tokens. Other forms of canvassing are not prohibited as such, but it should be emphasised that improper or oppressive methods of inducing debtors to enter into agreements may affect the Director General's decision as to the creditor's licence.

4.29   Canvassing off trade premises

It is an offence to canvass debtor–creditor credit off trade premises, under s.49(1) of the Act. This is clearly aimed at the peddling of unconnected loans on the doorstep. What constitutes canvassing is set out in s.48. It involves making oral representations to the prospective debtor, or any other individual, during an unsolicited visit for that purpose to any place other than the business premises of the creditor or owner, a supplier, the canvasser himself or his employer or principal or the prospective debtor. The premises referred to may be permanent or temporary. This means that it is not canvassing to solicit custom in relation to DC agreements from a stall at a trade fair, for example. In addition, it is not canvassing if the visit takes place at the prospective debtor's business premises. The oral representations need not be face-to-face discussions, nor need they be directed at the prospective debtor, provided they are the purpose for the visit. An oral or written request will suffice to make the visit a solicited one. However, if the request is not in writing and signed by the person making the request or a person on his behalf, the offence of soliciting is committed under s.49(2).

Two-party credit cards are unlikely to fall foul of these provisions as they are usually associated with the supply of goods or services and are consequently DCS agreements outside the scope of s.49. Three-party credit card agreements are potentially within the scope of the section, as they normally provide for the obtaining of cash as well as goods and services. In relation to the obtaining of cash, they are DC agreements. In practice, however, it is not normal to attract customers for credit cards by using the canvassing technique as described in s.48.

4.30   Circulars to minors

Of far more significance for issuers of credit cards is the provision in s.50 of the Consumer Credit Act, which places a prohibition on the sending of documents, with a view to financial gain, to a person under 18 years of age, inviting him or her to borrow money, obtain goods on credit or hire, obtain services on credit, or to apply for information or advice on borrowing money or otherwise obtaining credit, or hiring goods.

The prohibition is wide indeed and extends beyond merely regulated agreements. The invitation document must be sent, not personally delivered, if there is to be an offence. As most credit card issuers use the post to invite business, they are in danger of infringing this provision — it is easily done. It is a defence for the person charged to prove that he did not know, and had no reasonable cause to suspect, that the person was a minor (s.50(2)). The onus is on the credit card issuer to establish the defence on the balance of probability. However, s.50(3) provides that where a document is received by a minor at any school or other educational establishment for minors, a person sending it to him at that establishment knowing or suspecting it to be such shall be deemed to have reasonable cause to suspect that he is a minor. It is essential that those responsible for soliciting custom in this way have a system which attempts to prevent this type of situation from arising so as to be in a position to use this defence or the more general one in s.168 of the Act.

4.31   Unsolicited credit-tokens

By s.51(1) it is an offence to give a person a credit-token if he has not asked for it. Section 189(1) provides that 'give' means to 'deliver or send by post to'. The section is, therefore, wider than originally intended, as it was designed to prevent the mass mailing of credit cards. It should also be noted that it does not matter that the token is given under a regulated agreement or not. As a consequence, it would appear that a mass mailing of cards such as American Express or Diner's Club would infringe s.51(1). We have already seen that giving a document with no contractual force may amount to a credit-token (*Elliot* v. *DGFT*, para.3.04).

To satisfy s.51(1), a request must be contained in a document signed by the person making the request, unless the credit-token agreement is a small DCS agreement. In that case, presumably, no offence is committed where the request is oral only.

Two further practical exceptions are contained in s.51(3). Section 51(1) does not apply to the giving of a credit-token for use under a credit-token agreement already in existence, which is common sense as the making of the agreement is the necessary request for the purposes of s.51(1). Jones inclines to the view (p.45) that this would be a defence where the credit card issuer gave a credit-token to the debtor's spouse or child as an additional cardholder. This conclusion is not reached without some doubt, but it is suggested that, in these circumstances, the creditor would take the risk of any misuse by the recipient as the latter would be an unauthorised user (see Chapter 7).

The other exception in s.51(3) provides that s.51(1) also does not apply where the credit-token is given in renewal or replacement of a credit-token previously accepted under a credit-token agreement which continues in force, whether varied or not. This again is of immense practical importance in view of the frequent renewal of credit cards. Banks and building societies which issue cheque guarantee cards to customers must be wary when inviting the customer to take in the future a multi-function card combining a guarantee and credit card, for example. They must ensure that they have a request in writing before issue of the new card.

The consequences of a breach of s.51(1) are limited to a criminal infringement only: the validity of any subsequent agreement is not affected. However, there is the ever present threat that any breach of the section, whether inadvertent or not, may have consequences for the unfortunate creditor's licence on renewal.

Paragraph 15.1 of the Code of Banking Practice reinforces the effect of s.51(3) by providing that card issuers are to issue cards to customers only when they have received a request in writing or to replace or renew existing cards already issued.

4.32   Quotations and display of information

Section 52 of the Consumer Credit Act provides that regulations may be made governing the form and content of quotations to prospective customers informing them of the creditor's terms of business. Section 53 gives the power to make regulations concerning the display of information at the premises of the creditor to which the public have access. No regulations have been made under s.53, but the Consumer Credit (Quotations) Regulations 1989 (SI 1989 No.1126) have been made under s.52. It is not proposed to discuss these at any length as it is rare for credit card business to be conducted in such a way as to fall within their purview.

The Regulations came into force on 1st February 1990 and they impose a duty on a trader or credit-broker to give a quotation wherever a request to which the Regulations apply is received. To be within the Regulations (reg.4), the request must be made to a trader or a person acting on his behalf, by a customer or a person acting on his behalf, requesting a document providing information about the terms on which the trader is prepared to do business with the customer and the request must either be in writing, or made orally in the presence of the trader or person acting on his behalf, on premises where he carries on a business, or on the telephone in response to an advertisement which gives the number by means of which requests may be made as indicated by the trader. A trader is a person who carries on, for example, a consumer credit business. Generally, a customer includes any individual except a corporate body. The request must be for information in writing, otherwise it is outside the Regulations, as it will also be if it is not made in accordance with one of the three specified forms of communication. So, for example, if the request is made during a telephone call initiated by the customer, the trader need not comply with the request at all. The Regulations do not apply to requests where they relate to transactions in respect of which a quotation was given to the customer within the period of twenty-eight days prior to the request, or the request is made by or on behalf of a person living outside the UK at the time, or where it is made by or on behalf of a minor. The Regulations also do not apply where, within a reasonable time after receipt of the request, the trader informs the customer, or the person acting on his behalf, by notice in writing that he does not intend to do business with that customer (reg.6).

If the request does not conform as discussed above, the trader need not respond to it. However, if the trader does in fact volunteer written information about his terms of business, the document must comply with the Regulations (reg.5).

The information to be given is broadly the same as that to be given in full credit advertisements. However, one or two provisions are added which are of particular concern to those issuing credit cards. In the case of a quotation relating to fixed-sum credit under a DCS agreement or under a credit-token agreement, the quotation must state the amount of credit which may be provided under the agreement. In addition, in relation to running-account credit, the quotation must specify the credit limit expressed as a sum of money, include a statement that the credit limit will be determined by the creditor from time to time and notice will be given to the debtor, or a sum of money with a statement that the creditor may vary the limit in accordance with the agreement, giving notice to the debtor of any variation, and in any case not falling within the above, either a statement as to how the limit is to be calculated with notice to the debtor or indicating that there is no credit limit (Sch.1, paras.7 and 8).

4.33 Conclusion

In this chapter we have seen the many and varying controls over precontractual statements and activities imposed by the common law and statute. From the creditor's point of view, seeking business leading to the issue of a credit-token is a highly regulated affair and it pays to be fully conversant with the range of controls, particularly in the light of the possibly severe implications concerning the renewal, suspension or revocation of a consumer credit licence.

CHAPTER 5

Formalities of the Agreement

5.01 Introduction

In the previous chapter we saw how tightly regulated the credit card issuer is when seeking customers. Once a customer has been persuaded to enter into a contract with the issuer for the supply of a credit card under a regulated agreement, there is little let-up in the strictness of the controls exerted by the Consumer Credit Act 1974. Indeed, as we shall see in this chapter, the pitfalls and obstacles facing the creditor are as plentiful post-contract as they are in the precontractual period. Part V of the Act is as severe on the creditor as is Part IV. Where the agreement is regulated and not exempt from the controls in Part V, the form of the document embodying the agreement is highly prescribed by the Act and various regulations made thereunder. Not only is the document to be in a certain form, but the debtor must be supplied with a copy or copies, depending on the circumstances, and in accordance with strict time limits. These rules apply to credit-token agreements as they do to other types of consumer credit agreement, but there are slight, but nonetheless important modifications for credit-token contracts. Where an agreement is cancellable (see Chapter 6), the creditor has the burden of compliance with the rules concerning the serving of notices relating to statutory cancellation rights. The consequences of failing to comply with the formalities and the copy and cancellation rights notices are dire for the creditor. The final topic in this chapter concerns the statutory rules relating to the acceptance of credit-tokens, and the issue of PINs under the Code of Banking Practice.

5.02 Formalities of agreement

The Code of Banking Practice (Part B) exhorts its subscribers, card issuers, to express the terms and conditions of a card service in plain language and to provide a fair and balanced view of the relationship between the customer and themselves. The first of those objectives may appear difficult to realise in the light of the highly regulated nature of the form of a regulated credit agreement. Section 55 of the Consumer Credit Act gives the power to make regulations requiring specified information to be disclosed in the prescribed manner to a debtor before a regulated agreement is made. An agreement is not properly executed unless such regulations are complied with before the agreement is made. Fortunately, it has not been thought necessary to make any regulations under this provision. This is presumably because the precontractual disclosure rules discussed in the previous chapter are considered sufficiently demanding to protect the prospective debtor adequately. Those controls are in one major sense much wider than any regulations under s.55 might be, as they are not restricted to the disclosure of information in respect of regulated agreements only, as would be any s.55 regulations. However, a breach of any s.55 regulations would affect the enforceability of the subsequent agreement, whereas a breach of the regulations discussed in the previous chapter would result only in criminal sanctions.

5.03 Exemptions from Part V

Section 74 of the Act contains a number of exclusions from the provisions of Part V. An agreement exempt in this way will not be subject to the formality requirements under the Act and regulations, as well as the seemingly onerous burden of the cancellation provisions. Apart from s.56, Part V does not apply to a non-commercial agreement (s.74(1)(*a*)). Apart from ss.55 and 56, Part V does not apply to a small debtor–creditor–supplier agreement for restricted-use credit (s.74(2)). It should be noted that not all small agreements as defined in s.17 and discussed in Chapter 2 are exempt under this provision. However, Part V does not apply (with the exception of ss.55 and 56) to a small credit-token agreement.

Section 74(1)(*b*) exempts from Part V debtor–creditor agreements enabling the debtor to overdraw on a current account. By s.74(3), however, the exemption operates only where the Director General of Fair Trading so determines. His determination may be made subject to such conditions as he thinks fit. The Director may make a determination only if of the opinion that it is not against the interests of debtors. Where, however, the creditor is the Bank of England or a bank within the meaning of the Bankers' Books Evidence Act 1879, as amended, the Director must make a determination unless it would be against the public interest to do so. Such a determination has been made (21st December 1989), but one of the conditions is that the creditor should have informed the Office of Fair Trading in writing of the creditor's general intention to enter into the types of agreement covered by the determination. Thus, a bank which has satisfied this and other conditions will not have to comply with Part V solely because it allows a customer to overdraw on a current account. It should be noted that in circumstances where a customer has been issued with a debit card and a PIN and the use of the card overdraws the account, the card is in this instance a credit-token, irrespective of whether Part V applies to the agreement, and even irrespective of whether the agreement is regulated under the Act (see Chapter 7). It appears that the Director's determination requires amendment to bring it into line with the EC Directive on Consumer Credit (87/102/EEC (OJ L42, 12th February 1987) dated 22nd December 1986). This requires that the consumer is to be informed, either before or at the time of making an agreement, of the credit limit, the annual rate of interest, the charges applicable from the time the agreement is concluded and the conditions as to when these may be amended and the procedure for bringing the agreement to an end. This information is required to be in writing. Changes in the rate of interest or charges are to be communicated as soon as they occur. In any event, under the Code of Practice (paras.14.1 and 14.4), the terms and conditions of a card service, it would seem, must be in writing as we have seen and information as to variation of rates and other matters have to be in writing or in notices in stores or the press.

The final exemption relates to debtor–creditor agreements to finance the making of payments that arise on death, e.g. inheritance tax. This is unlikely to apply in the credit card context, but the exemption is again dependent on a determination by the Director (s.74(1)(*c*) and (2)).

5.04   Form and content of the agreement

The Secretary of State is under a duty to make regulations relating to the form and content of documents which embody a regulated agreement. The regulations are to contain such provisions as appear to him to be appropriate with a view to ensuring that the debtor is provided with information as to the rights and duties conferred or imposed upon him by the agreement, the amount and rate of the total charge for credit, the protection and remedies available to him under the Act, and any other matters the Secretary of State thinks it desirable he, the debtor, should know (s.60(1)). The regulations may require specified information to be included in the prescribed manner in documents and may exclude other specified material. They may contain requirements to ensure that speci-fied information is clearly brought to the attention of the debtor, and that one part of the document is not given insufficient or excessive prominence compared with another (s.60(2)).

Under s.60(3) the Director may, on application by a person carrying on a consumer credit business, if it appears to him to be impracticable for the applicant to comply with any requirement of the regulations made by the Secretary of State in a particular case, direct that the requirement be waived or varied in relation to such agreements, and be subject to such conditions (if any) as he may specify. To give a direction under this provision, the Director must be satisfied that such waiver would not prejudice debtors (s.60(4)). Goode (I[1220]) suggests that 'impracticable' does not mean just more expensive or inconvenient; equally, it should not be taken to mean impossible. If a reasonable businessman would not incur the expense or the extra effort of compliance, that should be enough to satisfy the Director.

5.05 Agreements Regulations — general requirements

The Consumer Credit (Agreements) Regulations 1983 (SI 1983 No. 1553, as amended by SI 1984 No.1600 and SI 1985 No.666) prescribe the form, content, legibility and signature of regulated consumer credit agreements. There are five heads of prescribed information: a descriptive heading specifying the legal nature of the document; the name and postal address of the parties; financial and related matters; other information; and forms of statement concerning the protection and remedies available to the debtor under the Act.

The information requirements vary according to the type of agreement. Schedules 1 and 2 to the Regulations govern the information to be included in regulated consumer credit agreements. Where items under 'financial and related matters' are not capable of being ascertained precisely, documents embodying the agreement must contain estimated information based on such assumptions as the creditor may reasonably make in the circumstances. Information as to the assumptions made must also be incorporated. The financial and related matters information must be shown together as a whole and not interspersed with other information. In the case of documents embodying regulated consumer credit agreements, the prescribed statements of the protection and remedies available to the debtor must be shown as a whole with the financial and related information. The appropriate statutory forms are set out in the Schedules and no alteration or addition is allowed other than very minor ones set out in the Regulations. Footnotes are permitted but they are not obligatory. Where a footnote contains an instruction for something to be omitted or deleted, this must be complied with.

The Regulations permit some flexibility in legibility. They state that the lettering of the terms of the agreement included in the document referred to in s.61(1)(*a*), containing all the prescribed terms of the agreement, and of the information in that document for the purpose of complying with the Regulations, is, the signature apart, to be easily legible and of a colour which is readily distinguishable from that of the paper. It is the readability of the lettering which is important here and this will involve a consideration of matters such as the size, spacing, colour and length of a line of print.

Prominence is also an issue. The Regulations state that the heading showing the nature of the document must be displayed prominently on the first page. Additionally, the APR must be given no less prominence than any of the other financial and related information and the statement of protection and remedies of the debtor. Words shown in capitals in any of the prescribed forms in the Schedules to the Regulations, though they need not necessarily be reproduced in capitals, have to be given more prominence than other lettering in the form and no less prominence than that given to any other information except the heading, APR, trade names, names of parties and lettering inserted in handwriting. The Regulations mention three ways of affording prominence: capital letters, underlining and large or bold print, but this does not exclude other means such as colour, italics and so on.

5.06   Agreements Regulations — detailed requirements

Schedule 1 of the Regulations contains the detail of the requirements for consumer credit agreements, but not all are applicable to credit-token agreements. The rules for running-account credit are generally less severe than those for fixed-sum credit. The following matters must be included in a credit-token agreement:

(1)   a heading stating 'Credit Agreement regulated by the Consumer Credit Act 1974' and the names of the parties to the agreement;

(2)   details of any amount payable in advance by the debtor, e.g. a payment for the issue of the token itself;

(3)   a statement of the credit limit, with details of how this might be varied (if at all);

(4)   a statement of the rate of interest and other items in the total charge for credit;

(5)   the amount of the repayments, their frequency and the date of the first payment;

(6)   the APR: if the creditor reserves the right to alter the rate of interest, the agreement must state that the APR has been calculated

excluding this possibility and specify the basis for the use of the power to vary;

(7) although not often employed in the credit-token context, if the creditor wishes to include default charges, full details must be given.

All the above information must be included in the agreement and is designed to enable the debtor to appreciate his financial responsibilities under it. Equally important, however, are the details of the protection and remedies for the debtor which Sch.2 to the Regulations requires to be inserted. In appropriate cases a cancellation notice may have to be inserted in the document embodying a credit-token agreement. This will be discussed below. A notice giving details of the debtor's right to early settlement (Chapter 12) of the agreement has to be included, together with a notice concerning the possibility of obtaining compensation from the creditor if there has been a breach of contract by the supplier of the goods and services acquired by the use of the token (see Chapter 9). Finally, and possibly most importantly, the agreement must contain a notice regarding the extent of the debtor's liability in the event of loss or misuse of the credit-token (see Chapter 7). In this context, it would be wise for the creditor to include the name, address and telephone number of a person to whom notice is to be given under s.84(3) of loss, theft or possibility of misuse of a credit-token. If the creditor wishes to exercise his right to impose limited liability on the debtor in such circumstances, then the credit-token agreement must contain such detail prominently displayed and easily legible (s.84(4) and the Consumer Credit (Credit-Token Agreements) Regulations 1983, SI 1983 No.1555). Of course, failure to include such information does not render the agreement improperly executed, but merely means that the creditor cannot take advantage of the limited liability provision imposed on the debtor under s.84 of the Act.

5.07 General requirements of the Consumer Credit Act

So far we have considered the general and detailed formality requirements specified by the Agreements Regulations made under the power in s.60. The Act itself also specifies a number of general requirements which require close consideration. Section 61(1) provides that an agreement is not properly executed unless:

(1) a document in the prescribed form itself containing all the prescribed terms and conforming to regulations made under s.60(1) is signed in the prescribed manner both by the debtor or hirer and by or on behalf of the creditor or owner; and

(2)   the document embodies all the terms of the agreement, other than implied terms; and
(3)   the document is, when presented for signature, in such a state that all its terms are readily legible.

Paragraph (1) refers to the Regulations made under s.60 (discussed above), which prescribe the form and some of the terms to be included in the agreement. To comply with this paragraph, the agreement must itself contain the prescribed terms, so that a reference to another document containing them will not suffice. An agent cannot normally sign for the debtor. If there is more than one debtor, both must sign. According to the Regulations, the signature should be in a box with a statutory warning as to the legal consequences of signing.

Paragraph (2) appears to cover the situation where the agreement does not contain all the terms itself, but refers to another document which does. If, however, the agreement or any document under para.(2) does not contain all the express terms of the contract, the agreement will be improperly executed. Section 61 prevents what used to be a common practice of obtaining the debtor's signature to a blank form, the detail being filled in later by the dealer or creditor. This would now render the agreement improperly executed.

5.08   Copy requirements

The copy requirements are an equally important aspect of the formalities imposed by the Act. There would be little point in insisting on strict control over the form of the agreement, without equally strict regulation of the supply of copies of it to the debtor.

Sections 62 and 63 of the Consumer Credit Act are designed to ensure that the debtor is given ample opportunity to consider the terms of the agreement into which he has entered or is about to enter. The sections normally require two copies of the agreement to be supplied to the debtor, namely, a copy of the unexecuted agreement, and at some later stage a copy of the executed agreement. An 'executed' agreement is a document signed by or on behalf of the parties, embodying the terms of a regulated agreement, or such of them as have been reduced to writing. An 'unexecuted' agreement is a prospective regulated agreement, i.e. it has not yet been signed by or on behalf of both parties (s.189(1)). It may have been signed by one of the parties, but it is still unexecuted.

Section 62(1) provides that where the unexecuted agreement is presented personally to the debtor for signature, but, on the occasion when he signs it, the document does not become executed because it has not yet been signed by or on behalf of the creditor, a copy of the unexecuted agreement, and of any other document referred to in it, must be delivered to the debtor there and then. As a follow up to this, s.63(2) provides that a copy of the executed agreement, and of any other document referred to in it, must be given to the debtor within the seven days following its making. The agreement is executed once it has been signed by or on behalf of the creditor in the circumstances under discussion.

A number of points are to be noted here. First, when the agreement is signed by the debtor it is unexecuted and at this stage there is no contract between the parties. The debtor has, by signing the credit card agreement, or as the case may be, made an offer to enter into it. Until acceptance by the creditor there is no concluded contract, under basic principles. This point is explored further in the next chapter when we consider withdrawal from an agreement. Secondly, it should be noted that the second copy (a copy of the executed agreement) must be sent within seven days of the 'making' of the agreement, not within seven days of the execution of the agreement (i.e. the creditor signing). This distinction is of no significance in the case of credit-token agreements, as s.63(4) provides that the copy of the executed agreement (the second copy) need not be sent within those seven days provided it is given before or at the time of the credit-token is given to the debtor. In practice, therefore, as long as the copy of the executed agreement arrives with the credit-token itself, there should be no problem for the creditor. Thirdly, if either the unexecuted copy or the second copy rules are not complied with the agreement is improperly executed. Finally, if the agreement in question is cancellable (see Chapter 6), the second copy must be sent by post.

It is highly likely that when the credit card agreement is signed by the debtor, it will at that stage remain unexecuted in which case the analysis above will apply. The position would not differ if the agreement were sent to the debtor for his signature and it remained unexecuted after he signed. Section 62(2) provides that in those circumstances a copy of the agreement and of any other document referred to in it must be sent at the same time. Similarly, s.63(2) provides for the second, executed copy to be sent in just the same way as where the agreement is presented personally to the debtor. Section 63(4), as before, relaxes the seven-day rule in the case of a credit-token agreement.

There are exceptions to the two-copy rule. If the agreement is presented to the debtor personally, or is sent to him for signature, and in either case it becomes an executed agreement on his signature, there is no need to send a further copy, and the copy under s.62(1) or (2) will suffice. There would be little point in sending the second copy as the debtor, once the document was signed by him, would have a complete document in his possession. In one further situation there is no need to supply two copies. If the application for credit is freely available on display to the public, and it is completed and signed by the debtor and sent to the creditor, then in this type of case the creditor need send only a copy of the executed agreement under s.63(2); if it is a credit-token agreement, this need only be sent with the token itself as we have already seen.

According to the Consumer Credit (Cancellation Notices and Copies of Documents) Regulations 1983 (SI 1983 No.1557) every copy of an executed agreement, security instrument or other document referred to in the Act and delivered or sent to the debtor under any provision of the Act must be a true copy. It seems that this will extend also to an unexecuted copy. This does not mean an exact copy, although it should be recalled that there can be little room or scope for deviation from the strict requirements in the Agreements Regulations, bearing in mind the legibility, prominence and presentational obligations imposed upon the creditor. Some minor deviations are allowed.

There are other situations, peculiar to credit-token agreements, when a further copy of the executed agreement must be given to the debtor. Section 85 of the Consumer Credit Act states that whenever, in connection with a credit-token agreement, a credit-token (other than the first) is given by the creditor to the debtor, the creditor must give the debtor a copy of the executed agreement (if any) and of any other document referred to in it. This is clearly designed to remind the debtor of the terms of the agreement on a replacement or renewal of the token. It would seem that this is also meant to cover the situation where the supply is of an additional card for an authorised user. In this situation, the copy, presumably, must be given to the debtor and there is no obligation to give a copy to the authorised user as such. By s.185(1)(*a*), where there are joint debtors, a copy must be served on both of them. Any copy sent must contain the current terms of the agreement, whether varied or not (Consumer Credit (Cancellation Notices and Copies of Documents) Regulations 1983). The Act is strangely silent on when the copy must be given, so it seems that it need not necessarily accompany the token itself, although this normally happens and is good practice. Failure to comply with s.85 prevents the creditor from enforcing the agreement while the default continues. If it continues for one month, the creditor commits an offence. This is perhaps an indication of an appropriate time scale for the delivery of the s.85 copy. The requirement under s.85 does not apply to small agreements (s.85(3)).

5.09 Cancellation notices

When discussing the detailed requirements under the Agreements Regulations earlier in this chapter, it was mentioned that in some instances it is necessary to include a cancellation notice in the agreement. Such a notice must be included in every copy of a cancellable agreement, whether executed or unexecuted (s.64). The notice must be in the prescribed form, advising the debtor of his or her right to cancel the agreement, how and when that right is exercisable and the name and address of a person to whom notice of cancellation may be given. The prescribed form is set out in the Consumer Credit (Cancellation Notices and Copies of Documents) Regulations 1983.

If the agreement becomes an executed agreement when signed by the debtor, s.63(2), as we have seen, requires only one copy of the agreement to be given. If the agreement is cancellable under s.67 (see next chapter), that copy must contain the prescribed notice of cancellation rights. In addition, however, s.64(1)(*b*) requires that a further notice of cancellation rights in the prescribed form must be sent by post to the debtor within seven days of the making of the agreement. It should be noted that a full copy of the agreement need not be sent and that the seven-day period runs from the making of the agreement, not its execution. For credit-token agreements, the seven-day rule is relaxed, provided the notice is sent by post either before the token is sent or together with it. Note that it must be sent by post, as must a second copy of the agreement if it is cancellable (s.63(3)). This second copy or separate notice of cancellation rights is important for another reason. As we shall see in the next chapter, the receipt of one of these triggers the operation of the cancellation period. There is power to exempt by regulation certain agreements from the burden of the separate notice of cancellation rights under s.64(1)(*b*). Regulations have been made but they do not affect credit-token agreements, only credit by mail order at present.

Finally, a failure to comply with the provisions of s.64 will render the agreement improperly executed. As we shall see, the consequences of this are extremely serious for the creditor.

There are different prescribed forms for use in respect of cancellation notices depending on whether the notice is in a copy of the unexecuted or the executed agreement, or whether it is the separate notice under s.64(1)(*b*). Each notice must be in a box, which must contain nothing else. Where the notice of cancellation rights does not appear prominently on the first page of any copy agreement delivered or sent to the debtor, there must be a box on the first page containing a statement specified in the Schedule to the Regulations. In addition to the notice, each copy of the executed agreement must contain as a distinct item a cancellation form for use by the debtor if he so wishes. Likewise, where the separate notice is sent under s.64(1)(*b*), there must be a similar cancellation form. In this instance, however, it must be an integral part of the form and on a single piece of paper. If the notice covers only one side of the paper, the form must also be on that side. If the notice runs over the page, at the foot of the text the word and symbol 'over' must appear.

5.10   Effect of non-compliance

As mentioned above, ss.61, 62(3), 63(5) and 64(5) all state that non-compliance with their respective provisions renders the agreement improperly executed. Section 65(1) takes this one step further by stating that an improperly executed agreement is enforceable against the debtor only by order of the court; it is enforceable by the debtor against the creditor without the need for the court's approval.

Generally, it is likely that a court would be prepared to make an enforcement order in favour of the creditor. The language of the Act is such that a court may refuse an enforcement order if, but only if, it considers it just to do so, having regard to any prejudice caused to any person by the contravention in question, and the degree of culpability for it. The court is also to consider its powers conferred on it by s.127(2) and ss.135 and 136. Section 127(2) enables the court to make an order and at the same time compensate the debtor for any prejudice suffered by him as a result of the breach of the formality provisions, by reducing or discharging any sum payable by him or a surety. Sections 135 and 136 give the court wide powers to impose conditions or suspend the effect of any order and vary agreements and securities respectively. There ought to be few circumstances in which a court would refuse to make an enforcement order in favour of the creditor, bearing in mind these wide powers. A mere technical infringement with minimal culpability should cause no difficulty.

However, there are three cases in which the court is not able to make an enforcement order. Section 127(3) provides that the court has no power to grant an order under s.65(1) if s.61(1)(*a*) (signing of agreements – see (1) in para.5.07) was not complied with unless a document, whether or not in the prescribed form and complying with regulations under s.60(1), itself containing all the prescribed terms of the agreement, was signed by the debtor, whether or not in the prescribed manner. The effect of this is to emphasise that compliance with s.61(1)(*a*) is essential, in that the creditor must ensure that the debtor has signed a document containing the prescribed terms, if nothing else. A failure to observe the other formalities in s.61 is redeemable and is not a total bar to an enforcement order. Section 127(5) allows the court to disregard terms omitted from the document signed by the debtor but only when making an enforcement order under subs.(3).

Section 127(4) provides that a court shall not make an enforcement order under s.65(1) in the case of a cancellable agreement if a provision of s.62 or 63 was not complied with, and the creditor or owner did not give a copy of the executed agreement, and of any other document referred to in it, to the debtor or hirer before the commencement of the proceedings in which the order is sought, or if s.64(1) was not complied with.

It seems from this that a failure to comply with the copy requirements under ss.62 and 63 is capable of being redeemed, but that a failure to follow the cancellation notice procedure in s.64 makes the agreement permanently unenforceable. Where the court does refuse or is not able to make an enforcement order, the creditor is obviously in a difficult position. Any attempt to terminate the agreement or claim any money and interest outstanding under it will clearly be an enforcement. In the context of a credit-token agreement, clearly the creditor cannot sue for repayment by the debtor where the card has already been used. Is the creditor allowed to prevent further use of the card by the debtor and, furthermore, is the creditor entitled to reclaim the card if the issue of ownership of the card has been covered in the agreement itself? With regard to the first issue, it would surely be the case that a court would not regard this as enforcement of the agreement. As to the second, this might amount to enforcement, although it might be possible to bring the action for the recovery of the card in the tort of conversion. The creditor would be using the term in the contract to establish his better right to the card over the debtor, but would not strictly be enforcing the contract. However, if the creditor is permitted, as seems likely, to cut off the source of the credit, the card itself will be virtually worthless and the creditor will have achieved the major objective.

5.11   Acceptance of credit-tokens

The final topic in this chapter concerns the issue of precisely when the debtor becomes liable for the use of the credit-token. This ties in to some extent with the discussion in Chapter 7 on the debtor's liability for loss or misuse of the credit-token. It is discussed here because in a sense the issue under the 1974 Act is one of formality, as we shall see. The agreement between the creditor and debtor might specify that the liability of the debtor starts immediately on the making of the agreement, or at some later stage, for example, when the token is sent to or received by the debtor. All these alternatives place the risk of the token falling into the wrong hands and being misused firmly upon the debtor. For regulated agreements, the Act intervenes and postpones the debtor's liability until such time (if ever) as the token is 'accepted' by him or her under the provisions in s.66. The debtor accepts a token when it is signed, or a receipt for it is signed, or it is first used, either by the debtor himself or by a person who, pursuant to the agreement, is authorised by the debtor to use it.

The first point to note is that this section applies only where the token is issued under a regulated credit-token agreement. Therefore, although a credit card might fall within the definition of a credit-token in s.14 of the Act if it is otherwise unregulated by the 1974 Act, the debtor's liability for its use will depend on the terms of the contract, which are likely to favour the creditor, or in certain circumstances reference may be made to the Code of Banking Practice (see below) although this of marginal utility in these circumstances or so it appears.

Secondly, it is not sufficient for the creditor to prove that the debtor has received the token. One of the three positive acts must be established and the burden is clearly on the creditor (s.171(4)) to show that the token was lawfully supplied to the debtor and accepted by him, should the creditor wish to bring proceedings under the agreement. This raises one particular difficulty where the creditor wishes to sue on a term of the agreement which is operational before acceptance takes place. For example, the agreement might specify that on the making of the agreement the debtor shall make an advance payment. This might be a fee for the issue of the token. If by oversight this is not paid, but the token is still issued and the debtor does not accept it in accordance with s.66, it would seem that the creditor cannot bring proceedings for the fee because it cannot show that the token has been accepted. This would be unfair, as the acceptance rules are merely designed to place the risk of misuse of the token on the creditor until acceptance, rather than prevent the enforcement of the other terms of the contract by the creditor. It would seem to be in the creditor's interests to keep the period between the making of the contract and the issue of the token as short as possible, or to use secure techniques to ensure that the card cannot be used or tampered with before being received by the debtor. In the case of two-party store cards this is relatively easy, as the debtor can be invited to collect the card from a conveniently placed store, or the creditor can provide that the card be validated (electronically or otherwise) before first use and on proof of identity by the debtor.

Thirdly, the need for acceptance by the debtor under s.66 will arise every time a replacement or renewal card is issued. Additionally, where the debtor arranges for further cards to be issued to authorised users, acceptance has to take place for each of the additional cards before any liability on the debtor can arise from its use. The creditor, therefore, runs the potential risk of loss on several occasions under one credit-token agreement.

Fourthly, acceptance under s.66 is clearly one of fact. Where the debtor signs for a package containing the credit-token, it is suggested that this is not a receipt for the token within s.66 as the receipt must relate specifically to the token itself. The Act provides that the acceptance need not be by the debtor but may be by an authorised user on first use of the token. If the debtor does not sign the card, or a receipt for it, and allows another person to use it, even though that person is not a declared authorised user, it is suggested that this would constitute first use by the debtor (but see Jones, p.145).

Fifthly, it seems that once the card has been accepted by the debtor, e.g. by signing it, the debtor is liable on it, subject to what is said in Chapter 7, even though it may not be in force until some time in the future.

Finally, s.66 is the starting point of the debtor's liability under the credit-token agreement. It would seem to override the provisions in s.84 of the Act where there is any conflict or overlap between them.

5.12 Card security and the Code of Banking Practice

The Code of Banking Practice contains several provisions designed to ensure card security. Initially, card issuers are to satisfy themselves about the identity of a person seeking to open an account or obtain a card and are to provide customers with details of the necessary identification (para.13.1 and 2). We have seen that card issuers will issue cards only when requested in writing or to replace or renew cards already issued (para.15.1). Card issuers are to tell customers whether a card issued by them has more than one function. There has been some controversy where card issuers have insisted on issuing PINs against the wishes of the customer. They are now obliged to accede to the customer's request (para.15.2).

PINs are to be issued separately from the cards and the PIN is to be advised to the customer only (para.16.1). These last provisions go beyond the statutory rules in s.66, and as they appear in a non-statutory code are not binding on a court. However, they are intended to be examples of good banking practice and a court will no doubt be willing to listen to arguments based on them should a relevant point arise in litigation. This might be the case irrespective of whether or not the credit card issuer was a subscriber to the Code. Certainly, the Banking and Building Societies Ombudsmen will give great weight to the Code's provisions in matters within their terms of reference (see Chapter 13).

5.13   Conclusion

In this chapter it has been seen that the credit-token agreement, like nearly all other regulated consumer credit agreements, is a highly and intensively controlled relationship. The penalties for failing to comply with the formalities in the Act and regulations made thereunder are visited without fear or favour upon errant creditors. We have seen that the form of the agreement and its contents are subject to detailed regulations, and that the copy and cancellation notice requirements are severe on the creditor in the light of the enforcement powers of the court. Furthermore, the Act places a substantial burden of risk on creditors because of the unfavourable rules on acceptance contained in s.66. As with the rules on seeking business, described in the preceding chapter, it pays to approach the formality requirements correctly.

CHAPTER 6

Cancellation and Withdrawal from Credit Card Agreements

6.01 Introduction

This chapter discusses the debtor's rights to withdraw from a prospective agreement and to cancel an agreement. Frequently, a debtor may be pressured in some way into signing a document which relates to a credit transaction, which he or she later, sometimes almost instantly, regrets for one reason or another. If all the normal elements of a contract are present and there is a concluded contract, at common law little can usually be done to enable the unfortunate debtor to extricate himself or herself from the agreement. Traditionally, the common law has taken the view that once a contract is made, then however bad the bargain is for one of the parties, there is no way out for that party in the absence of fraud, duress or other vitiating factor.

The credit field, however, has long been recognised as a special case, high-pressure sales techniques that persuade debtors to get into debt way above their heads being considered socially undesirable and detrimental to the family unit. The Hire-Purchase Acts contained provisions whereby in certain circumstances a debtor could cancel what would otherwise have been a binding contract. This right was narrow in that it applied only to certain types of credit agreement, in the main (but not exclusively) hire-purchase agreements. On the other hand, the aim of the provisions was to minimise the perceived harmful effect of doorstep sales in which the high-pressure sales techniques were used with considerable success for the creditors but often resulted in abject misery for the debtor. The wording of the provisions, however, was sufficiently wide to catch other transactions. The Consumer Credit Act 1974 sought to meet these imperfections by widening the scope of the cancellation provisions to include other means of providing credit, thus taking in credit card agreements, and at the same time narrowing the coverage by restricting the provisions to face-to-face situations where the agreement was signed away from the business premises of the creditor and those associated with him.

Withdrawal from a prospective agreement is governed by the common law in the main. It is merely the right of an offeror to withdraw his offer to contract before that offer has been accepted. Having said that, the 1974 Act does contain specific reference to the right to withdraw in an attempt to tidy up some loose ends left by the common law.

The right to cancel is generally one of the most important given to debtors by the 1974 Act. Its importance in the context of credit cards is perhaps not as great as in relation to, say, the hire-purchase agreement. One reason for this is no doubt because there is in practice less chance of a credit card agreement being cancellable, particularly where it is common for the communications leading to the making of the contract to be conducted through the post rather than face to face. Even where it can be classified as cancellable, the debtor's position under a credit card agreement is likely to be less dire than that of the reluctant hire-purchaser who finds the contract too expensive. After all, there is usually no obligation actually to use the card and incur any debt. Nonetheless, situations can arise where the debtor may have the right to cancel and wishes to exercise that right.

The discussion will start with the rules about withdrawal from a credit card agreement. We then consider when an agreement is cancellable, how and when the right is exercisable and, finally, the consequences for the parties of both withdrawal and cancellation.

6.02   Withdrawal

Withdrawal of an offer to enter into a regulated credit card agreement is possible, in just the same way as it is possible to withdraw or revoke an unaccepted offer in respect of any type of contract. The right to withdraw arises, as mentioned in the preceding section, under the common law rules on offer, acceptance and revocation of offers. Section 57 of the 1974 Act was inserted to resolve a few issues relating to credit agreements untouched by the common law. The section does not replace the common law; rather, it builds upon the common law rules.

The general rule is that a person may withdraw an offer to contract at any time prior to its valid acceptance by the offeree, unless the offeror has bound himself to keep the offer open, either under seal or by means of another contract, namely, a binding option. Section 59(1), however, provides that an agreement is void if, and to the extent that, it purports to bind a person to enter as a debtor into a prospective regulated agreement. This means that the debtor cannot be made to enter into a regulated agreement by virtue of a term in another agreement, although this is not likely to happen in practice in the credit card context. Section 59(2) provides that regulations may be made to exempt agreements from the prohibition in s.59(1). Regulations have been made but they are not relevant to credit-token agreements. It should be noted that s.59(1) does not prevent a creditor from agreeing to enter into a regulated agreement.

Withdrawal from a prospective agreement is possible in the credit field, although prospective debtors may mistakenly believe that once they have signed a document they have concluded a binding contract and cannot extricate themselves. More often than not, the signing of the document in question will amount in law to an offer by the prospective debtor to enter into an agreement, an offer capable of being withdrawn before acceptance by the creditor has taken place. If the credit card issuer sends the agreement to the debtor for signature, it is unlikely that the creditor has at this stage executed it. If it is then signed by the debtor and returned to the creditor, there is still no actual contract in existence. This occurs only when the document is executed by the creditor and the approval letter is sent with the copy of the executed agreement to the debtor. The position would be the same if the agreement, on being presented personally to the debtor for signature, remained unexecuted after signature by him. Until such time as the creditor does send by post the letter of approval, the debtor is free to withdraw from the transaction. On the other hand, if in the two situations envisaged above, the agreement is executed as soon as it is signed by the debtor, the contract is concluded there and then. The debtor cannot withdraw his offer and, if wishing to extricate himself from the contract, must rely on the right of cancellation, if any. It must be emphasised that the right of withdrawal is a common law right and applies to any credit agreement, irrespective of whether it is one to which the statutory right of cancellation applies, a point sometimes overlooked. This distinction is further highlighted when the effects of a withdrawal are considered. The Act provides that a withdrawal is to have the same effect as if the agreement had been made and then cancelled, irrespective of whether the agreement was a prospective cancellable agreement (s.57(4)).

6.03 Mode of withdrawal

At common law an offer may be withdrawn in a variety of ways provided the withdrawal is communicated before there is a valid acceptance. There is no required formality and this approach is adopted in the 1974 Act itself. Section 57(2) provides that notification of withdrawal from a prospective regulated agreement can be either written or oral. It does not matter how it is expressed as long as it plainly indicates that the debtor does not wish to go ahead with the transaction.

Normally, at common law the communication of withdrawal must actually reach the offeree, which will usually be the credit card issuer, before it is effective. The 1974 Act provides for a far wider category of persons to whom notification of withdrawal may be effectively communicated. Section 57(3) deems the following persons to be the agent of the creditor:

(1) a credit–broker or supplier who is the negotiator in antecedent negotiations; and

(2) any person who, in the course of a business carried on by him, acts on behalf of the debtor or hirer in any negotiations for the agreement.

A supplier who introduces a debtor to a credit card company will be a deemed agent to receive notice of withdrawal under para.(1), although at common law he would not be regarded as such. Paragraph (2) seems strange, in that it deems a person who has acted on behalf of the debtor to be the agent of the creditor in this particular context. Clearly, at common law such a person would be regarded as the agent of the debtor in most instances. The type of person falling into this category might be a solicitor, accountant or mortgage broker acting for the debtor. To fall within the provision such a person must be actively involved in the negotiations which are to lead to the prospective agreement. This would seem to put the creditor at a serious disadvantage, but s.175 of the Act provides that the deemed agent has a contractual duty to transmit the information as to withdrawal forthwith, i.e. as soon as is reasonably practicable. A breach of this section gives rise to an action for damages by the creditor against the deemed agent. A credit card issuer who suffered loss because of the lack of communication by the person falling within s.57(3), could recover it as long as it was not too remote under normal contractual principles, namely, within the reasonable contemplation of the parties. If the creditor, unaware of the withdrawal by the prospective debtor, were to proceed to issue a credit-token and this was used by the debtor or by an unauthorised user, this loss, if the money could not be recovered, would be recoverable from the deemed agent.

6.04 Consequences of withdrawal

The primary effect of a valid withdrawal is, of course, that there is no concluded contract between the creditor and the debtor. Section 57(1) provides further:

'The withdrawal of a party from a prospective regulated agreement shall operate to apply this Part to the agreement, any linked transaction and any other thing done in anticipation of the making of the agreement as it would apply if the agreement were made and then cancelled under section 69.'

Despite the roundabout wording of the subsection, its clear effect is to apply all the provisions of ss.68 to 73 relating to the consequences of cancellation of an agreement to a withdrawal from a prospective agreement. As we saw earlier, this means that the debtor has the advantage of the rules in those sections even in situations where the prospective regulated agreement was non-cancellable (s.57(4)). The debtor therefore benefits from the rules on cancellation of linked transactions, withdrawal of offers to enter into linked transactions, recovery of payments made by the debtor and the return of part-exchange goods or the part-exchange allowance. These are all matters about which there is much uncertainty at common law, although the recovery of monies paid in respect of an agreement which never comes into being would normally be recoverable on the basis of a total failure of consideration. The detail of these rules is explored below in the discussion of the consequences of cancellation, but it is worth emphasising at this stage that the creditor must repay any sums paid to him by the debtor, for example to cover precontractual expenses (even if actually incurred), irrespective of what the parties may have actually agreed, e.g. that the sum is not refundable in any event.

The final point on withdrawal is that there are special formality rules in respect of withdrawal from prospective land mortgages which are designed to obviate the need for statutory cancellation of such agreements with all the practical problems that this would involve. These are contained in s.58 of the Act, which gives the prospective debtor under such an agreement a precontractual period for reflection before signing the agreement. This need concern us no further as it is scarcely relevant in the credit-token context.

6.05 Cancellation

As mentioned in the Introduction, this is an extremely valuable right for the person who has second thoughts about the credit agreement fairly soon after signing it. It is not available at common law unless the agreement itself contains a cancellation clause, which will be rare in most consumer credit agreements, the credit card agreement no less so. Some issuers do, however, when including the required statutory notices in relation to cancellable agreements in their contracts, state that if the agreement is not cancellable under the Act, the agreement itself will confer such a right. Statutory cancellation rights are also seldom given and, in this particular context, not every regulated consumer credit agreement is, so far as the debtor is concerned, subject to such privileged status. The aim of the cancellation rights in the Act is to strike at those practices associated with high-pressure selling on the doorstep, although, as will be seen, the provisions do catch transactions that could hardly be said to be conducted on the doorstep. The Act creates a category of agreements which are considered to be cancellable. The right of cancellation is conferred by s.67, which reads:

'A regulated agreement may be cancelled by the debtor or hirer in accordance with this Part if the antecedent negotiations included oral representations made when in the presence of the debtor or hirer by an individual acting as, or on behalf of, the negotiator, unless —

(*a*)   the agreement is secured on land, or is a restricted-use credit agreement to finance the purchase of land or is an agreement for a bridging loan in connection with the purchase of land, or

(*b*)   the unexecuted agreement is signed by the debtor or hirer at premises where any of the following is carrying on any business (whether on a permanent or temporary basis) —

   (i)   the creditor or owner;
   (ii)   any party to a linked transaction (other than the debtor or hirer or a relative of his);
   (iii)   the negotiator in any antecedent negotiations.'

6.06   Exemptions from cancellation

Apart from the major exemption in respect of agreements secured on land as specified in s.67(*a*), these provisions apply only to regulated agreements and therefore there is no statutory right to cancel an exempt agreement such as American Express or Diner's Club. Other agreements not caught are those specified in s.74 as being generally exempt from Part V of the Act, i.e. non-commercial agreements, current account overdrafts and agreements to finance payments on death, as discussed in para.5.3, above. Also, s.74(2) provides, as we have already seen, that some small agreements are outside the scope of Part V, namely, small debtor–creditor–supplier agreements for restricted-use credit. The effect of this is to exempt small credit-token agreements, among others, from the scope of Part V. This still remains the position after the introduction of s.74(2A) by the Consumer Protection (Cancellation of Contracts Concluded Away from Business Premises) Regulations 1987 (SI 1987 No.2117). This is of marginal impact so far as credit card issuers are concerned, but nonetheless requires some explanation.

The 1987 Regulations are a result of the EC Directive on doorstep selling (85/577/EEC (OJ L372, 31st December 1985, p.31) dated 20th December 1985) and are made under s.2(2) of the European Communities Act 1972. They give a consumer a right of cancellation entirely distinct from that in the 1974 Act, for example where a consumer enters into a contract with a trader for the supply of goods and services during an unsolicited visit by a trader (not necessarily the one with whom the contract is made) to the home of the consumer or to the home of another person or to the consumer's place of work. Among other things, the Regulations do not apply where the total payment under the contract does not exceed £35 or to credit agreements where the credit does not exceed £35. Agreements which are cancellable under the 1974 Act are not cancellable under the Regulations. However, credit agreements not cancellable under the Act are cancellable under the Regulations if they otherwise fall within the Regulations. Section 74(2A) provides, in a rather clumsy fashion, that in the case of a credit agreement falling within the 1987 Regulations, the reference in s.74(2) to a small agreement is to be construed as if the relevant figure was £35 rather than £50. The effect of this is that the small credit-token agreement where the credit limit is less than £35 is cancellable under neither the Act nor the 1987 Regulations. Where, however, such agreement provides for credit over £35 but not exceeding £50 and the agreement would fall within the ambit of the 1987 Regulations, the agreement may be cancellable under the Act, assuming the conditions in s.67 are satisfied. It should also be noted that the 1987 Regulations may apply to credit agreements which are otherwise not cancellable, either because they enjoy exemption from Part V under the other provisions in s.74, or they are exempt under s.16 or the credit exceeds £15,000.

6.07   Antecedent negotiations

The meaning of 'antecedent negotiations' is vital to the working of the cancellation provisions in s.67. It is also of extreme significance in the context of the deemed agency provisions in s.56(2) of the Act, considered later in Chapter 10. The definition is contained in s.56(1) and (4).

Section 56(1) provides that 'antecedent negotiations' means any negotiations with the debtor or hirer:

'(*a*) conducted by the creditor or owner in relation to the making of any regulated agreement, or

(*b*) conducted by a credit-broker in relation to goods sold or proposed to be sold by the credit-broker to the creditor before forming the subject matter of a debtor–creditor– supplier agreement within section 12(*a*), or

(*c*) conducted by the supplier in relation to a transaction financed or proposed to be financed by a debtor–creditor– supplier agreement within section 12(*b*) or (*c*), and "negotiator" means the person by whom negotiations are so conducted with the debtor or hirer.'

Section 56(4) states that, for the purposes of the Act, antecedent negotiations shall be taken to begin when the negotiator and the debtor or hirer first enter into communication (including communication by advertisement), and to include any representations made by the negotiator to the debtor or hirer and any other dealings between them.

The precise width of these provisions is explored in Chapter 10. Suffice it to say at this stage that the term is extremely wide and includes advertisements and any other dealings between the parties. For present purposes it is important to be able to define antecedent negotiations in the first place, before going on to consider whether those negotiations included oral representations, as required by s.67 if the agreement is to be cancellable. It is also crucial to be able to identify a person who may be regarded as a 'negotiator' for the same reason.

6.08 Negotiator

The oral representations must be made to the debtor by a person who falls into one of the three categories in s.56(1). Falling within para.(*a*) would be the situation where, in a two-party card arrangement, the employee of the creditor, namely, the store issuing the credit-token, discussed the matter with the debtor, whether at the store or elsewhere. The negotiator here would be the creditor itself, not the employee. The position would be the same if the discussions were carried on by a person who was, at common law, the agent of the creditor. If, for example, a credit card issuer authorised a store or bank with which it otherwise had no connection to discuss applications to the creditor for credit-tokens, the store or bank would be the creditor's agent and the negotiator would be the creditor. This type of situation must arise very rarely, but if it did the three-party card agreement would fall into this paragraph as well as the two-party one.

Paragraph (*b*) applies only to s.12(*a*) DCS agreements (namely, hire-purchase, conditional and credit-sale agreements) and as the usual credit-token agreement can be a DCS only under s.12(*b*), this need be discussed no further in this context.

Paragraph (*c*) contemplates that a supplier might be a negotiator, and Goode states (I[1433]) that this will include a supplier selling goods against a credit card. This statement is not without some controversy and will be returned to later in Chapter 10. For present purposes, if a supplier has an arrangement to accept a particular credit card and becomes involved in promoting the card with customers, then discussions by the supplier with the prospective debtor may be antecedent negotiations, the supplier being the negotiator. This situation does not arise often, however, if at all.

As mentioned above the negotiations begin at the first point of contact between the debtor and the creditor, and, as they are expressed to be 'antecedent', it is safely assumed that they finish at the point when the regulated agreement comes into being. Post-contractual statements are not capable of being antecedent negotiations.

6.09   Oral representations

Having decided what amounts to the antecedent negotiations, for the purpose of s.67 and its operation, it is necessary to see whether they contain any 'oral representations' and, equally important, were those representations made when in the presence of the debtor, i.e. face to face? If there have been no such representations, the agreement is not cancellable.

The representations need not relate to the credit agreement directly, but might relate to the goods and services which might be supplied using the credit agreement as the finance (see to the contrary, Jones, p.128). They need not constitute misrepresentations and, as Goode points out (I[1436]), the expression is much wider than the common law meaning attributed to a 'mere representation'. It includes any condition or warranty, and any other statement or undertaking, whether oral or in writing (s.189(1)), including matters of opinion, statements intended to be terms of the contract and statements not intended to induce a contract at all. Whilst it does not seem to matter whether the representations are directed specifically at the debtor, they must be made in his presence. This excludes telephone, telex, fax and any other form of instantaneous communication. Finally, it should be noted that it does not matter where the oral representations take place as long as they are in the debtor's presence. If the discussions, for example, take place at the business premises of the creditor, this does not prevent their being oral representations for the purpose of s.67. The place where the agreement is signed by the debtor is relevant for s.67.

6.10   Place of signature by debtor

The cooling-off provisions in the Act do not apply if the agreement is signed by the debtor at the business premises of the creditor, any party to a linked transaction (other than the debtor or a relative of his) or the negotiator in the antecedent negotiations. The premises need not be permanent. If the agreement is, for example, signed at a stand at an exhibition or at a mobile caravan belonging to the creditor or one of the other parties mentioned in s.67, the agreement will not be cancellable. Signature at the business premises of the debtor or some other place of business falling outside the categories in s.67 will not preclude the cancellation provisions. It seems that it is for the creditor to prove that the agreement was signed at appropriate business premises, as it is the creditor who wishes to take advantage of the exception in s.67. Where the agreement is to be entered into by joint debtors, it seems that if just one of them signs away from appropriate business premises the agreement will be cancellable.

6.11   Notice of cancellation rights

Cancellation notices were considered in the preceding chapter (para.5.9) as an element in the formalities to which a regulated cancellable agreement is subject. Because of the dire penalty of unenforceability of a cancellable agreement in circumstances where the cancellation notice procedure was omitted, creditors sometimes insert such a notice in cases of doubt, to be on the safe side. In that situation, if it transpires that the agreement is non-cancellable, the creditor is probably conferring a contractual right of cancellation upon the debtor. In the event of a change of mind, the debtor may exercise that right. How, when and to whom this may be done will depend on the terms of the contract, but it may well be the case that by inserting the unnecessary clause, the creditor will have incorporated into the contract the statutory rules on cancellation in ss.68 to 73 for the benefit of the debtor.

Jones (p.134) states that sometimes the creditor puts the onus on the debtor to decide whether the agreement is cancellable, by explaining that if oral statements were made to the debtor and the agreement was signed away from the creditor's premises, the debtor should ask for another form of application. The creditor runs a serious risk adopting this practice, particularly if the original form of application is badly worded, difficult to understand or simply just not read by the applicant for the credit-token. Any attempt to exclude the cancellation rights by asking the debtor to sign a clause stating that no oral statements were made face to face is likely to be unsuccessful (see s.173(2) and (3)).

6.12 Mode of cancellation

Assuming that it has been established that an agreement is cancellable, to whom is notice of cancellation to be given and how? Section 69 provides the answers by stating that the right is exercisable by notice in writing (see s.189(1)). The notice need not be in any particular form, as long as it indicates the debtor's intention not to proceed. The debtor need not use the cancellation form required to be inserted by the creditor under s.64(1) and the Regulations and the notice may be expressed in any form of words as long as the debtor's intention can be ascertained from it. It must be served by the debtor in the prescribed time on:
(1) the creditor; or
(2) the person specified in the s.64(1) notice as the person to whom notice of cancellation may be given; or
(3) a person who (whether by virtue of s.69(6) of the Act or otherwise) is the agent of the creditor.
The first two of these are straightforward enough. The reference to s.69(6) needs explanation. This is a similar provision to that met already in the earlier discussion on withdrawal. It is a deemed agency provision which includes, as does s.57(3), a person acting on behalf of the debtor in the negotiations leading up to the agreement as a person on whom notice of cancellation may be served. As with s.57, there is a contractual duty to transmit the information concerning the cancellation to the creditor as soon as is reasonably practicable. The notice may be served on a person who is, at common law, the agent of the creditor. The public often mistakenly assume that a person who introduces them to a creditor is the latter's agent. But if the person served is not the agent under the general law, the situation should, more often than not, be covered by s.69(6)(*a*).

It was stated above that the notice of cancellation, unlike notice of withdrawal, must be in writing. It will normally be sent by post by the debtor. In this event, s.69(7) provides that whether or not received by him, a notice of cancellation sent by post by the debtor to an appropriate person shall be deemed to be served on him as soon as it is posted. The debtor is here given the advantage of a rule akin to the postal acceptance rule in the general law of contract. By way of contrast, the point was made earlier that normally in case of withdrawal of an offer, this must be communicated to the creditor or his agent under the common law or s.57(3).

6.13   The cooling-off period

The cooling-off period, as it is commonly known, is the time during which the debtor may consider his position and is provided for in s.68 of the Act. There are three possible situations.

(1)   Where the agreement remains unexecuted after signature by the debtor, because the credit card issuer has not yet signed it, the creditor, as we have seen, must send by post a copy of the executed agreement containing the notice of cancellation rights under s.64(1)(*a*). In the case of credit-token agreements, this need not be within seven days of the making of the agreement, as long as it is posted before the credit-token is sent or with the token itself. The cancellation period is triggered by the arrival of this copy. The debtor has five clear days from receipt of the second copy to cancel, the day of receipt being ignored. For example, if the second copy is received by the debtor on 1st July, he has until midnight on 6th July to serve his written notice of cancellation. It should be recalled that under s.69(7) the notice is deemed to be served, if posted, at the time of posting. If the notice is posted on 6th July, it is effective to cancel the contract, even though it will arrive outside the cooling-off period, if at all. Even if it does not arrive, it is still effective on proof of posting.

(2)   Where the agreement is executed on signature by the debtor, as well as receiving a copy of the executed agreement immediately, he must also be sent by post a separate notice of cancellation rights under s.64(1)(*b*). Again, there is a similar relaxation of the seven-day rule where the agreement is a credit-token contract. The receipt of this separate notice commences the cooling-off period, again five days. The comments made under (1) above with regard to the calculation of the period apply equally in this situation.

(3)   It was mentioned in para.5.9 that s.64(4) empowers regulations to be made exempting certain agreements from the rigour of the need to serve a separate notice under s.64(1)(*b*). At present, the regulations made under this power do not affect credit-token agreements. If the notice is dispensed with, the cancellation period, according to

s.68(*b*), is fourteen clear days from the date of signature of the unexecuted agreement by the debtor.

In the case of the majority of cancellable agreements, the all-important time will be the receipt of the second copy under (1) or of the separate notice under (2) above. What is the position of a debtor who does not receive the one or the other as appropriate? If it is a failure by the credit card issuer to comply with s.62, 63 or 64 as the case may be, the agreement is improperly executed and unenforceable subject to s.127 of the Act (s.65). If the formalities have been met, there is no question of the agreement being improperly executed, but it seems that the debtor has an indefinite right of cancellation should the copy or notice go astray in the post, for example. Goode (I[1452]) takes the view that if the creditor discovers outside the time for serving the copy or notice that it has gone astray, he cannot rectify the situation by serving a fresh copy or notice as this does not satisfy the statutory requirements in s.63 or 64. It appears that all that the creditor may do in these circumstances, if it comes to enforcement of the agreement, is hope that the debtor does not exercise the right to cancel.

6.14   Effects of cancellation

The consequences of the service of a valid cancellation notice by the debtor are set out in ss.69 to 73 and they are many and varied. Some will rarely apply in the case of credit-token agreements, others will be extremely important as far as both parties, and in some cases the supplier, are concerned. The most obvious effect of the notice is to cancel the credit-token agreement immediately. In addition, the notice operates both to cancel any linked transaction and to withdraw any offer to enter into such a transaction by the debtor or a relative (s.69(1)). An agreement or transaction cancelled as above is treated as though it had never been entered into (s.69(4)), although there are exceptions to this, namely, ss.70(5) and 71.

Broadly, the Act provides that the debtor is released from liability for payment under the agreement and is entitled to repayment of any sums paid under the agreement or linked transaction, recovery of goods offered in part exchange or the allowance made for the same and has the benefit of a lien over the goods he has received (if any) under the agreement pending repayment of any sums due to him. The process is not entirely one way, as the debtor has to restore goods received under the contract, subject to his right of lien, and to take reasonable care of them.

6.15   Recovery of payments

The debtor or his relative is entitled, on cancellation of a regulated agreement or linked transaction, to recover all payments made under or in contemplation of the agreement or transaction, including any item in the total charge for credit (s.70(1)(*a*)). There are a number of qualifications to this. First, if the total charge for credit includes a fee or commission charged by a credit broker, the amount repayable to the debtor on respect of that item will be the excess of the fee or commission over £3 (s.70(6) and the Consumer Credit (Increase of Monetary Amounts) Order 1983, SI 1983 No.1571). In addition, if the total charge for credit includes any sum payable or paid by the debtor to a credit broker otherwise than in respect of a fee or commission charged by the broker, the sum is to be treated as if it were a fee or commission. Secondly, the debtor is entitled to repayment of any sum paid by him or to be released from liability to pay any sum for the issue of a credit-token, only if the token is returned to the creditor or is surrendered to the supplier (if any) (s.70(5)). Thirdly, there is an exception in respect of sums covered by s.71 of the Act, discussed below (s.70(5)).

Fourthly, normally the repayment to the debtor must be made by the party to whom the money was originally paid. If the debtor has paid money directly to the supplier under a linked transaction partly financed by the credit-token agreement, then normally the supplier has to refund the money to the debtor. However, if the agreement is a DCS agreement under s.12(*b*), the creditor and the supplier are jointly and severally liable to the debtor for repayment (s.70(3)). For example, suppose that the debtor agrees to buy an item costing £500 from the supplier, paying £200 in cash with the balance provided under the cancellable credit-token agreement with the creditor. On cancellation, the debtor is entitled to recover the £200 from either the supplier or the creditor as the agreement is a s.12(*b*) DCS agreement. Note that this rule applies only where the agreement is a DCS under s.12(b) (restricted-use), *not* s.12(*c*) (unrestricted-use). All is not lost for the creditor, unless the supplier is in liquidation, because the creditor is entitled, subject to rules of court, to have the supplier joined in any proceedings brought against the creditor under this provision (s.70(3)). Also, the creditor, subject to any agreement between them, is entitled to be indemnified by the supplier for any loss suffered by the creditor in satisfying the liability under this provision, including costs reasonably incurred in defending any proceedings. Of course, in the example given above the creditor may well, before cancellation, have paid the £300 to the supplier. In this event, as it is a s.12(*b*) DCS, the creditor is entitled to recover this sum from the supplier (s.70(1)(*c*)). The joint and several liability provision works both ways, in that if the debtor has paid a sum to the creditor before cancellation, e.g. a fee for the issue of the token, it seems that this can be recovered from the supplier. The draftsman obviously envisaged it being only a one-way process, i.e. the creditor having to pay for the supplier's misdeeds or misfortunes, as there is no provision for indemnity or to permit the creditor to be joined in any action brought by the debtor against the supplier for recovery of any sum under s.70(3).

6.16   Release from liability to pay

A further consequence of cancellation is that the debtor or his relative ceases to be liable to pay any sum, including any item in the total charge for credit, which but for the cancellation is or would or might become payable under the agreement or transaction (s.70(1)(*b*). There are two major exceptions to this, contained in ss.69(2) and 71 respectively. The former states that in the case of a DCS agreement for restricted-use credit (which includes as we have seen a credit-token agreement) which finances either:

(1)   the doing of work or supply of goods to meet an emergency; or
(2)   the supply of goods which, before service of the cancellation notice, had by the act of the debtor or his relative become incorporated in any land or thing not comprised in the agreement or any linked transaction,

different provisions are to apply. In these two instances, the cancellation notice operates to cancel only such provisions of the agreement and any linked transaction as relate to the provision of credit, require the debtor to pay an item in the total charge for credit or subject the debtor to any obligation other than to pay for the work or the goods, as the case may be.

If the debtor, in an emergency, used the credit-token within the cancellation period to pay for work done to his home and then served a notice of cancellation, the token agreement and any obligations related to the credit agreement would no longer operate. If the creditor had not yet paid the supplier on receipt of the relevant voucher, the creditor would be entitled to refuse to pay (s.70(1)(*c*)), presumably on the basis of a set-off. The debtor would nonetheless remain liable under the contract with the supplier for the contract price. If the creditor had paid the supplier, the creditor would be entitled to recover the amount from the supplier, the debtor once again remaining liable to the supplier for the price.

The other exception concerns unrestricted-use agreements, in which case the debtor is not released from liability for repayment of a loan still subsisting under s.71(1) and not yet repaid under s.71(2) (s.70(5)). Where a credit-token agreement permits the debtor, as most do, to obtain cash loans over the counter or from an ATM, this situation would fall within the exception. There would be an obligation to repay the loan in accordance with s.71 (but see Goode, I[1476] and the discussion below on s.71).

6.17   Part-exchange goods and allowances

Frequently — particularly, but not exclusively, in relation to hire-purchase agreements — the debtor's initial payment may consist, either entirely or partly, of part-exchange goods. In such circumstances, the document recording the agreement will normally have made an allowance in cash terms representing the value of the goods offered by the debtor in part exchange. This type of situation may not be so frequent in transactions financed by a credit-token agreement, but it is nonetheless a possibility to be considered.

Where, in the antecedent negotiations, the negotiator (usually the supplier) agreed to take goods in part exchange, the goods have actually been delivered to the negotiator and the agreement is cancelled, s.73(2) applies. This provides that, unless within the period of ten days beginning with the date of cancellation, the part-exchange goods are returned to the debtor in substantially the same condition as when they were delivered to the negotiator, the debtor shall be entitled to recover from the negotiator a sum equal to the part-exchange allowance. The latter is the sum agreed as such in the antecedent negotiations, or if no figure has been agreed, a reasonable sum to allow in respect of the goods offered in part exchange (s.73(7)(*b*)). Sometimes the part-exchange figure in the agreement is inflated by the supplier for one reason or another. Whatever the legality of this practice, the supplier is bound by the figure in the agreement for these purposes in the absence of fraud or duress by the debtor. According to Goode (I[1416]) this does not confer an option on the supplier either to return the goods or pay the allowance. Nor does the language of the section suggest that the debtor is entitled to insist on either the return of the goods or claim the allowance. Section 73 is non-committal on these issues and the outcome may well depend on any terms in the agreement expressly dealing with these points. Goode continues by suggesting that usually the passing of the property in the part-exchange goods will be conditional on the coming into being of the regulated agreement, in which case refusal to deliver by the supplier would amount to conversion. On the other hand, it is common practice for the supplier to dispose of the part-exchange goods fairly quickly, either by sale or sometimes, in the case of old items, destruction. It surely makes sense that, in such circumstances, the supplier will be required only to pay the allowance after the ten-day period has expired.

In the case of a s.12(*b*) DCS agreement, which of course includes a credit-token agreement, there is joint and several liability on the supplier and the creditor in respect of the payment of the allowance under s.73(2) (s.73(3)). The creditor is entitled to an indemnity from the supplier for loss suffered in satisfying such liability, including costs reasonably expended defending proceedings started by the debtor (s.73(4)). In addition, the creditor is entitled to have the supplier/negotiator made a party to the proceedings subject to the rules of court (s.73(8)). Finally, where the debtor recovers a sum representing the part-exchange allowance from the supplier or creditor, or both of them jointly, the property in the goods vests in the supplier on the recovery of the sum, if it has not already done so (s.70(6)). This could work harshly against the creditor if the supplier is insolvent. The part-exchange goods will belong to the receiver and the creditor will merely rank alongside the supplier's other unsecured creditors on the basis of the statutory indemnity mentioned above. However, this was precisely why the joint and several liability provision was included: to protect the debtor from the supplier's insolvency and place the risk of that occurring on the creditor.

6.18 The debtor's lien

A provision of immense value to the cancelling debtor is the statutory lien accorded to him in circumstances where goods have been transferred to him under the regulated agreement or linked transaction. Sections 70(2) and 73(5) respectively provide that the debtor or his relative is entitled to exercise a lien over these goods in relation to either sums repayable to him under s.70(1) or the return of the part-exchange goods or the allowance. Once the ten-day period has expired in relation to the latter, the supplier cannot insist that the debtor accepts the return of the part-exchange goods and must tender a sum equal to the allowance in order to discharge the lien. This is a possessory lien and it is lost if the debtor voluntarily returns the goods to the supplier.

6.19 The duties of the debtor in respect of the goods

The debtor may have acquired goods from the supplier by using the credit-token under an agreement which is cancellable. If the debtor exercises his right to cancel in a valid manner then, as one would expect, the goods must in normal circumstances be returned to the supplier.

Section 72 sets out the debtor's statutory responsibility in respect of the goods while in his possession. The section applies where there is a restricted-use DCS agreement, or a linked transaction to which a debtor or a relative of his is a party and the agreement is cancelled. Section 72(3) provides that during the period before cancellation and after acquiring possession of the goods the debtor or his relative, as the case may be, is deemed to have been under a duty to retain possession of the goods and to take reasonable care of them.

As to the position after cancellation, the possessor is under a duty to return the goods, subject to any lien he may have, but he is not under any duty to deliver the goods, except at his own premises and pursuant to a written request signed by or on behalf of the other party (namely, the person from whom the possessor acquired possession) and served on him either before, or at the same time as, the goods are collected from his premises. The possessor in the meantime is still under a duty to retain possession of the goods and to take reasonable care of them (s.72(4) and (5)). Section 72(6) states that if the debtor or his relative decides not to wait to hear from the other party as above, and delivers the goods (whether at his own premises or elsewhere) to any person on whom notice of cancellation could have been served (except, of course, those persons mentioned in s.69(6)(*b*)), or sends the goods at his own expense to such a person, the duties of retention or delivery are discharged. Where the goods are delivered (s.72(6)(*a*)), the obligation to take reasonable care ceases at that point. If, however, the debtor sends them, as permitted by s.72(6)(*b*), he is under a duty to take reasonable care that they are received by the other party and not damaged in transit, but otherwise the duty to take care will cease (s.72(7)). Presumably, the debtor will satisfy this by using a reputable carrier for the goods and in appropriate cases ensuring that the goods are properly packaged and labelled.

The duty of care ceases after a period of twenty-one days from cancellation, unless the debtor unreasonably refuses a request to return the goods made under s.72(5), in which case the duty will continue until such time as the goods are sent or delivered in accordance with s.72(6). After the twenty-one days, the duty of the debtor will be the common law one not wilfully to neglect them. The other party (usually the supplier) takes the risk of accidental or careless damage to the goods in that event. Breach of any duty in s.72 is actionable as a breach of statutory duty (s.72(11)).

These provisions do not operate where the goods are perishable, or by their nature consumed by use and were so consumed before cancellation, or were supplied in an emergency, or had become incorporated in any land or thing not comprised in the cancelled agreement or linked transaction (s.72(9)). It seems that in respect of the first two situations the debtor does not have to pay anything for the goods and has no duties under s.72 in respect of them. With regard to the other two, we have already seen that the debtor is not exempted from the obligation to pay the cash price for them just because he has cancelled the credit agreement (s.69(2)).

Many of the problems facing a creditor in this regard, and those discussed above with regard to joint and several liability with the supplier for repayment of money or the part-exchange allowance, may be avoided by ensuring that the cancellation period has expired before the credit-token is sent or delivered to the debtor or authorised user. This entails sending the second copy of the agreement or the separate notice of cancellation rights, say, at least seven days before the token is sent. To be on the safe side, allowing for a possible postal delay, another two or three days would make sense. Once the cooling-off period has passed, the creditor is safe from the deliberately unfavourable consequences of the provisions in ss.70 and 73 in particular. The creditor under a two-party credit-token agreement is more likely to be affected by the provisions relating to the effects of cancellation than is the creditor under a three-party agreement. Consequently, it would make even more sense to adopt the precaution outlined above.

6.20 Unrestricted-use agreements

Special rules have been inserted in the Act in respect of unrestricted-use loan agreements which are cancelled by the debtor. These are punitive as far as the creditor is concerned and are designed to discourage the creditor from handing over the loan money to the debtor before the expiry of the cancellation period. Section 71, which we have referred to already, provides that on cancellation an unrestricted-use loan agreement shall continue in force so far as it relates to the repayment of the credit and the payment of interest. For example, if the debtor uses the token to obtain a cash advance, the agreement is here being used as one for unrestricted-use. If the debtor cancels the token agreement, he is still under an obligation to repay the credit obtained and any interest. However, s.71(2) provides that if the debtor, in this situation, repays the whole or a portion of the credit either before the expiry of one month after service of the notice of cancellation or, in the case of credit repayable by instalments, before the date on which the first instalment is due, no interest shall be paid on the amount repaid. This is an important provision because, in respect of cash advances obtained by use of a credit-token, interest is usually charged immediately from the time of the advance. The interest-free period is designed to discourage the creditor, as mentioned above. The way to avoid this problem is that outlined in para.6.19. Repayment is deemed to be duly made if it is made to any person on whom a notice of cancellation may be served, except those mentioned in s.69(6)(*b*) (s.71(4)).

If repayment in full has not been made by the time specified in s.71(2), the debtor is not liable to repay any of the credit except on receipt of a written request in the prescribed form, signed by or on behalf of the creditor, stating the amounts of the remaining instalments (recalculated by the creditor as nearly as may be in accordance with he agreement and without extending the repayment period), but excluding any sum other than principal and interest. This last part prevents the creditor from making any kind of administration charge to recoup any loss of interest he might incur on the application of the provisions in s.71(2) and (3).

6.21   Other matters

Cancellation of a regulated agreement also operates to nullify any security provided in relation to the agreement and entitles the debtor to the return of any property lodged with the creditor solely for the purposes of that security (s.113(3)). This will rarely be the case in relation to a credit-token agreement. One further point, again of only marginal significance in the context of credit-token agreements, is that not all linked transactions are automatically cancelled on service of the cancellation notice. The Consumer Credit (Linked Transactions) (Exemptions) Regulations 1983, SI 1983 No.1560, exempt any linked transactions comprising any contract of insurance, any other contracts in so far as they contain a guarantee of goods, and any agreement relating to the operation of a deposit or current account, including a savings account, from cancellation under s.69 of the Act.

6.22   Conclusion

Withdrawal from and cancellation of a regulated credit-token agreement are rights which are not quite as important from the debtor's viewpoint as they are in respect of other types of regulated agreement, for example hire-purchase agreements. However, where a credit-token agreement is cancellable and the debtor chooses to exercise that right, the Act does contain a number of provisions which can be viewed as punitive from the creditor's position. It is worth emphasising that the creditor should try to ensure that no oral representations are made face to face with the debtor and that the agreement is signed by the debtor on appropriate business premises, thus removing it from the cancellable category. Alternatively, assuming the agreement is cancellable, the creditor should ensure that the statutory cooling-off period has expired before the token is delivered to the debtor. This will avoid the unpleasant consequences in ss.70 to 73 of the Act.

CHAPTER 7

Debtors' Liability for Misuse of a Credit-Token

7.01 Introduction

This chapter contains a detailed consideration of the debtor's liability for the use of a credit-token, in particular where the token has been lost, stolen or used without authorisation by a third party. The credit card issuer will naturally be interested in knowing whether it is entitled to debit the amount of money obtained by the unauthorised user to the debtor's account. This will depend upon the terms of the credit card agreement, the Consumer Credit Act 1974 and possibly the Code of Banking Practice — the last being more important in relation to cash cards where there is no element of credit involved in the supply of the cash obtained. That this is seen as an important issue is highlighted by the fact that Parliament decided to include specific limitations on the liability of the debtor where there is misuse of a credit facility by means of the use of a credit-token. The provisions in ss.83 and 84 of the Act deal with the issue in terms which are usually extremely favourable to the debtor, and consequently deleterious as far as the creditor is concerned. Notwithstanding this provision, which is hardly concerned with preventing the loss, merely with shifting it as between creditor and debtor, over the years misuse of plastic cards other than credit cards has increased, presumably in direct proportion to the significant number of them now in circulation. It is hardly surprising that fraud has reached such epidemic proportions. After consultation, and considerable pressure from consumer organisations such as the National Consumer Council, strongly supported by the impartial Banking Ombudsman, the banks were persuaded to include in their Code provisions similar to those in s.84 of the Act. These aspects of the use of cards other than credit cards are considered in depth in Chapter 13.

The problem of fraud and other misuse is unlikely to diminish significantly until some better way of preventing it is introduced, whether involving the introduction of photographs onto cards or some sophisticated technology such as a device for detecting and differentiating thumbprints. The annual reports of the Banking Ombudsman for 1988/89 and 1989/90 reveal that complaints relating to the use of ATMs formed the single largest category of complaints in each of those years. The latest report available (1990/91) shows that such complaints had fallen to third place in the complaints league table. This falling trend is also borne out to some extent by the latest report of the Building Society Ombudsmen (1990/91), where complaints about ATMs had slipped to second place. In all cases, the actual figures in terms of number of complaints and percentages of the overall complaints figures had fallen. However, the complaints concerning the use of ATMs prove beyond a shadow of doubt to be the most intractable for the Banking Ombudsman. In his latest report, the complaints league table has been divided into two parts: 'immature' and 'mature' complaints. The former are screened and the latter are investigated following screening, on the basis that they have not been resolved satisfactorily at the initial screening level. Many complaints naturally do not develop beyond the 'immature' stage for one reason or another. Whatever the reasons, complaints concerning the use of cards and ATMs form a very high proportion of the complaints achieving maturity (38.4%, the next highest category in the table reaching only 9.7%). Unfortunately, the figures do not show the breakdown as between disputes concerning credit-tokens and other forms of plastic card, so it is not possible to see just how effective the provisions in the Act are in relation to misuse.

We shall consider issues relating to debit and cash cards further in Chapter 13 as that chapter looks at the Code of Banking Practice and its impact on such cards where there is no misuse of a credit facility. Where there is misuse, the creditor must turn to the terms of the Consumer Credit Act to resolve the issue of liability for any losses incurred. This point has perhaps not been so readily appreciated by some institutions, in that the Banking Ombudsman in his latest report felt it necessary to repeat in full a list of examples where he thought that the Act applied. These were originally contained in a separate Guidance Note which he had circulated to all member banks during the year. It seems that his rather brief mentions of ss.83 and 84 in his two previous reports had failed to bring home the message to the various institutions that the Act could apply to a cash or debit card in circumstances where there was misuse of a credit facility. The examples discussed below in the context of what is meant by 'credit facility' lean heavily on the Ombudsman's guidance as set out in the latest report. Without doubt the provisions of the Act on the issue of misuse are not totally free from ambiguity and difficulty, as will become evident from the discussion below. There is a complete absence of case law on the two sections to be considered and, thus, the Ombudsman's suggestions are of great value. After all, in cases which come before him he is the final arbiter, and his decisions will no doubt influence the result in later complaints on similar issues of interpretation of the two sections.

We shall first consider the general effect of s.83 of the Act, which provides protection for the debtor where there is misuse of a credit facility available to him. The major exceptions to this are those in s.84(1) and (2), although at times it is difficult to describe that in s.84(1) as a true exception, in that the debtor's liability is limited to a current paltry maximum of £50. It seems to be the case that debiting the customer's account with such a figure when the overall loss to the creditor may far exceed this amount is often not worth the trouble, a view sometimes taken by the credit card issuer. Bearing in mind the new provisions in the Code of Banking Practice in relation to debit and cash cards, which impose similar restrictions on the right to recovery by the card issuer as against the customer, the pendulum has swung a long way in favour of the debtor or customer. It seems that the creditor or card issuer is considered better able to stand loss in such cases.

7.02   Debtor's liability for misuse

The debtor is, of course, normally liable for the use of the credit-token by himself and by any person authorised by him to use it. This will be a term of his contract, whether express or implied. It will include the use by a joint cardholder, in which situation both holders are jointly and severally liable for use of the card. This situation must be distinguished from that where the cardholder requests additional cards for members of the family. The cardholder is liable to the creditor for their use, although there may be some difficulties concerning use which exceeds the principal cardholder's permission. We shall return to this shortly. Also, it might be the case that the debtor allows another person to use his (the debtor's) card, in circumstances where the debtor's signature is not required, e.g. telephone transactions or at an ATM with the PIN. At common law the other person would no doubt be regarded as the agent of the debtor in such a case, or at least be deemed to be such on the basis of a form of estoppel.

The terms of the contract may, however, go much further than just stating the obvious: that the debtor is liable for normal use. They may attempt to render the debtor liable for all misuse no matter how it arises. Section 83 was inserted precisely to deal with such an eventuality.

Section 83 provides that a debtor under a regulated consumer credit agreement shall not be liable to the creditor for any loss arising from the use of a credit facility by another person not acting, or to be treated as acting, as the debtor's agent. It seems that the section is merely stating what the position would be at common law in respect of the debtor's liability for the acts of his agent, whether actual or ostensible. What it does do is to prevent the creditor from imposing liability going beyond this on the debtor. Section 83 overrides anything in the agreement which might have this effect, for example a clause which made the debtor liable for all misuse made of the facility irrespective of who misused the credit-token. Any clause in the agreement which tried to avoid the effect of s.83 would be void in so far as it was inconsistent with the protection of the debtor in that section (s.173(1)).

It should be appreciated that s.83 applies to any credit facility, whether a credit-token agreement or not. For example, misuse of an overdraft facility by a third party who is neither the authorised nor deemed agent of the debtor is covered by s.83, as long as the agreement forming the basis of the facility is a regulated consumer credit agreement. As it is concerned only with regulated agreements, by definition s.83 does not apply to exempt agreements under s.16 or the Regulations made thereunder. This conclusively rules out agreements such as American Express and Diner's Club which, as we have seen, are so exempt. These two types of agreement may be credit-tokens for some purposes in the Act (see paras.3.02 and 4.31), but it seems that the rules in s.84, in particular the £50 limit on the debtor's liability in certain circumstances, are not applicable, as this section is closely tied to the wording of s.83, as we will see below. However, the Code of Banking Practice does impose a similar limit (para.18.3) and will apply if the credit card issuer is a subscriber to the Code.

It is important to remember that agreements which are exempt only from Part V of the Act are still regulated agreements. For example, if a debtor is provided with an overdraft facility as an adjunct to his current account, whilst the creditor does not have to comply with the formalities in Part V, ss.83 and 84 could nonetheless apply to the agreement as it is otherwise regulated under the Act. The sections would apply only in relation to the credit aspect of the agreement, however. This point is considered in more depth below, but before turning to this, there are one or two further preliminary matters to mention. First, s.83 does not apply to a non-commercial agreement (s.83(2)). This is rarely likely to be an issue in a credit-token context, but the effect of the provision is to leave it to the parties to such an agreement to agree where the liability should fall in the event of misuse or, failing express agreement, to the common law of agency discussed briefly above. Secondly, s.83 does not apply where the misuse comes about by means of a cheque, the matter being regulated by the common law and the cheques legislation, which need not concern us here (s.83(2)).

7.03   Credit facility

As mentioned above, s.83 applies only where there is the misuse of a credit facility, and not, for example, the misuse of a current account which is in credit and the misuse relates to the credit balance. The point has caused some confusion, or so it appears from the Banking Ombudsman's reports referred to earlier. As Goode states (I[2268]), the purpose of s.83 is to give the debtor immunity only from liability, not to indemnify him for any losses, e.g. the credit balance on his current account. Clarification of this point has been achieved by the Guidance Note issued by the Banking Ombudsman, the essential text of which is set out in para.10.06 of his 1990/91 report. By identifying certain cases as misuse of a credit facility under a regulated agreement, the Ombudsman has been able to resolve some of his more problematical complaints, although perhaps not as many as he might wish.

Case 1 in the report concerns an agreed overdraft limit of £250 and the account is £20 in debit. Misuse by means of the debtor's cash card and PIN by an unauthorised person in these circumstances is misuse of a credit facility; consequently s.83 applies (and s.84, as we shall see shortly). In Case 6 the agreed overdraft limit is once again £250, but this time the account is £60 in credit. A third party, without authority, abstracts £150 by means of the debtor's cash card and PIN. As s.83 (and also s.84) does not operate in respect of the credit balance, the creditor will be entitled to debit the debtor's account with the £60 without any problem in normal circumstances. As to the £90, the extent of the overdrawn amount, ss.83 and 84 will apply as this is misuse of a credit facility.

Case 9 raises the point mentioned in para.3.03 concerning the use of an ATM belonging to an institution other than the one issuing the cash card. It was suggested that this does not amount to the provision of credit, and this conclusion is adopted by the Ombudsman. In his example, the debtor's account is always in credit, and £100 is taken from an ATM of a building society which has a networking agreement with the card issuer. As this is not the provision of a credit facility, s.83 does not apply and neither does s.84 as the card is in any event not a credit-token. Case 10 illustrates the point that a card which has a number of functions, e.g. a cheque guarantee card, debit card and cash card combined may attract the provisions in ss.83 and 84 in circumstances where it is used in relation to a credit facility. If the debtor has an agreed overdraft and his account is already in debit, misuse by an unauthorised third party of the cash card to withdraw further amounts is covered by both sections, but in relation to that particular type of use only. If the card was, for example, used as a guarantee card to take money from the debtor's account, this would not be within the section, as it would not be misuse of a credit facility. In any event, if the withdrawal was made by a cheque, s.83(2) would apply, excluding reliance on s.83 by the debtor.

Staying with Case 10, the Ombudsman suggests that ss.83 and 84 cannot apply to a debit card when used as a means of payment for goods or services. His reason for this is that s.187(3A) exempts the use of debit cards in such circumstances from the Act. It is respectfully suggested that this is incorrect. Section 187(3A) has the effect merely of preventing it being argued that use of a debit card in this way can constitute a DCS agreement; thus, as a consequence, ruling out the possibility of the joint and several liability imposed by s.75 being visited upon the supplier and the creditor (see para.3.15). There is no reason at all why ss.83 and 84 cannot apply to a debit card used to pay for goods and services in this way, provided the misuse relates to a credit facility, as discussed above. This is supported by Goode (I[2271]) where, in his Example 2, a debtor is given an overdraft facility of £500. His debit card is stolen and used to purchase goods. In this situation Goode seems to have no doubt that s.83 will apply (see also Goode's Examples 3 and 4).

If the conclusion is that there is no misuse of a credit facility and therefore there is no room for application of s.83, it must not be assumed automatically that the creditor is entitled to debit the customer's account in respect of any misuse. Whether this can be done will depend on the terms of the agreement or the general law, particularly estoppel, whereby the debtor is prevented from denying the authority of the wrongdoer. An estoppel is not easily established and it must not be forgotten that there is no general duty on a person to safeguard his or her property. The fact that the card is stolen as the result of the debtor's negligence is unlikely to substantiate a contention of estoppel. In most cases the issue is likely to be resolved by the presence in the agreement of a clause making the debtor liable for such misuse.

One final point under this heading concerns the situation where there is no agreed overdraft facility or there is an agreed but limited facility before the misuse occurs, unlike the cases and examples cited above. It seems that s.83 may apply in circumstances where the credit facility is created by the creditor's decision to honour the withdrawal which results in a debit balance or an increase in the debit balance previously agreed. In the case of an ATM the decision of the creditor to honour a temporary overdrawing is made in advance by programming the machine, but it does not seem to matter that in other instances the decision is retrospective. Goode dismisses (I[2268.2]) the argument that such a decision by the creditor is non-consensual and not a misuse of a credit facility within the section. A creditor would not be permitted to evade the application of s.83 on that basis. Case 8 in the Ombudsman's list of examples illustrates the point. There is no agreed overdraft and the account is £46 in credit. The creditor marks the account with a £55 limit to avoid embarrassment to the debtor should he or she slightly overdraw. An unauthorised user withdraws £100. As the bank has permitted the withdrawal by, e.g. programming the ATM in advance to accept the card and pay the money, this amounts to misuse of a credit facility and is governed by s.83 (and as we shall see s.84 also).

7.04 Misuse of a credit-token

So far we have been considering in a general way the debtor's liability for misuse of a credit facility, for s.83, as explained above, extends beyond misuse by means of a credit-token. Section 84 of the Act contains further rules appertaining to the debtor's liability for misuse, but these are directed solely at misuse by means of a credit-token. Before concentrating on the detail of this section, it is worth reminding ourselves of the position under s.66 of the Act: that the debtor is not liable under a credit-token until it has been accepted by him, as discussed in para.5.11. Further, in any proceedings brought by the creditor to a regulated credit-token agreement, the onus is on the creditor to prove that the token was lawfully supplied to the debtor and accepted by him, and where it is alleged by the debtor that the use was not authorised, the creditor must prove either that the use was authorised or that the use occurred before the creditor was given notice as required under s.84(3) (s.171(4)(*a*) and (*b*)).

The main provisions in s.84 operate by way of exception to the general rule in s.83. A debtor may be liable in appropriate circumstances for the misuse of a credit-token by someone other than himself, his agent or a person deemed to be his agent. As we shall see, in one instance at least, the liability is kept at an extremely low level and may be negligible compared with the loss suffered by the creditor as a result of the misuse of the token.

The first situation giving rise to potential liability on the part of the debtor is contained in s.84(1). This provides that s.83 does not prevent the debtor under a credit-token agreement from being made liable to the extent of £50 (or the credit limit if lower) for loss to the creditor arising from the use of the credit-token by other persons during a period when the credit-token ceases to be in the possession of any authorised person and ending when the credit-token is once more in the possession of an authorised person. Section 84(7) provides that the debtor, the creditor and any person authorised by the debtor to use the credit-token are authorised persons for the purpose of s.84(1). Thus, the operation of subs.(1) ceases once the token is with any such person. The token, if lost, may not always be returned to the debtor. If it reaches the creditor first, the debtor's responsibility under s.84 is at an end for any further misuse until such a time as it, if ever, is out of his possession (or that of a person mentioned in s.84(7)). The return of the token to the creditor is more likely to happen because the creditor's name, address and telephone number will normally, as a matter of practice, be on the card itself.

The second instance where the debtor may be liable is covered by s.84(2). This states that s.83 does not prevent the debtor under a credit-token agreement from being made liable to any extent for loss to the creditor from use of the credit-token by a person who acquired possession of it with the debtor's consent. It does not matter whether the use by the person in possession of the card is permitted or not, or whether some permitted limit has been exceeded by the possessor. For example, the card may be given to another person for safekeeping only: s.84(2) applies and removes the barrier to liability contained in s.83. Alternatively, the card may be given to another person with permission to use it to buy a specific item in circumstances where the debtor's signature is not required, e.g. a telephone sale. If the possessor uses it for another, or additional, transaction(s) s.84 provides the way for the creditor to avoid the obstacle imposed by s.83. It seems that, even if the consent of the debtor is obtained by fraud, the subsection may still apply, although this is far from settled. Consent must be from the debtor; the consent of any other authorised user will clearly not suffice. It should be noted that this subsection does not provide any statutory limit as does subs.(1), so the debtor could theoretically be liable for all the loss until such time as the creditor was notified in accordance with s.84(3) of the possibility of misuse. It could be argued that s.84(2) adds little to s.83 and the common law. If the debtor consents to another person having possession of his card, it could be said that any misuse by the possessor will fall within the deemed agency situation referred to above, in which case this is provided for in s.83 itself.

If the creditor wishes to rely on the provisions in s.84 (whether subs.(1) or (2)) he must establish liability under the agreement or at common law. If there is nothing in the agreement covering loss by misuse in these circumstances, and the creditor cannot establish either an actual or deemed agency, s.84(2) is of no use to him whatsoever. It must be appreciated that s.84 does not create liability on the part of the debtor, it merely removes the obstacle placed in the way of recovery by s.83. To avoid any difficulty with this issue, the creditor must ensure that there is a suitable clause in the agreement which covers the question of loss in circumstances where the card is stolen or lost, or where it is given to a person with the debtor's consent. In the event that the debtor is held liable for any sum under s.84(1) or (2), s.84(6) provides that any money paid by the debtor for the issue of the credit-token, to the extent (if any) that it has not been previously offset by use made of the credit-token, shall be treated as paid towards satisfaction of any such sum.

7.05   Misuse of a credit facility

In the discussion on s.83, it was pointed out that the section operated only in respect of the misuse of a credit facility, and that this was the case even where there was not an agreed overdraft in place before the misuse occurred. We also saw that in a situation where a creditor temporarily honours drawings beyond the agreed credit limit, the misuse is within the scope of s.83. This must apply equally to the operation of the provisions in s.84, which are expressed as exceptions to s.83. As Goode comments (I[2271.1]), if there is no pre-existing agreement for credit, or if there is and the credit limit has already been reached, the debtor cannot be rendered liable under s.84. If the credit has been partly used up prior to the misuse, the debtor can be made liable only for the undrawn amount or £50, whichever is the lower.

Some illustrations from the Ombudsman's latest report may prove instructive. Case 1 we referred to earlier. There is an agreed overdraft limit of £250 and the account is £20 in debit. The thief withdraws the sum of £200 cash by means of an ATM using the PIN and the card. The creditor is entitled to debit the debtor's account only with the sum of £50 under s.84(1). Case 2 illustrates the point that if, instead of making one withdrawal of £200, the thief were to make two withdrawals, or two separate uses of the card, amounting to £200 in total, the result will be the same: the creditor can debit the account only to the extent of the statutory limit.

Case 3 again involves a credit limit of £250. Here, the unauthorised user of the card withdraws £200 or purchases £200 worth of goods. The account before this misuse was £90 in debit. The liability of the debtor, according to s.84(1), is £50 or the credit limit if lower. As the balance of the credit was £160, the lower figure of £50 applies. Case 4 has the same overdraft limit, but here the account is only £20 in debit. The thief makes two withdrawals, one for £200 and the other for £60. The creditor is again entitled to debit only £50 in respect of the two unlawful withdrawals. Case 6 we have considered briefly already. The agreed overdraft is again £250, but the account is £60 in credit. An unauthorised withdrawal of £150 is made, rendering the account overdrawn by £90. Sections 83 and 84 have nothing to say concerning credit balances, so the creditor is entitled to debit the £60 (but see the Code of Banking Practice, in Chapter 13). However, with regard to the further £90 (the extent of the overdrawing), the creditor is limited to a further £50 only under s.84(1). The creditor therefore must stand the loss of the remaining £40 and is not entitled to debit his customer's account for that amount.

Case 7 illustrates graphically the point that the creditor is not entitled to debit the debtor's account where the credit limit has been reached or already exceeded before the unauthorised transaction takes place. The agreed limit here is £1,000 but this has already been exceeded by £100. An unauthorised use of the card increases the overdraft by a further £200 to £1,300. The creditor has a standard term which provides that the cardholder is liable for all amounts drawn by use of the card including those while the account is overdrawn or those which make it overdrawn. As the credit limit has already been exceeded, the cardholder is not liable at all, because he is liable only for the lower of the credit limit and £50. As there is effectively no credit limit, there is nothing to be debited to the cardholder's account.

We considered Case 8 earlier. This concerned a credit balance of £46 with no agreed overdraft, although the creditor has put an anticipatory overdraft limit of £55 in the event that its customer might just stray into debit. When the thief withdraws £100, the creditor is entitled to debit the account with the £46 (subject to what is said in Chapter 13) and the sum of £50 (being less than the temporary credit limit of £55).

Two final points on s.84 require discussion in this context. First, s.84(8) provides that where two or more credit-tokens are provided under one credit-token agreement, the provisions of s.84 apply to each credit-token separately. It is not altogether clear whether this includes the situation where a debtor has additional cards for members of the family. Does each additional card amount to a credit-token so that s.84(8) applies? It would seem the make sense if they were to be so regarded, so as to render the debtor liable up to the £50 limit on each of those cards when out of the possession of an authorised user.

Second, it is implicit from the wording of s.84(1) that once the token is back with an authorised user, the £50 limit will apply once more should the token again fall into the wrong hands. The way in which this might operate is highlighted in Case 5, where there is an agreed overdraft of £1,000. The account is £400 in debit and the card is misused on three occasions, each for £100. The card is then returned to the customer, who uses it lawfully to withdraw £60. The card is taken once again and misused on two further occasions to withdraw £100 each time. The overdraft is now £960. The cardholder is liable for two separate £50s because of the break in the possession of the card between the first three unauthorised transactions and the final two. The creditor has to stand the remaining £400.

One hitherto unexplored point concerns the situation where the token is out of possession of an authorised user and it is used to pay for goods, costing say £200. The card is recovered by the authorities and handed over to the creditor. At that point s.84 ceases to operate, but the debtor is liable for £50 at this time. While the card is in the creditor's possession, s.83 prevents any liability being imposed on the debtor, which seems fair enough. However, if the creditor returns the token to the debtor, but it is intercepted in the post, for example, and subsequently misused, is the debtor liable under s.84(1)? It should be recalled that the creditor is an authorised person for the purposes of s.84(1). There is no provision similar to that in s.66, whereby the debtor is liable only after he has accepted the token, in this situation. However, it would seem inappropriate to make the debtor liable for a second £50 before the token is back in his actual possession. The creditor should consider adopting a procedure whereby the card could not be used until the debtor has acknowledged receipt of it, to avoid the risk of further losses.

7.06   Restrictions on liability

There are two restrictions on the creditor's ability to take advantage of s.84(1) and (2). Section 84(3) provides that subs.(1) and (2) do not apply to any use of the credit-token after the creditor has been given oral or written notice that it has been lost or stolen, or is for any other reason liable to misuse. The subsection does not require the notice to be given by the debtor or an authorised user. Goode (I[2272.1]) seems to infer that this does not prevent notice being given by an organisation which reports card losses to creditors on behalf of a debtor. This makes sense and it seems unlikely that a court would be prepared to say that a creditor may ignore notification of fraud in this way and expect the debtor to pay for at least part of the fraud. On the other hand, a creditor may indicate in the agreement that such notification will not be accepted. It seems unlikely that a court would give much weight to such a provision and, in any event, it might be argued that this is an attempt to oust the provisions of the Act, which is forbidden (s.173(1)).

Notice is not effective until it is received, so the onus is clearly on the debtor to ensure that the creditor is aware of the loss or liability to misuse. The notice may be oral and this may often be the method of communication, not just because it is quicker, but because the creditor will normally have included in the documents sent to the debtor an emergency telephone number for precisely this purpose. If the notice is oral, and the agreement requires confirmation in writing, the notice is of no effect unless so confirmed within seven days (s.84(5)). It is likely that the credit-token agreement will require notification in writing and creditors should ensure that such a clause is in their standard form of agreement. If the debtor does not confirm within the seven-day period, his oral notice does not have any effect and the debtor will be liable in accordance with s.84 for unauthorised use up to the time of receipt of the written notice (if any), subject to the £50 limit or the credit limit if lower in the case of s.84(1).

Finally, the creditor cannot take advantage of the provisions in s.84(1) and (2) unless the credit-token agreement contains, in the prescribed manner, particulars of the name, address and telephone number of a person stated to be the person to whom notice is to be given under subs.(3) (s.84(4)). As mentioned above, it is a useful precaution to include such particulars on the credit-token itself, although this is not mandatory.

7.07 Conclusion

It should be evident from the discussion above that liability for loss arising from the misuse of a credit-token is laid largely at the door of the creditor. Section 84(1), whilst appearing to give the illusion of being an exception to the obstacle placed by s.83 in the path of creditors attempting to pass losses to the debtor, fails by a good margin to be of any real assistance to creditors because of the low statutory limit set on the debtor's potential liability. Until such time as some better method of protecting against credit card fraud is devised, creditors need to be vigilant as to other ways of preventing misuse. They must exhort retailers to adhere strictly to verification procedures when accepting payment by credit cards, and debit cards as well, including close checks on signatures. Shop floor limits can be useful in reducing the impact of fraud, and the prohibition of telephone sales not requiring a signature would help, although this would prove highly unpopular with both the public and retailers.

Instructions to debtors concerning the risk of loss must be forceful as to signing of cards on receipt, keeping the card in a safe place, not handing it over to others, and destroying the PIN after memorising it. These comments apply to the issue of cash cards as well as to credit and debit cards, in the light of the limitation introduced by the Code of Banking Practice on the debtor's liability, thus shifting the burden of loss significantly in the direction of the card issuer, something we shall return to in Chapter 13.

CHAPTER 8

Matters Arising During the Currency of a Credit-Token Agreement

8.01 Introduction

The preceding chapter concentrated exclusively on one particularly important issue arising during the course of a credit-token agreement, namely, liability for loss caused by unauthorised use of the token. Other issues that arise during the currency of an agreement may be equally important. Principal among these are the joint and several liability of the supplier and the creditor and the deemed agency provisions, contained respectively in ss.75 and 56 of the Consumer Credit Act 1974. Both these topics merit a chapter in their own right (see Chapters 9 and 10). This chapter is concerned with a miscellaneous group of issues which are also regulated by the 1974 Act with the general aim of protecting the consumer. Some are concerned with the supply of information to the debtor, repeating the theme adopted by the Act on precontractual disclosure and the provisions of the Act dealing with the formalities. This is a theme adopted as a governing principle of the Code of Banking Practice, para.1.4(c) of which states that banks, building societies and card issuers will help customers to understand how their accounts operate and will seek to give them a good understanding of banking services. Paragraph 1.5 specifies that this is to be achieved by giving information to customers, particularly at the time of opening the account, but at other times on request by the customer. The Code contains more detailed provisions indicating how and what information is to be conveyed to the customer, which will be discussed as appropriate below.

The first part of this chapter is concerned with the rights to information of the debtor under a credit-token agreement within the Consumer Credit Act. This includes a discussion of the rights to regular statements of the account, to a settlement statement and, finally, to a termination statement. We then consider three more issues: appropriation of payments, variation of agreements and modifying agreements.

8.02   Information to be supplied on request

The information the debtor under a regulated consumer credit agreement is entitled to under the 1974 Act depends on whether the agreement is for fixed-sum or running-account credit. Section 77 deals with the former and need not be considered here, as we are concerned solely with the latter, covered by s.78 of the Act.

Section 78(1) provides that the creditor under a regulated running-account credit agreement, within the prescribed period after receiving a request in writing to that effect from the debtor and payment of a fee of 50 pence, shall give the debtor a copy of the executed agreement (if any) and of any other document referred to in it, together with a statement signed by or on behalf of the creditor showing, according to the information to which it is practicable for him to refer:

'(*a*)   the state of the account, and
(*b*)   the amount, if any, currently payable under the agreement by the debtor to the creditor, and
(*c*)   the amounts and due dates of any payments which, if the debtor does not draw further on the account, will later become payable under the agreement by the debtor to the creditor.'

The supply of information imposed by this subsection depends on action being initiated by the debtor in the form of the written request and the payment of the small fee. This compares with the automatic requirement to supply information in s.78(4), covered below. The prescribed period is twelve working days from the receipt of the written request (the Consumer Credit (Prescribed Periods for Giving Information) Regulations 1983, SI 1983 No.1569). A 'working day' is any day other than Saturday or Sunday, Christmas Day, Good Friday or the usual bank holidays (s.189(1)). When giving the requisite detail under paras.(*a*) and (*b*), the creditor is entitled to assume that no further drawings have been made, as the subsection talks of the statement being given 'according to the information to which it is practicable for him to refer'. In addition, the creditor may not be in a position to give in precise terms the information required under para.(*c*), referring as it does to the future. There may be a provision in the agreement, as there invariably is in a credit-token agreement, for the variation of the interest rate charged by the creditor. In these circumstances, s.78(2) states that if the creditor does not have sufficient information to ascertain the amounts and dates as required by subs.(1)(*c*), he may comply with the requirement if he gives the basis on which they would fall to be ascertained under the agreement. The agreement might specify that the rate will vary with the interest base rate, perhaps 2% or 3% above this figure. This formula will be acceptable as complying with the duty under s.78(1).

Section 78(1) does not apply to an agreement under which no sum is, or will or may become payable by the debtor (s.78(3)(*a*)). Nor does it apply to non-commercial agreements (s.78(7)). Also, the creditor need not respond to a request made less than one month after a previous request under subs.(1) relating to the same agreement was complied with (s.78(3)(*b*)). It seems that where there are joint debtors, despite s.185(1), which requires that where there are joint debtors to an agreement anything required to be done by or under the Act shall be done in relation to each of them, the subsection would not apply in the situation where a second request was made in the period by a different debtor under the agreement (Jones, p.150). However, when complying with the original request by one of the joint debtors, s.185(1) would require the necessary information demanded by s.78(1) to be supplied to the other joint debtor within the twelve working days.

A statement supplied under s.78(1) is binding on the creditor by virtue of s.172(1). However, the court is empowered to give such relief to the creditor as appears just in circumstances where it is sought to rely on a statement in any proceedings and it is shown to be incorrect. The court would no doubt grant relief where the error was purely typographical and an obvious mistake. On the other hand, if the debtor has acted to his detriment in cases where the error is not so obvious, the court may be reluctant to grant relief, or the debtor may be able to use an estoppel-based argument.

The sanctions for failure to comply with s.78(1) are that, while the default continues the creditor is precluded from enforcing the agreement, and if the default continues for a month an offence is committed (s.78(6)). We shall see below that there is a glaring omission to provide a sanction in respect of a breach of s.78(4). Finally, s.108 of the Act provides that where an agreement is secured, the creditor is required after receiving a request from a surety to give similar information to the latter. This is rarely applicable to a credit card agreement as it is unlikely to be secured.

Part B of the Code of Banking Practice, para.19.1, states that card issuers will provide customers with a written record on their statement of account of all payments and withdrawals made. In addition, the card issuer is in many cases to be provided with an immediate written record. The imprecision of this compared with the obligations on the creditor under the Act is striking and should be noted accordingly. There is nothing specific as to the types of cases in which the 'immediate' record is to be given. No time limits at all are mentioned in the first part of the paragraph.

8.03   Automatic supply of information

Section 78(4) goes one step further than s.78(1) by providing for the automatic supply of information by the creditor to the debtor. The subsection states that where running-account credit is provided under a regulated agreement, the creditor shall give the debtor statements in the prescribed form, and with the prescribed contents:

'(*a*)   showing according to the information to which it is practicable for him to refer, the state of the account at regular intervals of not more than twelve months, and

(*b*)   where the agreement provides, in relation to specified periods, for the making of payments by the debtor, or the charging against him of interest or any other sum, showing according to the information to which it is practicable for him to refer, the state of the account at the end of each of those periods during which there is any movement in the account.'

We can see immediately that this provision is of significance in the context of regulated credit-token agreements. For such agreements falling outside the scope of regulation, the Act does not impose any duty to supply any information of the kind mentioned in either subs.(1) or (4), although there may be terms in the agreement which bind the creditor to do this. In relation to credit cards, it is more likely that s.78(4)(*b*) will be applicable, as the majority of agreements will provide for repayment by the debtor and the charging of interest by the creditor on a monthly basis. It should be noted that the creditor is relieved of the duty to supply any such statement if there has been no movement on the account during the relevant period, e.g. a month. However, it would seem that movement may include matters other than further drawings by the debtor or the adding of interest charges to the account by the creditor. Jones (p.151) suggests that this would include a refund of money, e.g. in respect of faulty goods on a store card, and include drawings by the debtor which left the account in credit. Both of these would be a movement and would fall within s.78(4).

The information must be supplied, according to s.78(5) within the prescribed period after the end of the period to which the statement relates. The Consumer Credit (Running-Account Credit Information) Regulations 1983, SI 1983 No.1570, set out some rather complex rules for calculating the prescribed period. Where the statement includes a demand for payment from the debtor, the time allowed for the supply of the statement of information is one month after the end of the period to which it relates. Where, however, there is no such demand, and the statement does not show a debit or credit balance at the end of the period to which it relates, the creditor is allowed twelve months from the end of the period to which it relates. Alternatively, if there has been no debit or credit balance at any time during the relevant period, the creditor has twelve months after the date on which there is first a debit or credit balance following the end of the period in question. In other situations not covered under the above, the time allowed is six months from the end of the relevant period.

The first statement, given under s.78(4) must, according to the 1983 Regulations, refer to a period starting on or before the date of the first movement in the account. Subsequent statements must cover a period starting from the end of the period covered by the statement immediately preceding.

8.04   Prescribed form and contents under s.78(4) of the Consumer Credit Act

The Schedule to the 1983 Regulations prescribes the contents of the s.78(4) statement. It must contain:

(1)   Any opening balance on the account at the beginning of the relevant period and the balance at the end of that period.

(2)   The date of any movement on the account during the period and the date of the end of the period in question.

(3)   The amount of any payments made into the account by, or to the credit of, the debtor during the period.

(4)   The amount of any drawing on the account by the debtor during the period, with enough information to allow the debtor to identify the drawing.

(5)   The amount of any interest or other charges payable by the debtor and applied to the account during the period, whether or not the interest or other charges relate to that period.

(6)   Where the statement indicates that interest has been charged to the account during the relevant period:

    (a)   sufficient information to enable the debtor to check the way in which the interest was calculated; or

    (b)   the rate of interest which has been used to calculate the amount of the interest or, if the rate has varied, each rate which has been used and the time during which each rate was employed; or

(c)   a statement that the rate, or each rate, which has been used to calculate the amount of interest will be provided by the creditor on request, together with a clear explanation of how the amount of interest has been calculated.

As to the form of the statement, the Regulations prescribe that it must be in writing, and the lettering (including figures and symbols), the signature apart, easily legible and of a colour readily distinguishable from the colour of the paper.

8.05   Other points on s.78(4)

The duty under s.78(4) is totally separate from that under s.78(1). The automatic sending of statements by the creditor under subs.(4) does not do away with the obligation to comply with a valid request by the debtor under subs.(1). Another difference is that subs.(4) does not apply to a small agreement whereas subs.(1) does (s.78(7)). Similarly, a statement under subs.(4) is not regarded as binding under s.172(1), as is one under subs.(1) (as we have seen). A debtor might nonetheless be able to set up an estoppel in appropriate circumstances. The provisions are treated differently in relation to joint debtors. The duty under s.185(1) to supply joint debtors with information may be dispensed with under s.185(2). This states that where running-account credit is provided to two or more joint debtors, any of them may by means of a signed notice authorise the creditor not to comply in his case with s.78(4). The dispensing notice is to have effect until revoked by a further notice given by the debtor to the creditor. The provisos to this are that a dispensing notice shall not take effect if previous dispensing notices are operative in the case of the other debtor, or each of the other debtors, as might be the case, and any dispensing notices shall cease to be operative if any of the debtors dies. This dispensation is not available in respect of the duty under s.78(1).

A final, surprising difference concerns the failure of the Act to specify any sanction for the non-compliance with s.78(4), by way of contrast with s.78(1). Section 170 states that unless a sanction is expressly provided for, any breach of a requirement under the Act shall not incur any criminal or civil sanction. Of course, under s.170(2), the Director General of Fair Trading may take account of any such breach, notwithstanding the lack of sanction, when performing his functions under the Act, of particular importance when considering the fitness of applicants for a licence. Goode, relying on the power in s.170(3), suggests that a court might compel the creditor to supply a s.78(4) statement by means of a mandatory injunction (I[1713]). One similarity between the two subsections, by way of contrast with the previous discussion of the differences, is that neither duty applies to a non-commercial agreement.

8.06   Settlement statements

The right to early settlement of a regulated agreement is contained in s.94 of the Act. This is more conveniently discussed in Chapter 12, on default and termination of credit-token agreements. However, the right to a settlement statement is one that arises during the course of the life of an agreement and it is convenient to cover the issue in this chapter, along with the other rights to information in s.78.

There are some similarities between the right in s.97 to a settlement statement and the right to information in s.78(1). Section 97(1) provides that a creditor under a regulated consumer credit agreement, within the prescribed period after he has received a request in writing to that effect from the debtor, shall give the debtor a statement in the prescribed form indicating, according to the information to which it is practicable for him to refer, the amount of the payment required to discharge the debtor's indebtedness under the agreement, together with the prescribed particulars showing how the amount is arrived at.

Usually, a credit card agreement will provide a settlement figure as a matter of course in the monthly account sent to the debtor. Frequently, the debtor will discharge the full amount, as is his right under the agreement, and thus avoid interest charges. On the other hand the debtor may choose to pay by instalments, the minimum figure for any instalment also being included in the statement. Notwithstanding this normal situation, the debtor still retains the right to a settlement statement under s.97. Such a statement must be in writing and normally comply with the Schedule to the Consumer Credit (Settlement Information) Regulations 1983, SI 1983 No.1564, as to the required information. However, if within a month of receiving a request under s.97, the creditor supplies a statement of the account under s.78(4), the statement under s.97 need only say that the amount required to discharge the indebtedness of the debtor is the debit balance shown in the s.78(4) statement at the end of the relevant period covered by that statement.

Where the Schedule applies, the following information is to be included in the statement:

(1)   A description of the agreement to enable it to be identified.

(2)   The names and postal addresses of the debtor and the creditor.

(3)   The total amount required to pay off the debtor's indebtedness, without any deduction for any early settlement rebate.

(4)   The amount of any such rebate to which the debtor is entitled by virtue of the agreement or under s.95 of the Act (whichever is the higher) calculated on the assumption that early settlement takes place on the settlement date, or, as the case may be, that the debtor is not entitled to any such rebate. This latter option is likely to be the case in a credit-token agreement, as a rebate is normally applicable under s.95 only in respect of agreements where there is a fixed date for repayment of the loan. The credit-token agreement is also unlikely to include a clause providing for a rebate.

(5)   The total amount to settle after deducting any rebate.

(6)   The settlement date, which in the case of credit repayable by instalments will be the date of the instalment due immediately following the expiration of twenty-eight days from the creditor's receipt of the debtor's request under s.97. In other cases, the settlement date is the date of the expiration of twenty-eight days from the receipt of the request by the creditor.

(7)   Where the debtor is entitled to a rebate under the Act (not the agreement), a statement that the rebate has been calculated in accordance with the Consumer Credit (Rebate on Early Settlement) Regulations 1983, SI 1983 No.1562, and that information and advice about the operation of the Act and the Regulations may be obtained from the Office of Fair Trading and the local Trading Standards Department or CAB respectively.

Unlike s.78(1), the debtor need not send any fee with his request for a statement under s.97(1). However, in other respects the provisions are similar. The creditor need comply with the request under s.97(1) only once a month (s.97(2)) and the position is similar with regard to the provision of copies of the statement to joint debtors under s.185(1). There is no power to dispense with this as there is with s.78(4). In addition, s.172(1) makes the s.97 statement binding on the creditor subject to the court's power to grant relief as mentioned above. This is also subject to the possibility of an estoppel being raised by the debtor in equity. Finally, the same sanctions of unenforceability consequent on default by the creditor and the imposition of a criminal offence if this default continues for a month apply in relation to s.97(1) (s.97(3)).

8.07   Termination statements

Whilst the discussion of termination statements might have been conveniently left to Chapter 12, which deals with termination, it seems likely that if a debtor asks for a settlement statement under s.97, he or she is considering paying off the indebtedness under the agreement. It therefore seems appropriate at this stage to look at the further rights of the debtor consequent on the termination of the agreement. It should be remembered, however, that the right to a termination statement does not arise just on early termination of the agreement.

Section 103(1) provides that if a customer serves a notice on a trader stating that the customer was a debtor under a regulated agreement described in the notice, and the trader was the creditor under the agreement, that the customer has discharged his indebtedness to the trader under the agreement, the agreement ceases to be operative at all, and the notice requires the trader to give the customer a notice, signed by or on behalf of the trader, confirming that the statements are correct, the trader must, within the prescribed period after receiving the notice, either comply with it or serve on the customer a counter-notice stating that, as the case may be, he disputes the correctness of the customer's notice or asserts that the customer is not indebted to him under the agreement. The notices from the customer and trader must be in writing (s.189(1)). Where the trader disputes the accuracy of the notice, he is to give particulars of the way in which he alleges it to be wrong (s.103(2)). The prescribed period is twelve working days (Consumer Credit (Prescribed Periods for Giving Information) Regulations 1983, SI 1983 No.1569) and if the default continues for more than one month the trader commits an offence (s.103(5)). The trader does not have to comply with subs.(1) in relation to any agreement if he has previously complied with the subsection on the service of a notice under it with respect to that agreement (s.103(4)). It would seem that the request by one debtor would involve sending a notice or counter-notice to any joint debtors under the agreement (s.185(1)(*a*)). Section 103(1) does not apply to non-commercial agreements (s.103(4)). Finally, the notice or counter-notice given by the trader under s.103(1)(*b*), or a notice under s.103(1) that the debtor is not indebted to him under the agreement, is binding on the trader (s.172(2)), subject to the court's power contained in s.172(3) to give relief. It should be noted that there is no equivalent provision in the Code of Banking Practice on termination statements, other than the provision in para.19.1 discussed above.

8.08 Appropriation of payments

The common law rule on appropriation of payments allows a creditor owed money under two or more transactions by the same debtor, in the absence of any election by the latter, to appropriate any payment made as he sees fit. The credit-token agreement may itself have a specific provision expressly making an appropriation — no doubt to suit the creditor rather than the debtor. It will be rare for a debtor to be liable under two or more regulated credit-token agreements with the same creditor, although many debtors may have both a Visa and Access agreement at one and the same time. However, where the debtor does have two separate regulated agreements with the same creditor, the Consumer Credit Act 1974, s.81 provides that the debtor is entitled, on making any payment in respect of the agreements which is not sufficient to discharge the total amount then due under all the agreements, to appropriate the sum paid by him either in or towards the satisfaction of the sum due under one of the agreements, or in or towards the satisfaction of the sums due under two or more of the agreements in such proportions as he thinks fit. This gives the debtor complete freedom as to how the payment should be apportioned, if at all. It can all be used towards one of the debts, or be spread among the rest as he or she may wish to specify. If the credit-token happens to be secured, not a common event, s.81(2) provides that in the absence of any election by the debtor, the payment made shall be apportioned towards the satisfaction of the sums due under the several agreements respectively in the proportions which those sums bear to one another.

Section 81(1) applies only where there are two or more regulated agreements with the same creditor and debtor. Consequently, if there are two agreements and only one is regulated, the subsection is not applicable. In this situation the position is regulated by the common law, or the terms of the unregulated agreement. The situation appears to be the same where there are, say, two regulated agreements and one unregulated between the same parties. As between the two regulated agreements on the one hand and the unregulated on the other, the terms of the unregulated one will prevail on the issue of appropriation and s.81 is inapplicable. However, once the unregulated agreement has been discharged, s.81 would apply as between the two remaining regulated agreements. As between two or more *regulated* agreements, s.81(1) is non-excludable (s.173(1)) and applies whether or not the agreement is non-commercial.

One other interesting point concerns the concept of the multiple agreement. It will be recalled that it was suggested that the better view was that a credit-token agreement was an example of a unitary multiple agreement, namely, in essence one agreement. This is despite the fact that it will usually fall into at least two of the separate categories of the Act: a DCS restricted-use agreement and a DC unrestricted-use agreement. If this is a correct conclusion, then s.81 was not designed to cover this type of situation, although it may relate to other categories of multiple agreements. There also appears at first sight to be a conflict between s.18(4) and s.81. The former provides that any sum 'payable' under a multiple agreement, if not apportioned by the parties, shall be apportioned as the court thinks requisite. Goode's view (III[82]) is that s.81 applies to payments made or tendered, whereas s.18(4) is concerned with sums 'payable' under the multiple agreement.

Section 81 does not contain any sanction for non-compliance by the creditor. Consequently, a breach of the section is not actionable in a civil or criminal court (s.170(1)). Failure to comply with the section may be something for the Director General of Fair Trading to contemplate under s.25 of the Act in relation to the licensing provisions. Also, in any proceedings where the issue of payment by the debtor arises, any failure by the creditor to adhere to the provisions of the section would enable the court to reopen the creditor's appropriation and substitute that of the debtor in its place. Section 135 gives the court the power to suspend an order, for example, one in favour of the creditor allowing enforcement of an agreement, pending the occurrence of a specified act or omission by the creditor. It may be possible to persuade the court to suspend any such order, pending the creditor's giving effect to the debtor's wishes on appropriation.

8.09   Variation of agreements

At common law the courts are reluctant to intervene in any agreement made between the parties in the absence of such factors as fraud, duress or undue influence. The Consumer Credit Act 1974 provides numerous examples of statutory intervention in the contractual relationship between creditor and debtor, as we have already seen. The parties to a contract, however, are not normally permitted to make unilateral changes to what has been agreed by them. They are allowed to vary their existing contract provided this is consensual. Also, there may, and usually will, be a provision in a credit-token agreement which automatically adjusts the interest rate in line with base lending rate. This is not a variation of the original agreement, merely an application of it. On the other hand, there may be a clause in the agreement which does more than this and enables the creditor unilaterally to change one of the terms of the agreement. This is a variation, as is a change of the terms mutually agreed by both parties. This latter arrangement may be regarded as a modifying agreement for which there are special rules in s.82(2) to (6). Variation in the first sense, namely, a unilateral change of a term of the contract by a creditor is governed by s.82(1).

Section 82(1) provides that, where under a power contained in a regulated consumer credit agreement the creditor varies the agreement, the variation shall not take effect before notice of it is given to the debtor in the prescribed manner. The subsection does not apply to an unregulated agreement, which includes, of course, one exempt under s.16 of the Regulations. It does not apply to non-commercial agreements (s.82(7)), but it does apply to agreements which are partly exempt, namely, those (such as bank overdrafts) not caught by Part V of the Act. It does not apply to automatic variation as explained above and it does not apply to variation clauses in favour of the creditor beyond the regulated agreement. If, e.g., there was an insurance protection policy linked to the credit card agreement and the policy contained a variation clause, this would be outside the scope of the subsection.

The notice of variation demanded under the subsection must be in writing (s.189(1)) and must give the details of the variation, normally being served (see s.176(1) for what counts as proper service) on the debtor at least seven days before the variation takes effect (Consumer Credit (Notice of Variation of Agreements) Regulations 1977, SI 1977 No.328 as amended by SIs 1979 No.661 and No.667). There is an alternative procedure for service of notices. This applies where the variation concerns the rate of interest, and the rate is, both before and after the variation, calculated by reference to the outstanding balance established at daily intervals. The creditor may serve notice by publishing the variation in at least three daily newspapers, in each case the type being not less than 3 millimetres in height and occupying not less than 100 square centimetres, or if this is not reasonably practicable, to publish it in the *Gazette*. Further, if it is reasonably practicable to do so, the notice of variation is to be prominently displayed, so that it is easily read, in a part (if any) open to the public of the creditor's premises where the agreement to which the variation is maintained. This provision is designed to save the creditor from the expense and time involved in giving individual notices to debtors every time there is a change in base lending rates and relates particularly to overdraft facilities where the interest is calculated on a daily basis.

By the Consumer Credit (Cancellation Notices and Copies of Documents) Regulations 1983, SI 1983 No.1557 (as amended by SI 1984 No.1108 and SI 1985 No.666), where an agreement has been varied by virtue of s.82(1), every copy of the executed agreement given to the debtor (or a surety, if any) under any provision of the Act except s.85(1) must contain either an easily legible copy of the latest notice of variation given in accordance with s.82(1) relating to each individual varied term of the agreement, or an easily legible statement of the terms of the agreement as varied in accordance with the subsection. The latter alternative requires the terms of the whole agreement to be included, not just the varied terms. As to copies under s.85(1), which it will be recalled relates specifically to credit-token agreements, the Regulations prescribe that every copy of the executed credit-token agreement given under that subsection where the agreement contains a power of variation, must comprise an easily legible statement of the current terms of the agreement, whether or not varied under s.82(1).

A creditor may be tempted to include the power of unilateral variation in the credit-token agreement on a variety of matters, perhaps with a view to precluding the operation of s.82(2) to (6), as these are complex and to be avoided if at all possible. However, if the credit-token agreement contains a large number of variation clauses, it runs the risk of not being an agreement at all. This is something to be wary of when trying to draft the agreement.

The Code of Banking Practice also has provisions covering the issue of variation. Paragraph 14.1 provides that card issuers will tell customers how any variation of the terms and conditions will be notified, as well as giving reasonable notice before giving any effect to a variation. These provisions are clearly aimed at the type of variation under discussion, namely, the unilateral alteration of the terms under a power in the agreement. Card issuers are under an obligation under para.14.3 to issue to customers, if there are sufficient changes in a twelve-month period to warrant it, a single document providing a consolidation of the variations made to the terms and conditions over that period. Paragraph 14.4 provides that creditors will publish changes to their interest rates in their branches or stores or in the press or in statements of account sent to cardholders, or by all those methods when such changes are of immediate effect. These provisions allow a certain latitude to creditors in normal circumstances as to the method of notification. They are in general terms far less demanding than their counterparts in the Act and the Regulations.

8.10 Modifying agreements

A modifying agreement is one which varies or supplements an earlier agreement. It does not completely replace the earlier agreement in the first instance but merely adds, modifies or deletes terms in that agreement. An agreement which, at common law, completely replaces the earlier agreement is one of novation and is not regulated by s.82 of the Act. If the subsequent agreement does not have this effect it will be regulated by the Act. Section 82(2) provides that such an agreement shall for the purposes of the Act be treated as revoking the earlier agreement, and containing provisions reproducing the combined effect of the two agreements. The subsection also states that obligations outstanding in relation to the earlier agreement shall be treated as outstanding instead in relation to the modifying agreement. This is in effect a deemed novation.

The subsection is wide in that it is not just restricted to regulated agreements. Where the earlier agreement is regulated, however, but the modifying agreement is otherwise not, then unless the agreement is for running-account credit, the modifying agreement is to be regarded as regulated also (s.82(3)). The exemption for running-account credit is obviously crucial in relation to credit-token agreements. Unless the modifying agreement in relation to running-account credit is itself regulated, then the Act, apart from s.82(2), will have no application to it. One difficult question concerns the original agreement and any matters still outstanding under it. According to s.82(2) these are treated as outstanding under the modifying agreement. Are these outstanding obligations regulated by the Act as they were in the earlier agreement? According to s.82(2), apparently not, but this would provide opportunity for evasion of the Act's provisions and the better view would be that these remaining matters would continue to be regulated, as the case may be, by the other provisions of the Act (but see Goode, I[1757], Example (1)(b)).

We have met the provision in s.82(4) before, at para.2.19. This provides that, where the earlier agreement is for running-account credit and is regulated, and, by the modifying agreement, the creditor allows the credit limit to be exceeded on a temporary basis only, Part V of the Act (except the all-important s.56) shall not apply to the modifying agreement, thus obviating the need for the creditor to comply with the burden of the formalities in that Part of the Act. This is aimed principally at overdraft facilities, but covers credit-token agreements as well. This has the added effect of preventing the modifying agreement from being cancellable, as Part V contains the cancellation provisions. In any event a modifying agreement will rarely be cancellable. However, s.82(5) provides that if the earlier agreement is cancellable and the modifying agreement is made within the cooling-off period under s.68 in relation to that earlier agreement, then the modifying agreement, whether it would be cancellable or not apart from s.82(5), is deemed to be cancellable. A cancellation notice may be served under s.68 in accordance with the cooling-off period relevant to the earlier agreement (see para.6.13). Apart from this provision, a modifying agreement is not treated as cancellable (s.82(6)). These provisions will rarely be invoked. The rules on modifying agreements, in common with those under s.82(1), do not apply to non-commercial agreements (s.82(7)).

In respect of credit-token agreements there will be limited circumstances where the modifying agreement will be subject to the formalities of the Act. This will occur where both the earlier and modifying agreements (with the exception of s.82(4) situations) are regulated. Also, if the earlier agreement is unregulated, but the modifying agreement is partly regulated, then in so far as the regulated aspects are concerned, the formalities must be complied with (see s.18 and para.3.21).

Where the modifying agreement is required to comply, then it must contain information to enable it to comply with, in particular, the Consumer Credit (Agreements) Regulations 1983. These are discussed at para.5.5.

8.11   Conclusion

This chapter has been concerned with a number of small but important issues which may frequently arise under a regulated credit-token agreement. The creditor needs to have regard to his obligation to provide information in accordance with ss.78, 97 and 103, as well as remembering the duty to serve a notice of variation as appropriate under s.82(1). The creditor should perhaps try to avoid the perils of the modifying agreement rules, just discussed, by careful drafting of the credit-token agreement so as to ensure that the necessary rights of variation are included from the outset, rather than having to resort to obtaining the debtor's consent to a modifying agreement at a later date. The rules in s.82(1) are clearly less onerous than having to comply with the Agreements Regulations all over again.

CHAPTER 9

Joint and Several Liability of Creditor and Supplier

9.01   Introduction

One of the most innovative and significant provisions in the Consumer Credit Act 1974, a revolutionary piece of legislation in its own right, is that relating to the joint and several liability of the creditor and supplier created by s.75. No doubt the most controversial of the controls introduced by the Act, it has been under attack from creditors, the most prominent criticism being directed by the issuers of credit cards. Their ingenuity in seeking to interpret away its effect seems almost boundless and we shall be discussing the merits or otherwise of their attempts to reduce its scope in due course.

For the debtor, the most important problematical aspect during the currency of a credit agreement, other than the issue of repayment of the credit, will often be the quality of the goods or services acquired by means of the credit. The difficulty facing the debtor before the coming into force of s.75 was that in many transactions, on the face of it, there were two distinct agreements, one between the debtor and the supplier relating to the supply of the goods or services, the other between the debtor and the creditor for the supply of the credit. Frequently, where there was a problem with the goods or services, either because they were defective or had been misrepresented by the supplier, the debtor would be compelled to continue with the credit agreement which had financed the supply transaction, although he or she may have received little or nothing under the latter. Rights under the sale of goods or similar legislation were of little value if the supplier was insolvent, as sometimes happened. The debtor was obliged to pay for something which had little value, as the law failed to recognise any link between the supplier and the creditor. This link may now be recognised in suitable cases as we have seen, as evidenced by the cumbersome but effective concept of the debtor–creditor–supplier agreement (see paras.3.10 to 3.14). The clear policy behind the creation of this concept and the imposition of joint and several liability on the creditor and the supplier where the link is established was determined by the Crowther Committee in its influential report in 1971, the driving force behind the 1974 Act. Where a business connection could be established, the Committee (para.6.6.20 of the report) took the view that the creditor and supplier were engaged in a joint venture and had to share the responsibility as well as the profits. The creditor was to be liable for the misrepresentations and breaches of contract by the supplier in recognition of this sharing of responsibility. The debtor was seen as vulnerable in situations such as this, particularly at the hands of the supplier, and it was perceived that the creditor would normally have some control or power over the recalcitrant trader. In a sense the creditor was considered as being an insurer of the supplier's obligations, particularly so where the latter was insolvent or had otherwise disappeared from the scene.

In recent years, the value of the provision in s.75 has been admirably demonstrated in relation to holiday, leisure and travel companies. Where such a company goes into liquidation, typically at the height of the holiday season, many consumers are faced with losing considerable sums of money paid in advance for holidays and flights. For those stranded on the holiday at the time of the insolvency, the problem may be resolved under the ABTA or Civil Aviation Authority schemes. These schemes, however, are severely limited in their impact in many respects, but regulations soon to be made under an EC Directive will improve the holidaymaker's rights in this type of situation. It is clear that, in the meantime, s.75 has played a useful role in compensating consumers at least for some of their loss. There are, naturally, limitations on precisely what can be achieved using the section in this way and these will be explored below.

The section provides that the debtor shall have a 'like claim' against the creditor for the misrepresentation or breach of contract of the supplier. The creditor's liability, therefore, depends on the debtor establishing a claim under one of those headings against the supplier. The creditor's liability is meant to be the mirror image of that of the supplier; consequently, defences and valid exemption clauses which would avail the supplier if sued will also be available to the creditor. In such circumstances, credit card issuers must ensure that their claims staff are fully conversant with the provisions of the major consumer protection legislation, including the Sale of Goods Act 1979, the Supply of Goods and Services Act 1982 and the Unfair Contract Terms Act 1977, as well as having a good grasp of the law of actionable misrepresentation.

The first part of this chapter gives a brief overview of the potential liability of the supplier to the debtor under the supply contract. The remainder of the chapter considers the creditor's position as a result of s.75. The creditor may be liable for things done by the supplier independently of the section, for example under common law agency or the deemed agency created by s.56 of the Act. These are considered in the following chapter.

9.02 Misrepresentation by the supplier

The rules concerning actionable misrepresentation were discussed in reasonable depth in Chapter 4 in the context of the precontractual regulation of credit-token agreements. In general, we are here considering the supplier's misstatements relating to the qualities or other attributes of the goods or services supplied to the debtor. The possible liability of the supplier will be briefly summarised in this context.

Where the debtor is induced to contract with the supplier as a result of a false statement of fact by the latter, the debtor may have an action in fraudulent, negligent or innocent misrepresentation against the supplier. Fraud requires proof of dishonesty, but if established is actionable in the tort of deceit and damages may be awarded in respect of losses directly caused by the fraud, irrespective of foreseeability. The debtor who fails to prove fraud may be able to succeed in negligence either at common law under the *Hedley Byrne* principle or under the statutory action contained in s.2(1) of the Misrepresentation Act 1967. The common law action may succeed where the statement is one of opinion or advice, unlike the statutory action. However, the burden of proof under the statute is upon the defendant supplier to disprove negligence, whereas at common law it is normally upon the plaintiff debtor to prove negligence. If the debtor is successful under either of these two headings, he will be entitled to damages. At common law these will be based on the reasonable foreseeability principle, whereas under the statute the position is the same as if fraud had been established. If neither fraud nor negligence can be proved the misrepresentation is merely innocent and the debtor has no automatic right to damages. For all three types of misrepresentation, the debtor is entitled to rescind the contract with the supplier, subject in the case of innocent misrepresentation to the court's discretion to award damages instead (s.2(2) of the 1967 Act). The right to rescind may be lost in cases, e.g. of affirmation by the debtor and, sometimes, delay in purporting to rescind. It should be noted that where the debtor does rescind the contract, the debtor's claim for the return of the purchase price is a claim in restitution and not damages. This is often a point of some confusion and will be considered again later in the discussion on the scope of s.75 of the 1974 Act. It is possible that in some cases the debtor may be claiming both in restitution, i.e. for a refund of the price paid, and also for damages for consequential losses caused by the misrepresentation.

Liability for misrepresentation can be excluded only in so far as a clause satisfies the test of reasonableness in s.11 of the Unfair Contract Terms Act 1977 (s.8 of the 1977 Act).

9.03 Breach of express terms of the contract by the supplier

The potential breach by the supplier may fall under either the express terms of the contract, including statements in the precontractual negotiations which become incorporated in the contract, or under any relevant implied terms. The debtor's remedy for the former will depend on whether the term is considered to be a major or minor term of the contract (see para.4.5). The debtor may be entitled to repudiate the contract, recover the purchase price on a restitutionary basis, and at the same time claim damages on the grounds of what was in the reasonable contemplation of the parties under the normal contractual principle. Alternatively, the remedy may be damages only for breach of a minor term of the contract.

9.04 Breach of implied terms by the supplier under sale contracts

The majority of purchases made by means of a credit-token are probably made under contracts for the sale of goods. Essentially, this is a contract in which the supplier supplies goods in exchange for money only. In this type of contract, the Sale of Goods Act 1979 implies a number of valuable terms in favour of the purchasing debtor. Principal among these are the terms as to quality in s.14 of the Act, which, as we shall see, are non-excludable in consumer dealings.

The 1979 Act implies the following terms into sale contracts:
(1) a condition that the seller has the right to sell the goods or will have at the time the property in the goods is to pass to the purchaser, implied warranties that the goods are free from encumbrances and that the purchaser will enjoy quiet possession of the goods (s.12);
(2) a condition that where the goods are sold by description or sample, the goods will correspond with the description or sample (ss.13 and 15);
(3) where the supplier sells the goods in the course of a business, an implied condition that the goods are of merchantable quality, except as regards defects brought to the buyer's attention before the making of the contract, or, where the buyer examines the goods

before the contract is made, defects which that examination ought to reveal (s.14(2));

(4) where the seller supplies the goods in the course of a business and the buyer makes known, expressly or by implication, to the supplier any particular purpose for which the goods are being bought, an implied condition that the goods supplied under the contract are reasonably fit for that purpose, whether or not that is a purpose for which such goods are supplied, except where the circumstances show that the buyer does not rely or it is unreasonable for him to rely on the seller's skill or judgment (s.14(3)).

These implied terms are generally regarded as the cornerstone of consumer protection in the context of sale transactions, although their origins lay in the relationships between merchants in the nineteenth century rather than between traders and private consumers. A full exposition of their precise scope is not possible here, but it is worthwhile making a few observations on some salient points.

The implied terms as to title, correspondence with description and sample apply to all sale contracts irrespective of whether the goods are supplied by the supplier in the course of a business, unlike those of merchantable quality and fitness for particular purpose. This may have little impact in the case of purchases made by means of a credit-token, as it is unlikely that a private seller would have an arrangement with a credit card issuer. The implied term as to correspondence with description in s.13 of the 1979 Act is of only limited value to the debtor where the misdescription concerned relates to a matter which identifies the goods, something which is a substantial ingredient and is misdescribed. This normally rules out complaints about the quality of goods and many other aspects of misdescription. If the complaint is about the misdescription of some quality of the goods or some other aspect the debtor must use s.14 of the Act, or rely on an actionable misrepresentation.

The merchantable quality condition in s.14(2) of the 1979 Act and its definition in s.14(6) have caused endless problems for the courts over the years, particularly during the last twenty or so, where as a result of increased affluence and mass production consumer dissatisfaction with the quality of goods has risen rapidly. Most of the litigation brought by consumers has concerned new and second-hand vehicles. The courts have struggled with the problems of whether what are classed as 'minor defects' render a new car unmerchantable and what the appropriate level of consumer expectation should be in relation to a second-hand car. It is perhaps fair to say that the trend in the cases in the last few years has been more favourable to consumers.

The implied condition of fitness for particular purpose overlaps to some extent with the term of merchantable quality, in that goods may at one and the same time be both unmerchantable and unfit for their particular purpose. Where the provision comes into its own is the situation in which goods are merchantable because they are fit for one of their normal purposes but not fit for the buyer's particular purpose. If the buyer has expressly or implicitly informed the seller of his special purpose, the seller is deemed to confirm that the goods are fit for such purpose.

For a considerable time there have been proposals to amend the implied term as to merchantable quality. At one time these were contained in a Bill which was lost (Consumer Guarantee Bill 1990). There is a vague promise to reintroduce the amendments in the near future.

9.05 Implied terms in other types of contract

Whilst it is still true to say that the most common contract entered into by the debtor using a credit-token is one for the sale of goods, there are nonetheless many other contracts entered into by debtors and paid for by means of a credit card on a regular basis. These other types of contract include hiring agreements. For example, it is common to use a credit-token to pay for the short-term hire of a motor vehicle. The supplier's obligations in relation to implied terms in such a contract are to be found in ss.6 to 10 of the Supply of Goods and Services Act 1982. These implied obligations correspond, with suitable minor modifications, to those contained in ss.12 to 15 of the Sale of Goods Act 1979, discussed above. Hire-purchase agreements also have almost identical implied terms (ss.8 to 11 of the Supply of Goods (Implied Terms) Act 1973).

Similarly, in contracts for work and materials, ss.1 to 5 of the 1982 Act are modelled on the Sale of Goods Act implied conditions and warranties in relation to the goods supplied under the contract. For example, an agreement for the installation of central heating is commonly called a work and materials contract. If the goods under the contract, i.e. the boiler, radiators and piping, are defective, there may be a breach of one of the implied terms. It will often be the case that some part, if not all, of the work done under the agreement may be paid for by credit card.

By definition, work and materials contracts include an element of labour or services. There are also contracts which are pure services contracts, where no goods are transferred to the consumer. In both these situations, ss.13 to 15 of the 1982 Act imply in respect of the services aspect terms as to reasonable care and skill, reasonable time as to performance and reasonable charges. It may again often be the case today that services are wholly or partly paid for by credit-token.

9.06　Remedies

Equally important as the liability rules just discussed are those relating to remedies. After all, the debtor has a 'like claim' against the creditor and the liability decision, if favourable to the debtor, must be translated into a remedy. We have already discussed the possibilities in relation to actionable misrepresentation, namely damages and restitution.

Under the Sale of Goods Act 1979, where the buyer has received goods which are in breach of the implied terms, there are a number of possibilities. First, if the term is described in the Act as a 'warranty', the only remedy is a claim for damages based on contractual principles of remoteness and measure of damages. The rules are actually contained in the Act itself (ss.51 to 53). The buyer need not accept a credit note. Only a few of the implied terms in the Act are described as 'warranties', the majority being given the important label of 'condition'. They are major terms of the contract, breach of which normally entitles the buyer to repudiate the contract (reject the goods and claim back the purchase price on a restitutionary basis) and/or claim damages in respect of consequential losses. The buyer might, however, choose to carry on with the contract, thus treating the breach of condition as a breach of warranty, consequently restricting his remedy to one in damages only.

In addition, the buyer may be prevented from repudiating the contract on the ground that he has 'accepted' the goods under the statutory formula contained in ss.34 and 35 of the 1979 Act. The right to reject is currently lost in three situations where the contract is not severable and the buyer is deemed to have accepted all or part of the goods. The buyer is deemed to accept where he intimates acceptance to the seller, does an act inconsistent with the seller's ownership, or retains the goods beyond a reasonable time without rejecting them. The last of the three has proved the most problematic in consumer transactions in particular. It has been stated that the buyer merely has a reasonable time in which to test out the goods after they have been delivered; the time is generally short and is not geared towards the discovery of defects in the goods. One reason for this is that the buyer, on repudiation, is entitled to a refund of all money paid to the seller, without any deduction for use. Another is that when the goods are returned to the seller, they can no longer be lawfully sold as new, placing the seller in a difficult position. Whatever the merits of these arguments, the statutory rules on acceptance are tilted quite firmly in favour of the seller as they currently stand, although there are limited proposals to amend them to favour consumers more.

It should be noted that these rules apply only to contracts for the sale of goods, not to contracts covered by the Supply of Goods and Services

Act 1982, or to hire-purchase, hire agreements and conditional sale agreements, where the latter are consumer sale agreements. The issue of loss of the right to reject in these types of contract is governed by the more generous common law concept of affirmation. This states that a buyer loses the right to reject (where rejection is a theoretical and practicable remedy) only when he is fully aware of the breach. In circumstances where affirmation occurs, however, the buyer may not recover everything paid in a restitution claim, as the supplier may be able to set off a deduction for any use the buyer has had from the goods.

9.07   Exemption clauses

Just as the creditor may explore the ambiguities and difficulties in the liability and remedial rules outlined above, he may also rely, in proceedings brought against him under s.75 of the Consumer Credit Act, on a valid exclusion clause or notice employed by the supplier. Consideration must therefore be given to the issue of what constitutes a valid exclusion clause, a task made much more arduous for the supplier, and consequently the creditor, following the Unfair Contract Terms Act 1977.

At common law, the courts had attempted, with varying, but essentially limited degrees of success, to control what were perceived to be unfair exclusion clauses. The doctrine of incorporation by reasonable notice, the use of the *contra proferentem* rule of construction and the ill-fated fundamental breach principle (finally relegated to the status of a rule of construction) are all symptomatic of the judicial dislike of some exemption clauses. The common law rules are still with us and are occasionally useful in challenging the validity of a clause not struck down by the 1977 Act. However, in the context of the present discussion, it is more likely that the Act will affect any reliance on such a clause.

The definition of an exemption clause is given a very wide meaning by s.13 of the 1977 Act. It includes, for example, clauses which seek to impose arbitrary time limits on reporting complaints about defects, or seek to change rules of evidence or procedure or restrict the use of particular remedies.

9.08   Clauses excluding the implied terms as to quality

The Unfair Contract Terms Act takes different approaches to exemption clauses, depending on the type of liability sought to be excluded. As we shall see, some clauses are valid provided they are reasonable. Others are irrebuttably presumed to be unreasonable and are absolutely prohibited and declared void from the start.

Any attempt to exclude the implied obligations as to title in sale or other supply contracts, including hire-purchase, is void. As against a consumer, any attempt to exclude the liability for the implied terms as to correspondence with description or sample, merchantable quality and fitness for particular purpose is void. As against a person not dealing as a consumer, the exclusion clause must satisfy the reasonableness test (ss.6 and 7 of the 1977 Act). A person deals as a 'consumer' if he does not make or hold himself out as making the contract in the course of a business, the other party does make the contract in the course of a business and, where the contract in question involves the supply of goods, they are of a type ordinarily supplied for private use or consumption. The burden of proof is with the person who is claiming that the transaction is not a consumer dealing, namely, the supplier. A sale by auction or competitive tender is not a consumer dealing (s.12). A clause on display on retail premises, for example, stating that refunds of the purchase price are not permitted would fall foul of s.6 of the 1977 Act. To display such a notice would, in addition, constitute a criminal offence by the retailer under the Consumer Transactions (Restriction on Statements) Order 1976, SI 1976 No.1813, as amended by SI 1978 No.127. Whilst there is no suggestion that a creditor could be liable for an offence in these circumstances (s.75 of the Consumer Credit Act is concerned only with civil claims), the fact of a criminal offence in addition to the attempt to include an ineffective clause may be something the Director General might consider on renewal of a licence. It should be recalled that the supplier/retailer in this situation is regarded as the associate of the creditor.

9.09   Clauses seeking to exclude negligence

The judges did their best to restrict the use of clauses which sought to exclude contractual or tortious negligence claims, relying predominantly on the *contra proferentem* rule. The Unfair Contract Terms Act prevents the exclusion of negligence-based claims, whether contractual or tortious, as long as the claim arises in a business context and results in death or personal injury. Any other losses may be excluded provided the clause passes the reasonableness test (s.2). This provision may well be relevant where the supply contract is one wholly or partly for the supply of a service, e.g. installing central heating. A clause in the written agreement, for example, which purported to exempt the installer from liability for injury to the other contracting party should the installer or its employees be negligent would be void. It should be noted that s.2 differentiates clauses on the basis of the type of harm inflicted, not according to whether the transaction is a consumer dealing or not, by way of contrast with ss.6 and 7.

9.10 Exclusion of contractual liability in general

The 1977 Act also seeks to regulate other types of clause which attempt to exclude contractual liability which falls outside the categories described in paras.9.08 and 9.09 above. Section 3 applies where one of the parties to a contract deals as a consumer (para.9.08), or on the other's written standard terms of business. This latter phrase is not defined, but is clearly intended to include within the scope of s.3 a large number of contracts where both parties are businesses. For our purposes, it certainly includes a person dealing as a consumer and will be applicable to the majority of transactions under consideration in this book. Section 3, where it applies, provides that the other party cannot by reference to any contract term, when in breach of contract himself, exclude or restrict any liability of his in respect of the breach, unless the clause is reasonable. Nor can he claim to be entitled to render a contractual performance substantially different from that which was reasonably expected from him or, in respect of the whole or any part of his contractual obligation, to render no performance at all, unless the reasonableness test is fulfilled.

An example of where s.3 would apply would be a contract to service a washing machine on a particular day. If there was a clause in the agreement which attempted to prevent the consumer from suing if the contract was not performed on the due date, such a provision would have to be reasonable to survive.

9.11 The reasonableness test

The burden of establishing the reasonableness of any clause rests with the person seeking to rely on it. Section 11 of the 1977 Act provides that the reasonableness of the clause has to be tested in the light of the circumstances which were, or ought reasonably to have been, known to or in the contemplation of the parties at the time of making the contract. The wider an exemption, the less likely it is to be successful, bearing in mind the statutory guidelines in Sch.2 to the Act. Strictly speaking, by some strange anomaly, the guidelines in the Schedule apply to the reasonableness test only when it arises under ss.6 and 7. However, no doubt a court will consider the matters listed when deciding the issue of reasonableness imposed under ss.2 and 3. The Schedule provides that the following shall be considered:

(1) the relative strength of the bargaining power of the parties, taking into account, among other things, the availability of other means of meeting the customer's requirements;

(2) whether the customer received an inducement to agree to the term, or could have made a similar contract with someone else, without having to agree to a similar term;

(3) whether the customer knew or ought reasonably to have been aware of the existence of the term, taking into account, among other things, the customs of the trade and any previous course of dealings between the parties;

(4) where the term excludes or restricts any relevant liability if some condition is not complied with, whether it was reasonable at the time of the contract to expect that compliance would be practicable;

(5) whether the goods were manufactured, processed or adapted to a special order of the customer.

There has not been an abundance of case law on this test. In one of the very earliest cases on the reasonableness test (*Mitchell* v. *Finney* [1983] 2 AC 803), the House of Lords made it extremely clear that the appeal courts did not wish to see a flood of cases before them. It was stated that the test is a factual matter for the judge at first instance and an appeal court would be extremely reluctant to interfere with the trial judge's view. The underlying principle is the relative strength of bargaining power. Any inequality affecting the customer may well result in an adverse decision for the supplier. The elements of negotiation and ability to insure against the possible loss following any breach have been perceived to be decisive factors so far.

9.12 Joint and several liability

So far in this chapter we have considered the possible liability of the supplier to the debtor for misrepresentation and breach of contract. As pointed out earlier, this is necessary to appreciate just what the creditor might be found liable for under s.75 of the Consumer Credit Act, where it applies. Section 75(1) provides that, where a debtor under a DCS agreement falling within s.12(*b*) or (*c*) has, in relation to a transaction financed by the agreement, any claim against the supplier for misrepresentation or breach of contract, he shall have a like claim against the creditor, who is jointly and severally liable with the supplier. The wording is clear: the debtor's claim against the creditor stands or falls with that against the supplier. There is some overlap here with the agency liability created by s.56 of the Act. This is considered in the following chapter, when the two sections are compared.

A number of important and controversial points are raised by s.75(1).

9.13 Claim by debtor

Section 75(1) talks of a claim by the debtor only. This apparently has one major unforeseen consequence. The debtor is the person receiving the credit under a consumer credit agreement or the person to whom that person's rights and duties under the agreement have passed by assignment or operation of law (s.189(1)). The debtor is the person who is obliged by the terms of his agreement to reimburse the creditor for the credit facility. Consequently, a person who, at the request of the debtor, is provided with an additional card for his or her use is not a debtor. He or she is not liable for the repayment of the credit to the creditor, but also he or she cannot take advantage of s.75 when it might otherwise apply. If the person to whom the additional card was issued was made a joint account-holder, the problem would be resolved, for as a joint debtor s.75 would apply to his or her use of the card.

In the absence of a joint account, the authorised card user is in a difficult situation. He or she has a contract with the supplier but is unable to use the section and claim from the creditor. The debtor (the account-holder) has no contract with the supplier, because the supply contract is between the supplier and the additional card user. Therefore, the debtor cannot use s.75 because he has no claim against the supplier. The debtor is obliged to repay the creditor the credit and has no right of set-off. This will be particularly anomalous if the parties (the debtor and the authorised user) belong to the same household, as is often the case.

It might be possible to put forward an argument based on agency, namely, that the authorised user is the agent of the debtor, although its strength is doubtful. In any event, such an argument would be of minimal value, if any at all, where the goods acquired turned out to be defective and damaged the property of the authorised user. The agency argument would prevent him or her suing the supplier in contract and the debtor would have no claim because he had not suffered any loss. In that situation the authorised user would have to rely on the strict liability provisions in the Consumer Protection Act 1987, Part 1, provided the value of the property damaged exceeded the statutory minimum of £275, or possibly the common law relating to negligence.

Another rather ingenious argument on the debtor point has been put forward by credit card issuers. It has been remarked upon before that account-holders often repay the whole amount of the credit on receipt of the monthly account sent to them by the creditor. In such circumstances, it has been argued that once a debtor has repaid the amount of credit in respect of any particular item, he is no longer a debtor in relation to that supply. If the product in question failed to function or because of a latent defect caused harm to the debtor or his property after that date, he could not bring a claim against the creditor. He would have to pursue the claim against the supplier alone. This seems a technical argument with very little merit. Section 75 is concerned with the supplier's misrepresentation and breach of contract and the policy objective of sharing the liability between the creditor and supplier. By definition, misrepresentation takes place before the supply contract is concluded. In addition, an express term of the contract may be based on a representation which has become incorporated into the contract. It is also highly probable that a breach of an implied term will take place at an early stage after the delivery of the goods or supply of the service. Moreover, the essence of a claim for a breach of an implied term is that the defect in the goods or service existed at the time the contract was performed, by delivery or otherwise. Thus, at the time when the Crowther Committee, in its wisdom, considered that the debtor was highly vulnerable, namely, at or before the making of the supply agreement, the impact of things done by the supplier is also at its strongest. At this stage the creditor cannot deny that the account-holder is a debtor within the meaning of s.75. It seems therefore that the cardholder's rights under the section are in no way impeached by early payment. Jones suggests (p.203) that s.14(3) of the Act appears to apply to deem credit to be provided even if the account-holder pays off the account at the end of the settlement period. It would seem an arbitrary anomaly to extend the protection of s.75 to those who have availed themselves of the extended credit under a credit card agreement, and not to those who have not.

The most compelling argument against the interpretation suggested by credit card issuers is that it would deprive the debtor of the right to make a restitutionary claim against the creditor under s.75. That such a claim may be made where the supplier is guilty of misrepresentation or a serious breach of contract is seemingly beyond doubt. If the debtor could not use s.75 if he had repaid the credit, his claim for restitution would fail. He cannot bring such a claim unless he has paid the creditor, but if he does pay, he loses the benefit of s.75. This surely cannot have been intended when the section was incorporated into the Act.

9.14   Debtor–creditor–supplier agreements under s.12(*b*) or (*c*) of the Consumer Credit Act

We have already met a limited form of joint and several liability under the Act in relation to the return of deposits and payment of part-exchange allowances under cancellable agreements (paras.6.15 and 6.17, respectively). The liability was imposed there only in respect of DCS agreements under s.12(*b*) (restricted-use agreements only). Section 75 applies whether the DCS is under s.12(*b*) or (*c*). This means that it is applicable solely to those situations in which the creditor and supplier are different persons. If the creditor and supplier are one and the same person, as may be the case with a store or budget-type card, the agreement is a DCS under s.12(*a*), any claim for misrepresentation or breach of contract may be made against the creditor directly, as there is a contractual relationship between the creditor and the debtor for the supply of goods or the service. Occasionally, a department store may set up an associated but legally separate organisation to issue its in-store credit card. In this situation the agreement will be a DCS under s.12(*b*) and s.75 will apply.

Section 75 does not apply to a hire-purchase, conditional sale or credit sale agreement for much the same reason, as these are s.12(*a*) DCS agreements. The case of *Porter* v. *General Guarantee Corporation Ltd* [1982] RTR 384 suggests mistakenly that the section applies to a hire-purchase agreement, although the actual decision is not in any doubt. The creditor under the hire-purchase agreement was liable under the implied terms directly to the debtor. There was no need to rely on s.75 in those circumstances.

A credit card issuer may, however, be liable under a hire-purchase agreement in a sense. For example, the debtor may enter into a hire-purchase agreement with creditor A. The deposit is paid by means of a credit-token agreement issued to him by creditor B. In the event of a breach of the hire-purchase agreement, the debtor may sue creditor A, who in this situation is the supplier of the goods, or B, relying on s.75. The same would be true of a conditional sale or credit sale agreement in those circumstances.

9.15 Pre-existing arrangements

For there to be a DCS under s.12(*b*) or (*c*) of the Consumer Credit Act, some business connection must be shown to exist between the creditor and the supplier. We saw in Chapter 3 what the necessary business connection had to be and that it differed under s.12(*b*) from the requirement under s.12(*c*). If there is no such connection, there is no DCS agreement and, consequently, s.75 is inapplicable. We have also already seen that debit cards are expressly excluded from being DCS agreements because of the amendment to s.187 of the Act. The new s.187(3A) confirms what was probably the position anyway, that a card issued under EFTPOS arrangements does not constitute 'pre-existing arrangements'. This is so even in circumstances where the debit card enables the debtor to obtain credit, either where there is an agreed overdraft facility and the account is in debit already or will be following the transaction, or where the creditor temporarily allows an overdrawing. The effect of this is to prevent the debtor who acquires defective goods, for example, by using the debit card, from claiming against the issuer of the card. The debtor in that situation is restricted to a remedy against the supplier alone.

Barclaycard, one of the leading issuers of credit cards and a merchant acquirer, has put forward another argument in an attempt to reduce the impact of s.75. The company sought to argue that the section did not apply in transactions where the supplier in question had not been recruited to the Visa scheme by the company itself. Within the Visa scheme there are a number of merchant acquirers, of which Barclaycard was one. Each acquirer is entitled to recruit new suppliers into the scheme and would handle the business from that supplier, i.e. payments. Where the supplier was recruited by a merchant acquirer other than Barclaycard, the latter argued that even though its card was used to pay the supplier, there was no pre-existing arrangement between Barclaycard and the relevant supplier and therefore s.75 did not apply to the transaction. This again seems to be a technical argument without any merit. For one thing, the debtor is not in a position to know by which acquirer the supplier was recruited into the scheme. Second, it seems somewhat hypocritical of card issuers to suggest this, when consumers are often subjected to advertising and promotional literature which goes out of its way to stress the convenience of joining the Visa or Access scheme, with the vast number of outlets available for the use of either card. To suggest that members of the Visa or Access schemes are discrete entities runs counter to the professed image of the schemes themselves. The Office of Fair Trading disagreed with Barclaycard's view, but it seems that the matter has been resolved by a 1991 statement from Barclaycard to the effect that in practice it will not take the point in claims made under s.75.

9.16 Regulated agreement

As s.75 applies only to a DCS agreement under s.12(*b*) or (*c*), it also applies only to regulated agreements. Agreements outside the limits of the Act are obviously not covered, nor are exempt agreements. Therefore, the section does not apply to purchases made by American Express or Diner's Club cards. It does apply to those agreements, however, that are only partly exempt, namely, those exempt from Part V.

One controversy arose fairly soon after the coming into force of s.75 (1st July 1977). The card issuers took the view that a credit-token issued after that date but by virtue of an agreement already in existence on that date, did not attract the joint and several liability provisions. Goode (I[1576]) argues to the contrary on the basis that the agreement is a unilateral contract and that each use of the credit-token to pay for goods or services is in effect a separate acceptance of the standing offer by the creditor. He argues, therefore, that any use of the token after the relevant date does attract the provisions in s.75. This argument has not found favour with the card issuers. The Office of Fair Trading seems to take a similar view to Goode, although possibly on other grounds. The Office based its argument on the proposition that a new agreement is entered into on renewal of a token, once it has been accepted by the debtor under s.66. The disagreement has been settled by compromise, in that the banks have been persuaded to accept joint and several liability in respect of agreements entered into before the date in question. However, the liability under this compromise is only to the extent of the credit advanced under the transaction in dispute. It also seems to be the case that the card issuers expect the debtor to take action as far as is possible against the supplier before turning to them. There is evidence that the issuers have tended to honour the compromise, a good illustration being the Laker Airlines collapse.

9.17 Claim for misrepresentation or breach of contract by supplier

The claim of the debtor can be only in respect of a misrepresentation or a breach of contract by the supplier. In the discussion earlier in this chapter, the focus was upon the supplier's liability for actionable misrepresentation under the various headings and the possibility of action for breach of the express or implied terms of the contract in question. Section 75 of the Consumer Credit Act cannot be used where the basis of the action against the supplier lies in a breach of statutory duty, for example Part 1 of the Consumer Protection Act 1987. Such an action may be brought against a retailer who is an own-brander or where the retailer refuses to name his immediate supplier. This is clearly outside the scope of s.75. Also, it is not possible to bring an action in tortious negligence or fraud other than in misrepresentation. An action under common law negligence would not fall within s.75 (compare s.56, discussed in Chapter

10), unless the negligence related to a misstatement. On the other hand, contractual negligence, of whatever kind, is clearly covered.

The section's applicability is obviously based on the assumption that a supply contract has been entered into between the debtor and the supplier of the misrepresented or defective goods or services. This point may be easily overlooked in some situations. One such is where the debtor books a holiday with a holiday company through a travel agent. Agency law is somewhat ambivalent as to whose agent the travel agent is in these circumstances. It seems that he or she is probably an independent contractor, not the agent of either party. If the whole or part of the price of the holiday is paid to the agent by means of a credit-token, the debtor cannot rely on s.75, should the holiday company default under the contract or be guilty of misrepresentation. It would seem that the debtor is making a contract with the agent and if the latter fails to provide the service required, the debtor can sue the creditor for the travel agent's breach but not for that of the holiday company. Recently, Barclaycard did not take the privity point although it was legally entitled to do so (*Independent*, 29th July 1992, the Land Travel failure).

The creditor's liability is also restricted to those transactions financed by means of the use of the credit-token. Ancillary contracts are outside the scope of the section, unless they are also financed by the credit agreement. For example, the debtor pays for a fridge-freezer by means of a credit-token. He also enters into a maintenance agreement with the supplier. If there is a breach of this agreement, s.75 will not impose joint and several liability on the creditor unless the debtor paid part or all of the maintenance contract fee by using the token.

9.18   Scope of s.75 of the Consumer Credit Act

The debtor is given a 'like claim' against the creditor. As Goode (I[1578]) points out, the liability of the creditor to the debtor is 'co-terminous' with that of the supplier. The creditor is entitled to use any defences, including exemption or limitation clauses if valid, the supplier could employ in an action brought by the debtor. If the creditor tries to rely on a clause in the credit agreement purporting to exclude the debtor's rights against the supplier, this is not permitted, being caught by s.10 of the Unfair Contract Terms Act 1977.

It seems that the creditor can exercise a right of set-off vested in the supplier as well as any vested in him in his own right. Thus, if the debtor is liable to the supplier for sums under another contract, the creditor can set this off against the debtor's claim under s.75. Goode (I[1579]) argues that this is the sensible solution, as to decide otherwise would deprive the supplier of his right of set-off if subsequently sued under the indemnity provision (s.75(2)) by the creditor.

The debtor can maintain a restitutionary claim against the creditor. On rescission for misrepresentation, or repudiation for breach of contract, the debtor will be entitled to make such a claim, namely, for his money back. It seems beyond doubt that this is possible. It should be added that if the creditor is liable for restitution, he does not have any claim against any goods supplied under the contract. These revert to the supplier and the creditor's claim is monetary only by way of indemnity against the supplier.

One interesting point arises from the other case decided so far on the section. The fact that a debtor has the right to rescind or repudiate the supply transaction does not give him the right to rescind or repudiate the credit agreement. *UDT* v. *Taylor* (1980 SLT (Sh Ct) 28) decided to the contrary but the general consensus is that this is wrong (Goode, I[1580]; Dobson [1981] JBL 179; Davidson (1980) 96 LQR 343; Jones, p.208). The words a 'like claim' clearly refer back to the transaction financed by the credit agreement and not to a claim under the latter agreement itself. In relation to a credit-token agreement which may have been concluded sometime before, it would be a nonsense.

The claim against the creditor is a monetary claim, whether this has a basis in restitution or damages. The claim is not restricted to the amount of credit advanced by the creditor, or to the purchase price of the goods or services. If the supplier's breach results in personal injuries to the debtor, or substantial damage to his property, the creditor will be liable for this in the same way as the supplier would be.

The creditor retains his rights under the credit agreement despite the fact that he may be liable under s.75. Any rights he may have will, naturally, be subject to the debtor's claim. The debtor's claim may be less than is owed to the creditor under the agreement, in which case the debtor may exercise a right of set-off as against any payments due under the agreement. Alternatively, if the debtor's claim equals that of the creditor against him, the liabilities cancel each other out. If the debtor's claim exceeds the amount due to the creditor, the debtor would actively have to press the claim for the excess against the creditor.

As the liability is joint and several, the debtor may proceed directly against the creditor without any need to try to obtain satisfaction from the supplier beforehand. Indeed, this may be a useful tactic to persuade the creditor to bring pressure on the reluctant supplier to resolve the problem.

9.19 Exemptions

Section 75 of the Consumer Credit Act applies notwithstanding that the debtor, in entering the transaction under dispute, exceeded the credit limit by the use of the token or breached the agreement in some other way (s.75(4)). For example, the debtor has a card with a credit limit of £300. He is already £250 in debit and he uses the card to buy an item costing £150. Section 75 will still operate in respect of the purchase should the product be defective or misdescribed by the supplier.

There are, however, two situations where the section certainly does not apply. Section 75(3)(*a*) specifically exempts non-commercial agreements. Section 75(3)(*b*) provides a more difficult exemption. It states that the section does not apply in so far as the debtor's claim relates to any single item to which the supplier has attached a cash price not exceeding £100 or more than £30,000. Goode comments that this paragraph raises 'some tantalising problems' (I[1589]). So far there is no record of any difficulty with the phrase 'single item'. This may be particularly important at the lower end of the scale where a number of items are acquired by use of the token, all appearing on the same voucher. If the items are separate and are individually priced at amounts below £100, although the total bill exceeds £100, it seems that s.75 does not apply to any of them. However, where items are regarded as a set but may be acquired individually, s.75 would seem to apply. For example, a set of six dinner plates, individually priced at £30, sold as a set for £150, would seem to attract s.75 liability.

Another problem raised by Goode is the situation where an item costing £300 is entirely defective because of a defective part costing, say, £50 to replace. It would seem that this is within the section as the price of the single item is the reference point, not the cost of repair.

It should be noted that where the price of the item is above the lower figure but the debtor uses the token to pay only part of the total price, and the amount paid in this way is less than £100, this is still caught by the section. The section is not concerned with the amount of credit advanced but the price of the item.

9.20 Creditor's indemnity

Subject to any agreement between them, the creditor is entitled to be indemnified by the supplier for loss suffered by the creditor in satisfying his liability to the debtor under s.75(1), including costs reasonably incurred in defending proceedings brought by the debtor (s.75(2)). In addition, the creditor, in an action brought against him under s.75(1), is entitled, subject to rules of court, to have the supplier made a party to the proceedings (s.75(5)). The creditor may in any event have some express terms dealing with this issue in the contract with the supplier, which will displace s.75(2) in appropriate cases. It should be noted that the creditor need not wait to be sued by the debtor, but is entitled to settle the debtor's claim, if legitimate, and recover from the supplier any sum reasonably paid to the debtor.

9.21   Foreign element

The final topic on s.75 for discussion is whether the protective umbrella extends to purchases made abroad by the debtor by means of the credit-token. Publicity from the two main schemes once again extols the virtues of taking the card abroad in view of the many outlets in other countries. Barclaycard has taken the position that s.75 cannot be used in this type of situation. One reason given is that there are no pre-existing arrangements between the foreign supplier and the credit card issuer. It seems hard to believe that such an argument can be maintained in the light of the publicity and promotional literature put out by the issuers. The foreign supplier must have been recruited into the scheme, be it Visa or Access/Mastercard, and agreed to accept the card. This is an argument we have seen before and very little weight can be given to it in this context either.

Another argument is that unless the country in which the purchase is made has a similar rule to s.75 as part of its national law, s.75 does not apply. Section 75 does not say this, nor, with respect, does it seem possible to add a gloss of this nature to it. Arguably, the consumer needs no less, if not more, protection where the purchase is made abroad. It is still the position that the creditor, through its business connection, is in a better position to ensure the supplier's compliance with the relevant sales law than the debtor. This view is supported by Goode (I[1591]) and Jones (p.210). Apart from Barclaycard, the only other view to the contrary is that expressed by the Banking Ombudsman in his annual report for 1989–90 (para.5.3). He merely states that he is satisfied that Parliament never intended that s.75 should extend to foreign purchases in this way. No reason is given for the proposition which is, with respect, of dubious authority. It is perturbing to note that the Ombudsman has rejected those claims that have been brought to him on this point. It is respectfully suggested that this is an error of law.

The Ombudsman continued by saying that, in any event, he would have had to reject such claims as being outside his terms of reference on the basis that such matters concerned the supply of banking services outside the United Kingdom. To consider that the payment of a foreign supplier entails the banking services of the creditor taking place outside the UK seems to be taking a rather narrow view. The contract between the creditor and debtor is made in the UK, the majority of purchases will normally take place in the UK, the necessary statements will be sent and ordinarily received in the UK, and payment will be to the creditor in the UK. It is suggested that the Ombudsman is wrong on this point also.

The better view, therefore, is that s.75 does apply to purchases with this foreign element. It should be noted that if the supply law of the country in question is less favourable to the debtor than English law, the creditor may take advantage of this. However, English law will be applied to the supply contract, unless the creditor can prove, as a fact, the foreign law on the topic in question. It will be necessary to provide expert testimony to prove the foreign law, as well as properly pleading the issue.

9.22   Conclusion

Section 75 of the Consumer Credit Act 1974 is one of the most significant provisions in the Act in its radical approach to the issue of the liability of the creditor. We have seen that its scope is extremely wide in many respects and it is disliked, particularly by credit card issuers, for this reason. It should perhaps be remembered that a large number of credit-token transactions still fall below the £100 figure and are consequently outside the ambit of the section. Recently, however, in respect of claims falling below this threshold, Barclaycard indicated that even such claims would be considered (the Land Travel failure, 1992) on an ex gratia basis.

It should also be recalled that the creditor's liability mirrors that of the supplier. It is therefore imperative that persons in the field are not only aware of the provisions of s.75 itself, but are also well versed in consumer protection law, as outlined in the first part of this chapter.

CHAPTER 10

Agency of the Supplier

10.01 Introduction

In the three-party credit-token agreement, the three parties are generally independent of one another, although as seen in the preceding chapter, the Consumer Credit Act establishes the link between the supplier and the creditor in s.75 situations. Under that provision the creditor may be liable for the misrepresentation, among other things, of the supplier, as we have already observed. At common law the courts were reluctant to infer that the supplier was the agent of the creditor in all situations, even though at times it seemed to the layperson that he was. The problem typically arose in hire-purchase cases where the dealer transferred the goods to the creditor who then let them on hire purchase to the debtor. The liability of the creditor for the statements or acts of the dealer was non-existent at common law in this respect. The cases show that in respect of other matters in some instances the supplier was treated as the agent of the creditor, in others as the agent of the debtor and on other occasions he was not to be regarded as anybody's agent. The debtor would be stuck with a credit agreement which he may have been persuaded to enter into by the representations of the dealer. The dealer would normally not be liable, certainly before the *Hedley Byrne* cases in 1963, for the misstatement unless a collateral contract could be established. Any agency that might arise would depend on the particular facts. Often the typical hire-purchase agreement would include a clause making the supplier the agent of the debtor, thus forestalling any attempt to argue that he was the agent of the creditor. If any agency relationship of a broader nature could be established, the creditor would be liable for the acts of the agent acting within the scope of his actual, apparent or usual authority in accordance with normal agency rules. The Hire-Purchase Act 1965 contained a provision which made the supplier in the hire-purchase situation the agent of the creditor. This rendered the creditor liable for the misrepresentations of the supplier in the precontractual

149

discussions and prevented the creditor from contracting out or inserting clauses making the supplier the agent of the debtor. This was nonetheless an extremely limited provision, which certainly did not extend to the supplier who accepts a credit-token in payment for goods or services.

It was inevitable in the light of the radical nature of the proposals of the Crowther Committee that the 1974 Act would go much further in this regard than its predecessor, the 1965 Hire-Purchase Act. The provision in s.56, which we have discussed already in the context of cancellation (Chapter 6), is a far wider agency provision than had hitherto been introduced. It extends beyond the narrow parameters of the hire-purchase agreement to include all types of regulated credit agreement which fall within the DCS classification.

In the preceding chapter it was mentioned that there was some overlap between the s.56 deemed agency provision and the s.75 joint and several liability provision. After considering the scope of s.56, the chapter concludes with a comparison of the merits of the two sections.

10.02   Deemed agency

We saw in Chapter 6 that ss.57(3) and 69(6) of the Act create a limited form of deemed agency in respect of the persons to whom the debtor may give notice of withdrawal or cancellation respectively. Section 56(2) goes much further than this by extending the agency to all dealings of the deemed agent. The subsection provides that negotiations with the debtor in a case falling within s.56(1)(*b*) or (*c*) shall be deemed to be conducted by the negotiator in the capacity of agent of the creditor as well as in his actual capacity. Central to the agency provision is the concept of 'negotiator' which we also came across in Chapter 6 (para.6.8) in the context of cancellation. The discussion there focused on whether the 'antecedent negotiations' contained 'oral representations', being one of the factors in deciding whether an agreement was cancellable. The text of s.56(1) is set out at para.6.7 and the discussion in para.6.8 concerns the question of who is a negotiator. Section 56(2) refers to negotiations falling within s.56(1)(*b*) or (*c*). Subs.(1)(*b*) is concerned with the typical hire-purchase situation; for example, the supplier sells the goods forming the basis of the consumer credit agreement to the creditor. The goods are then let under the hire-purchase agreement by the creditor to the debtor. In this situation the supplier is the negotiator and, by virtue of s.56(2), he is the deemed agent of the creditor, who will be liable for, among other things, the misrepresentations of the supplier/negotiator.

We are more interested, however, in the provision in s.56(1)(*c*), which fits the supplier and credit card issuer situation, as was mentioned in Chapter 6. The supplier, having an arrangement with a credit card issuer to accept the latter's card at its outlets, is the negotiator within s.56(1)(c). The negotiations are conducted in relation to a transaction financed or proposed to be financed by a debtor–creditor–supplier agreement within s.12(b) or (c). Consequently, his negotiations are to be treated as negotiations on behalf of the creditor as well as in his own capacity.

Goode raises an important point in this context (I[1654]). It seems that by using the expression 'in the capacity of', the Act makes it unnecessary to consider whether what the deemed agent says or does is within or outside his usual or apparent authority. This would prevent the creditor from arguing that a person in the position of the supplier does not have usual or apparent authority in respect of certain acts or misrepresentations. To argue otherwise would destroy a large part of the benefit conferred by s.56(2). The debtor may, therefore, if in good faith accept the negotiations of the supplier as those of the creditor, 'however fanciful and extravagant they may be and whether or not they are of a kind which a person in the position of a negotiator would ordinarily be authorised to make by a person in the position of the creditor'. This means that the debtor is spared the niceties of agency law on the difficult issues of usual and apparent authority.

10.03   Duration of negotiations

We made the point in para.6.8 that the negotiations begin at the first point of contact between the negotiator and the debtor. According to s.56(4) of the 1974 Act, this includes communication by advertisement. The point at which the negotiations end is not covered in the Act, but as they are described as 'antecedent', it would seem logical to assume that they finish once the regulated agreement is made. Therefore, post-contractual dealings or communications are not capable of being 'negotiations', a point made in Chapter 6.

As was suggested in Chapter 6, this point is not without some difficulty in the context of running-account credit — in particular, for our purposes, the credit-token agreement. A very restrictive interpretation of the scope of s.56(2) has been promoted by some credit card issuers. It has been suggested that only those acts or statements by the supplier which precede the making of the credit agreement are within the scope of the deemed agency provision. This would have the effect of excluding statements made or things done by the supplier in relation to the supply of goods or services paid for under a credit card agreement concluded at some time prior to the relevant supply. As this will cover nearly all credit card transactions, it would have a remarkable impact on the scope of s.56(2): the debtor under a credit-token agreement which has been in existence for some time, who agrees to buy goods on the basis of a misrepresentation by the supplier, has no action against the creditor under s.56(2). If for some reason the debtor is not able to take advantage of s.75, his remedy is against the supplier only. On this interpretation, s.56(2) would avail the debtor only where the credit-token agreement is, for example, negotiated by a supplier who either makes a false statement about the credit agreement or, if the debtor makes a purchase at that time, about the goods or services then supplied. Only in those two narrow types of situation would the subsection apply.

The better view is that the s.56(2) applies to the dealings or statements by the supplier which may postdate the conclusion of the credit agreement, but which pre-date the making of the supply agreement. This is supported by Goode in his annotations to s.56 (III[57]). In his view, each fresh drawing on the typical credit-token agreement, constitutes 'on the commonly accepted analysis the creation of a new and binding extension of the credit agreement, to the extent of the drawing'. Therefore the 'negotiations' with a retailer preceding the supply transaction paid for by means of the credit-token are 'antecedent'. Goode refers to Sch.2, Example 3 to the Act. The example provides that discussions take place between a shopkeeper and a customer about the goods the latter wishes to acquire by using a credit-token under a regulated agreement. In his analysis, the draftsman states unequivocally that the discussions constitute antecedent negotiations within s.56(1)(c). This seems conclusive on the point.

The argument in favour of the wider interpretation is further strengthened by a consideration of the policy underlying ss.56 and 75. The nature of the joint venture between the supplier and the creditor and the vulnerability of the debtor at the points of supply of the credit or the items acquired by means of the credit have been referred to before. It would seem odd if that policy was to be deviated from, in the absence of some express statutory provision, in the case of credit-token agreements and other similar forms of running-account credit.

10.04   Effect of deemed agency

It seems that the effect of the provision in s.56(2) is to make the creditor liable to the debtor not only for the wrongful statements of the supplier but also, as we shall see, the latter's wrongful acts and omissions.

Section 56(4) states explicitly that the antecedent negotiations include any representations made by the negotiator to the debtor. This seems to be the normal interpretation of the word 'negotiation', and the consequence of making the creditor liable for the statements made by the supplier seems to go no further than the previous legislation (s.16 of the Hire-Purchase Act 1965), although that was restricted to a much narrower range of transactions than is s.56. 'Representation' is defined in s.189(1) to include any condition or warranty, and any other statement or undertaking whether in writing or not. According to Goode (I[1656]) 'representation' includes statements which are precontractual and non-promissory in nature and never become terms of the contract, but give rise in the alternative to an actionable misrepresentation along the lines discussed in Chapter 4. On the other hand, it will include a statement that was not a promise at the time it was made, but later became incorporated into the contract in some way or other. The third possibility is that the statement was intended from the outset as a promise, even though it may not appear in the contract when it is finally made. It is difficult to envisage a court holding that the negotiator intended a statement to be a contractual promise from the beginning, when the agency under s.56 is a purely notional one, but it must remain a possibility.

Goode continues by saying that 'representation' in this context goes much further than the normal meaning attributed to it at common law, by saying that it may be implied from conduct, 'and even silence may constitute a representation, as where the prospective debtor makes a comment concerning the apparent good quality of the goods in the presence of the negotiator, who says nothing to disillusion him'. This does seem a substantial departure from the normal meaning of the word, which must usually involve a positive statement. It may be safer to suggest that the example of silence by the supplier/negotiator might fall more happily into the category of 'other dealings' envisaged by s.56, discussed below.

However the statement is classified, the creditor will be treated as being responsible for it under s.56(2). The classification is nonetheless not redundant, as the scope and nature of the debtor's remedies may depend on whether the statement renders the creditor liable for a breach of contract or for an actionable misrepresentation. If it is regarded as the latter, the debtor will normally be entitled to rescind the supply contract, but this will not include the rescission of the credit-token agreement, if this was concluded before the negotiations for the supply contract commenced. Whilst it has been argued above that the creditor is liable for negotiations by the supplier prior to the entry into the supply contract, although after the making of the credit agreement, it would be going too far to suggest that the token agreement was rendered voidable in this way. If, on the other hand, the credit-token agreement was made at the same time as the supply contract, the debtor may rescind the credit agreement irrespective of whether the misstatement related to the credit agreement, the goods or any other aspect of the intended transactions. Notice of rescission may be given to the creditor or the negotiator (s.102(1)). On rescission the debtor may recover any monies paid from the party to whom they were paid and any goods part exchanged oɪ the allowance made in respect thereof. The debtor would have to return any goods received under the contract. The right to rescind may be lost in the usual ways, e.g. affirmation, delay and inability to restore the status quo. In a credit-token agreement, the debtor would presumably be entitled to set up a misrepresentation as a defence to a claim by the creditor for reimbursement of the payment made by the latter to the supplier. If the transaction involved payment of a deposit to the supplier or a part-exchange element, it is not clear whether the debtor can claim payments made to the supplier, such as the deposit, or the part-exchange allowance from the creditor or set either off against amounts owing under the credit agreement to the creditor, as is the case in cancellation (see Chapter 6, paras.6.15 and 6.17). If the supplier fails to honour his obligations to return payments or account for the part-exchange goods, it may be possible to include such amounts in the claim against the creditor in an action for damages for fraudulent or negligent misrepresentation under s.2(1) of the Misrepresentation Act 1967 or common law. Certainly, as the law stands at present, it would seem that in fraud or under the statutory action, the debtor would be so entitled.

Where the statement is a term of the contract because it was originally so intended, or has become so by incorporation, the debtor may take action against the creditor for breach. Whether the debtor is entitled to terminate the credit agreement will surely depend on the outcome of the earlier discussion. If the credit agreement is made before the supply contract, then whilst the debtor may be able to repudiate the contract of supply, this remedy will not extend to the credit-token agreement itself. The creditor would be liable in damages for the breach. However, the creditor may well be liable for the restitutionary claim of the debtor against the supplier for the price of the supply goods, or at least the debtor would be entitled to set up the breach as a defence to a demand by the creditor to be reimbursed. Whether there is a right of termination by the debtor for breach will depend on whether the term was considered to be a major or minor term at common law, or whether there was scope for an innominate term approach. One thing is certain: none of these difficulties has so far been judicially considered, and there is nothing in the Act dealing with them. Much of what is said above is consequently in the realms of speculation.

It should not be forgotten that in cases where the credit-token is used to pay for the supply of goods or services, the supplier is likely also to be liable in a personal capacity for the misrepresentation or breach arising from the precontractual negotiations. Section 56(2) makes this point specifically.

10.05 Other dealings

We have already remarked on the fact that s.56(4) refers to 'any other dealings' by the negotiator in the antecedent negotiations. This seems to cover any other act by the negotiator which has a bearing on or affects the regulated agreement. It includes ancillary contracts, for example maintenance agreements, installation of goods and the delivery of dangerous goods. This has wide implications, for it would seem to be the case that the creditor may be held liable in tort, i.e. negligence, in respect of the supplier's delivery of dangerous items which injure third parties. Equally, it would seem to include a breach of statutory duty by the supplier/negotiator, e.g. under the Consumer Protection Act 1987, Part 1. Just how wide this provision is may be illustrated by the case of *UDT* v. *Whitfield* [1986] CLY 375, although not a case involving a credit-token agreement. The creditor was held liable for the failure of the supplier to pay off an existing hire-purchase debt on the debtor's trade-in vehicle, as had been promised by the supplier.

It also seems to be the case that the creditor is liable for any precontractual injury inflicted by the supplier on the debtor. For example, if the supplier was to deliver dangerous goods to the debtor in the precontractual period and these caused injury to the debtor or damage to his property, once the agreement comes into being the creditor would be vicariously liable for the tort or breach of statutory duty of the supplier. If, however, no agreement was concluded, s.56 would have no application to the situation.

10.06 Exclusion of agency

Section 56(3) provides that an agreement is void if, and to the extent that, it purports in relation to an actual or prospective regulated agreement:

'(*a*) to provide that a person acting as, or on behalf of, a negotiator is to be treated as an agent of the debtor or hirer, or

(*b*) to relieve a person from liability for acts or omissions of any person acting as, or on behalf of, a negotiator.'

It seems that the effect of these provisions is merely to prevent the creditor from contracting out of his vicarious liability imposed by s.56, either by means of an exemption clause (para.(*a*)) or by a clause attempting to reverse the role of the supplier in the negotiations (para.(*a*)). The creditor is not prevented by the subsection itself from excluding his personal liability, although such attempts are severely constrained by other legislation, as we have seen, namely the Unfair Contract Terms Act 1977.

10.07   Sections 56 and 75 of the Consumer Credit Act compared

There are obvious similarities between actions under ss.56 and 75. It must be borne in mind that the overall policy of the provisions is to recognise the joint venture as between the supplier and the creditor in DCS agreements and that the law is seeking to redress the perceived imbalance of power in situations where the creditor and supplier are ranged together against the debtor. The objective of both provisions is to enable the debtor to take action against the creditor where there is a business connection between him and the supplier, and avoid hardship for the debtor where the supplier is insolvent or otherwise unable or unwilling to resolve the dispute. However, there are differences which may assume significance in certain cases. Overall, it seems that s.56 is favourable to the debtor in more instances than s.75.

First, s.56 does apply to non-commercial agreements, unlike s.75. This is likely to be of marginal significance in respect of a credit-token agreement.

Secondly, there are no monetary limits on the applicability of s.56, whereas it will be recalled that s.75 has the £100 and £30,000 limits. This will be of some importance in the credit card context, bearing in mind that many credit card transactions are below £100. Where s.75 is ruled out because of the limit, it may be that s.56 will fill the breach.

Thirdly, s.75 does not apply to ancillary contracts unless the whole or part of the ancillary contract itself is financed by the credit-token agreement. Section 56, as we have seen, applies to any other dealings, so long as they further the regulated agreement, which will probably include ancillary matters.

Fourthly, the debtor cannot rescind the credit agreement under s.75, whereas under s.56 this is clearly possible where the misrepresentation concerns the credit agreement itself, or the supply of goods or services at the time of the making of the credit agreement. Of course, as we saw in para.10.04, the right of rescission under s.56 is extremely limited in respect of credit-token agreements.

Fifthly, an action under s.75 is based on a breach of contract or misrepresentation by the supplier in respect of the goods or services supplied to the debtor. This includes breach of express or implied terms, whereas under s.56 there is no liability for the latter because they operate only when there is a contract. Section 56 is concerned with precontractual matters only. It is not correct, with respect, to say that s.56 is concerned only with liability in tort (Jones, p.216). A statement in the precontractual negotiations by the supplier may become incorporated into the contract as mentioned earlier. In such a situation, the debtor may have alternative actions in contract and for misrepresentation, the latter being considered tortious in nature so far as damages are concerned. Section 56 is wider than s.75 in that it covers other dealings, including liability in respect of negligent acts at common law or for breach of statutory duty.

Sixthly, s.75 creates joint and several liability as between the creditor and the supplier, whereas s.56 creates a separate vicarious liability. It is not at all clear whether the creditor can take advantage of defences or procedures available to the supplier, e.g. a right of set-off vested in the supplier, as would certainly be the case under s.75.

Finally, we saw in para.9.20 that s.75 provides for the creditor to be indemnified by the supplier in respect of claims made by the debtor using the section successfully. There is no such provision in s.56. Nonetheless, the creditor may be able to use the general law of agency or an express contractual provision in his contract (if any) with the supplier regulating what the supplier is permitted to do or say in antecedent negotiations and thus enable him to claim a contribution under the Civil Liability (Contribution) Act 1978. The creditor would be wise to insert a clause in his contract with the supplier concerning what the supplier is entitled to say or do in the precontractual discussions, as well as an express indemnity clause to cover the apparent statutory omission.

10.08 Conclusion

Very much like its counterpart in s.75, s.56 is a valuable aspect of the consumer protection afforded by the Consumer Credit Act 1974. Again like s.75, it appears to bring with it a succession of so far unresolved problems. There is no doubt that it is extremely wide in its effect and creditors must consider carefully the type and nature of the relationships they have with suppliers. There is no way of circumventing s.56, so attention must be given to the contract between the creditor and the supplier in order to provide for some form of indemnity if the supplier does anything which enables the debtor to invoke the section.

CHAPTER 11

Judicial Control of Credit-Token Agreements

11.01 Introduction

In this chapter we consider the powers of the court to intervene between the parties. The first part of the chapter is concerned with the ability of the court to reopen a credit agreement on the ground that the credit bargain is 'extortionate'. The courts have long had jurisdiction in equity to intervene between the parties to an agreement, but this was normally exercised only in favour of specially protected minority groups, or in situations of fraud, undue influence or duress. Generally, the law has been unsympathetic to the argument by one of the parties to the effect that he or she has made a bad bargain. The Moneylenders Acts 1900–1927 gave the courts the power to intervene in respect of certain types of loan and declare a transaction harsh and unconscionable. The court was empowered to reopen the agreement and interest rates exceeding 48% were presumed to be excessive. As the title of the legislation indicates, the provisions related only to loans by moneylenders, the definition of which excluded banks. The provisions, according to the Crowther Committee, were seldom used and, because of the major exclusion of banks from their remit, were largely ineffectual.

The Committee recommended that the power to reopen should be extended to all types of credit agreement, not just those involving moneylenders. This recommendation was accepted and the relevant provisions are in s.137 to 140 of the 1974 Act. It should be noted that the Insolvency Act 1986 contains very similar provisions, which enable transactions entered into by a debtor as an individual who becomes bankrupt to be challenged by the trustee in bankruptcy. Presumably, a court considering exercising its discretion under these provisions would take a similar approach as is adopted under the provisions in the 1974 Act. Some of the detail of the 1986 provisions will be discussed below.

Without doubt the court's power to reopen is extremely wide, as we shall see. However, the evidence of the sixteen years since the 'extortionate' credit bargain provisions came into force (May 1977) suggests that these provisions have been no more successful than their predecessors in the Moneylenders Acts. In a report published in 1991, *Unjust Credit Transactions*, the Office of Fair Trading found only twenty-three cases up to November 1990 which at first sight contained any reference to s.137 of the 1974 Act. On closer analysis, this was reduced to fifteen where there was any real discussion of the sections. The Office then discovered that in only four of these had the court exercised its discretion to intervene on behalf of the debtor. As a result the Office has recommended amendments to the provisions in an attempt to increase their effectiveness. This apparent trickle of cases suggests that debtors are reluctant to use or are unaware of the provisions. None of the cases has so far involved a credit card issuer, but it is necessary nonetheless to be aware of the impact of these provisions.

The second part of the chapter considers the court's powers to make time and other orders under ss.129 to 136 of the Act, although a number of these will be omitted as they clearly have no application to credit-token agreements.

11.02 Extortionate credit bargains

Under s.137(1), if the court finds that a credit bargain is extortionate, it is empowered to reopen the credit agreement so as to do justice between the parties. The credit agreement here means any agreement between an individual (the 'debtor') and any other person (the 'creditor') by which the creditor provides the debtor with credit of any amount (s.137(2)(*a*)). This is of immense significance as it widens the scope of the provision to include unregulated agreements which exceed the credit limit of £15,000 and agreements which are not regulated because they are exempt. This means that first mortgages are caught, as well as agreements such as American Express and Diner's Club cards and any other credit or chargecards where the debtor is obliged to repay the creditor in one payment. The only credit agreements remaining excluded are those where the debtor is a corporate body. Section 140 confirms the position that unregulated agreements are covered by ss.137 to 139. It provides that where the credit agreement is not a regulated agreement, expressions used in those sections which, apart from s.140 itself, apply only to regulated agreements, shall be construed as nearly as may be as if the credit agreement were a regulated agreement. The only such expression in those sections is 'linked transaction', but Goode (I[2909]) takes the view that s.140 applies to words such as 'creditor', 'debtor', 'security' and 'surety', these being words used in relation to consumer credit agreements.

11.03   Credit bargain

Whilst it is, on the face of it, only the credit agreement itself which is capable of being reopened, the court is entitled to look at the entire credit bargain to see if it is extortionate. The 'credit bargain' may consist only of the credit agreement itself, which will often be the case with a credit-token agreement. This is provided for in s.137(2)(*b*)(i), which states that the credit bargain, where no transaction other than the credit agreement is to be taken into account in computing the total charge for credit, means the credit agreement. Where one or more transactions are to be taken into account, credit bargain means the credit agreement and those other transactions taken together. The other transactions will include, for example, insurance and maintenance contracts which are taken into account when calculating the total charge for credit. The objective here is to prevent evasion by the creditor by keeping the terms of the credit agreement reasonable and imposing extremely onerous terms in these ancillary contracts. Some of these contracts may be linked transactions but contracts falling outside the definition of that term in s.19 may be relevant provided they are part of the total charge for credit as mentioned above.

It seems (Goode, I[2911]) that the word 'bargain' is not wide enough to cover prior loan transactions which are paid off by means of the credit under the agreement which is being challenged by virtue of the provision in s.137. The fact that these earlier agreements may be considered extortionate is not of itself a ground for opening up the later credit agreement. However, these earlier contracts can always be reopened by the court on application by the debtor, even though they have been settled.

We made the point above that the provisions in ss.137 to 139 apply to unregulated agreements such as American Express, Diner's Club cards, and so on. These agreements provide a very limited form of credit in that the debtor must pay off the amount due in one lump sum and does not normally incur any interest charges. In these circumstances it would be rare for a debtor to be in a position to argue successfully that any such agreement was extortionate. However, it is possible that there may be ancillary contracts attached to such an agreement: an insurance policy, perhaps, or a separate agreement relating to an annual fee for the issue of the chargecard. Such items would be part of the credit bargain.

It was mentioned above that the section talks of the credit agreement alone been opened up by the court. Section 139(2) appears to remedy the apparent anomaly by providing that the court has the power to set aside the whole or any part of the obligation imposed on the debtor by the credit bargain or any related agreement. Obviously, any ancillary contract falling within the meaning of a credit bargain can be dealt with by the court. Also any agreement not within that definition, as long as it is related, falls within the court's power. The Act does not define what is meant by a 'related' agreement, which leaves the court with a very wide discretion.

11.04   Meaning of 'extortionate'

Crucial to the impact of s.137 is the meaning of the word 'extortionate'. Section 138(1) provides that a credit bargain is extortionate if it either requires the debtor or a relative of his to make payments (whether unconditionally, or on certain contingencies) which are grossly exorbitant, or if it otherwise grossly contravenes ordinary principles of fair dealing. Section 138(2) provides that, in determining whether a bargain is extortionate, regard shall be had to such evidence as is brought before the court concerning interest rates prevailing at the time the bargain was made, other factors listed in subss.(3) to (5) (below), and any other relevant considerations. Factors specified in subs.(3) relate to the debtor and include his age, experience, business capacity and state of health. The court must also consider the degree to which, at the time of the making of the credit bargain, the debtor was under financial pressure, and the nature of that pressure. Subsection (4) sets out the factors relating to the creditor which are to be considered. These include the degree of risk accepted by him having regard to the value of any security provided, his relationship with the debtor, and whether or not a colourable cash price was quoted for any goods or services included in the credit bargain.

Subsection (5) provides that factors applicable under subs.(2) in relation to a linked transaction include the question how far the transaction was required for the protection of the debtor or the creditor, or was in the interest of the debtor.

The major criticism made by the Office of Fair Trading in its 1991 report was that the courts had been almost totally preoccupied with the meaning of the phrase 'grossly exorbitant' with reference to prevailing interest rates to the exclusion of other matters which might fall within the 'grossly contravening ordinary principles of fair dealing' criterion. All the cases investigated were concerned with the 'grossly exorbitant' test.

There has been a measure of inconsistency in the way in which these words have been interpreted. Goode comments (I[2913]) that the Moneylenders Acts referred to agreements being 'harsh and unconscionable' before being subject to reopening under that legislation, and extortionate 'would seem to mean much the same thing'. Diamond (p.71) expresses the view that it does not have a very precise meaning and that a court may take action if it feels 'sufficiently outraged', but continues that it 'probably means much the same as "excessive" and "harsh and unconscionable" in the Moneylenders Act 1900'. *Chitty on Contracts* (25th edn, 1983) states, more cautiously, that the decisions on the Moneylenders Acts may be of some guidance as to the principles upon which a court may act. The courts, on the other hand, do seem to have been heavily influenced by the approach taken in the old cases on the previous legislation, despite the fact that ss.137 to 139 were meant to mark a new departure. This is in spite of judicial pronouncements to the contrary by Foster J in *Ketley* v. *Scott* [1981] ICR 241 at p.245 and Edward Nugee QC in *Davies* v. *Directloans Ltd* [1986] 2 All ER 783 at p.789. In *Castle Phillips Finance Co Ltd* v. *Khan* (1978, unreported, Croydon County Court, cited in Goode, I[2913]), the judge commented that the meaning of 'extortionate' was the same as that given to 'harsh and unconscionable'.

It is not enough to show that the terms are onerous or unreasonable. It is suggested (Goode, I[2913]) that there must be some morally reprehensible behaviour by the creditor in taking a grossly unfair advantage of the debtor's circumstances. The position is aptly summed up by Lord Donaldson MR in *Wills* v. *Wood* [1984] CCLR 7 at p.15:

'It is, of course, clear that the Consumer Credit Act 1974 gives
and is intended to give the court the widest possible control over
credit bargains which, for a variety of reasons, might be
considered "extortionate". But the word is "extortionate", not
"unwise". The jurisdiction seems to me to contemplate at least a
substantial imbalance in bargaining power of which one party has
taken advantage.'

We now consider the terms of the agreement which may be relevant to decide the issue of whether the bargain is extortionate. This is followed by a discussion of the factors which are set out in s.138(2), (3) and (4) and some of the rather sparse case law as to the interpretation and emphasis laid on these matters.

11.05   Terms of the bargain

The court is to have regard to the terms of the credit bargain, namely, the credit agreement and any transactions falling within the definition in s.137(2)(*b*)(ii), at the time of the making of the credit agreement. Subsequent events are not relevant; for example; a drastic fall in interest rates since the making of the agreement is not something the court should be concerned with.

In the first instance, the court must consider the actual terms of the credit agreement and any other relevant transactions. The focus of attention may well be on the total charge for credit, but the court must have regard to any other terms which might be considered to render the bargain extortionate overall. Goode lists (I[2916]) a number of usual and useful matters that the court might wish to scrutinise in appropriate cases. Not all of these will necessarily be relevant to all or some credit-token agreements, but it is worthwhile noting them:

(1) The obvious one, the total charge for the credit, which, in accordance with s.138(2), must be weighed against interest rates prevailing at the time of the contract. In addition, the risk of default and the value of any security (if any) taken by the creditor are to be put in the balance (s.138(4)(*a*)). Just how this has worked out in practice is considered below in the discussion on the statutory guidelines.

(2) The severity of any default provisions: the court may well concentrate on issues such as the nature and gravity of the events which are particularised as giving rise to any such default provision becoming operative. A minor occurrence which is visited by a serious penalty by the creditor may be regarded as an indication of oppressiveness. Also, the court might be interested in the monetary liability imposed on default and any provisions for forfeiture, for example non-returnable deposits or enforcement of security.

(3) The amount of rebate on early settlement or on refinancing may be considered, although this is likely to apply only rarely to a credit-token agreement.

(4) The duration of the commitment under the contract is a factor, but once again this should not be an issue in a credit-token agreement. As we have noticed before, there is usually no obligation on a debtor under such an agreement to use or continue using the card to obtain credit.

(5) The extent to which the debtor is required, either as a term of the credit agreement, or as a condition of the grant to him of credit, to enter into or continue with ancillary contracts which are onerous to him.

Once the debtor has raised the issue of the extortionate nature of the credit bargain, there is no doubt that the court, in exercising its statutory discretion, will subject the agreement and other transactions to a close and detailed scrutiny.

11.06   External statutory factors

The relevant statutory factors were set out in para.11.04. These are the factors which a court must consider in applying the test to a credit bargain, although this should not be seen as an exhaustive list of matters that might receive judicial recognition.

Interest rates are obviously a major consideration. The Moneylenders Acts, it will be recalled, presumed that a rate exceeding 48% was unconscionable. There is no such presumption in the 1974 Act, despite the recommendation of the Crowther Committee. As indicated earlier, the majority of the cases have been concerned with the interest rate issue, and very few have been decided in favour of the debtor. It should not be forgotten that the debtor must take the initiative and raise the issue, it is not for the court to do so of its own motion or for anyone else, e.g. the local Trading Standards Department or the Office of Fair Trading, to start proceedings to challenge bargains on behalf of debtors as a group or individually. Under proposals submitted by the Office of Fair Trading in its 1991 report *Unjust Credit Transactions*, this would be the case.

Another problem is that the cases favourable to the debtor are not reported in the mainstream law reports, if reported at all. In one case, *Shahabinia* v. *Gyachi* (1989, cited in the OFT Report), the county court judge had reduced the flat interest rate on each of three loans to 15%. The agreements specified interest rates of 18%, 104% and 156% respectively. On appeal, the Court of Appeal increased the flat rate to 30% on each loan so as to do justice between the parties. This seems to have been an exceptional case, as other cases illustrate graphically the court's reluctance to intervene on behalf of the debtor.

In *Ketley* v. *Scott* [1981] ICR 241, the High Court judge was unable to find for the debtor where there was an interest rate of 48%. The defendant debtor had exchanged contracts on a property but was unable to complete the transaction because of a shortage of funds. He obtained a loan for £20,500 secured by a legal charge to enable him to complete. The interest rate was expressed as 12% over three months. The judge did not consider the bargain extortionate, despite the security. There was, however, a suggestion that the defendant had not disclosed all information required by the creditor. This may have been a conclusive factor against the exercise of the court's discretion. In *Davies* v. *Directloans Ltd* [1986] 2 All ER 783 the interest rate was nearly 26%, whereas usual rates were in the region of 20%. This was not considered extortionate in the circumstances. This conclusion harks back to the statement by Lord Donaldson MR, quoted above, to the effect that simply because a credit bargain is 'unwise' from the debtor's point of view does not on that ground alone render it extortionate. In *Coldunell* v. *Gallon* [1986] 1 All ER 429 the court considered that there was nothing unusual about the loan, the interest rate was reasonable and the plaintiffs (the creditor) had acted as one would expect a normal commercial lender to act. These cases indicate clearly that where interest rates are considered reasonable, the debtor's urgent need for the loan under pressure from extraneous circumstances will not be enough to persuade a court to exercise its discretion in favour of the debtor.

Still on the subject of interest rates, it is often the case that the creditor will set standard tariffs of interest rates or other charges on the grounds of efficiency. These, naturally, will not be established with the personal characteristics of debtors in mind. Generally, the rates will be set in accordance with external factors. It would seem that this practice, which is particularly prevalent in relation to credit-token agreements, would not, of itself, render the individual credit bargain based on such a tariff extortionate.

11.07   Characteristics of the debtor

It will be recalled that the court must consider the age, experience, business capacity and state of health of the debtor and also the degree to which at the time of the making of the bargain he was under financial pressure and the nature of that pressure. The question for the court is whether the creditor is taking advantage, for example, of the debtor's lack of experience, senility or the fact that he is under pressure to obtain a loan urgently. Jones (pp.238–9) argues rightly that the Act does not say that the creditor need know of the various factors relating to the debtor before a court can take them into consideration. However, the creditor who did not obtain information about age and some other factors would be imprudent and it is therefore likely that most of such information will be sought before the loan is made. In addition, there has to be some morally reprehensible conduct by the creditor. The court, in deciding this, needs to establish what the precise state of the creditor's knowledge was concerning the matters mentioned. Obviously, if the financial pressure was being exerted by the creditor himself, this would more easily lend itself to a finding by the court that the creditor had taken a grossly unfair advantage of the debtor in the circumstances. 'Has the creditor imposed terms that go far beyond what might be called fair and reasonable to protect himself?' is one question to ask in this situation. In most of the cases mentioned above, the debtor was clearly under financial pressure of varying degrees. It seems that this did not sway the court in favour of the debtor. In *Davies* v. *Directloans Ltd* the judge commented that the plaintiffs had been warned by both independent solicitors and the defendant that the arrangement would be costly. The judge took the view that any financial pressure on the plaintiffs was an inevitable consequence of the decision to buy the house. In *Wills* v. *Wood* Fox LJ thought that the defendant was really complaining about being lent the money in the first place. He continued:

'But if Miss Wood acted to her detriment in borrowing these sums, that may be because she was not properly advised by her solicitors or because she chose to act on her own judgement. It was, however, not because of any unfairness of dealing between herself and Mr Wills. She was of full age and capacity; she wanted loans on reasonable terms and that is what she got. Mr Wills had no contact with her and had no knowledge of her private circumstances. Nobody acting on his behalf misled her or induced her to grant the mortgages.'

In *Ketley* v. *Scott* the judge was of the opinion that the bargain was not extortionate because, among other things, the defendant was not under real financial pressure merely through the possibility of losing the purchase and having his deposit forfeited, and having regard to his business experience, he knew what he was letting himself in for at the time the loan agreement was made.

In *Barcabe* v. *Edwards* (1983, unreported, cited in the OFT Report 1991), the county court substituted a 40% rate for a flat interest rate of 100%, the judge taking into account the lack of business capacity, the illiteracy of one of the debtors and the lack of any unusual risk. This case illustrates well the point that the court must perceive that the creditor is taking unfair advantage of the debtor's personal characteristics in what is otherwise a normal situation. The evidence suggests that such cases will rarely be established by the debtor.

11.08   Factors relating to the creditor

The degree of risk assumed by the creditor is often the crucial factor. This has to be viewed in the light of and value of any security taken by the creditor. In *Barcabe* v. *Edwards* we saw that the lack of any unusual risk in the transaction was a factor militating in favour of a finding that the bargain was extortionate. In *Ketley* v. *Scott*, on the other hand, the creditor acted often as a lender of last resort, took exceptional risks and charged accordingly.

The requirement of security must be very rare in a credit-token agreement. On the other hand, a high degree of risk is inherent in such an agreement. The control of the risk is, however, in the hands of the creditor when setting the credit limit and it is unlikely that the degree of risk would be accepted as a weighty factor in any challenge relating to a credit-token agreement under s.137 of the Consumer Credit Act.

The court is also to have regard to the creditor's relationship to the debtor. Presumably, the court would be concerned to see whether the dealings were at arm's length, although it is not clear which party would benefit from a finding on this issue. If the creditor was in a fiduciary relationship to the debtor, perhaps a court might be more willing to declare the bargain extortionate. If the creditor is close to the debtor, it may be easier to infer that he was taking advantage of the debtor's incapacity or otherwise.

A further factor in relation to the creditor is whether or not a colourable cash price was quoted for any goods or services included in the credit bargain. If the cash price of an item is inflated by the creditor so as to make the credit transaction appear more reasonable or less oner-ous, this is a factor a court may consider in exercising its discretion. The effect of quoting a cash price that would *never* be charged renders the total charge for credit misleading. The court may consider the cash price of any ancillary contracts in the same way as long as they are included in the credit bargain. This factor may be relevant in credit-token agree-ments only very occasionally. Often the cash purchaser is at a disadvan-tage in relation to a debtor acquiring goods or services under a credit-token agreement. The banning of the 'no discrimination' clause fre-quently found in agreements between suppliers and creditors may eventually swing the pendulum back in favour of the cash purchaser.

11.09   Other relevant factors

It is clear that the guidelines are not exhaustive of the matters a court may take into account. Section 137(1)(*b*) enables the court to consider whether the creditor has grossly contravened ordinary principles of fair dealing, as well as monetary matters. Section 138(2)(*a*) entitles the court to take notice of any other relevant considerations.

In a credit-token arrangement it must not be forgotten that the creditor will often be paid from two separate sources. If the debtor takes advantage of the extended credit available to him by paying the creditor by instalments rather than paying off his indebtedness every month, the creditor will receive interest from that source. In addition, he will pay the supplier the amount of the transaction less an agreed discount. No doubt this might be another consideration for the court when assessing the harshness of the credit bargain. This may, of course, be offset by the risk factor involved in paying the supplier before receiving any payment from the debtor. This would not appear, on the other hand, to be an unusual risk.

As to other matters, the court may be interested in whether the debtor understood adequately the terms and nature of the bargain. A related question would be whether he received independent or impartial advice, or it was recommended to him by the creditor that he should obtain such advice. This was clearly a factor in *Davies* v. *Directloans Ltd*, where the judge commented specifically on the fact that the debtors had received advice from independent solicitors as well as from the creditor about the expensive nature of the transaction.

The court would no doubt take into account whether the debtor was offered inducements to enter into the bargain. For example, in *Wills* v. *Wood* the judge commented that there was an absence of any such inducement, which confirmed him in his view that the debtor had exercised her own judgment in entering into the arrangement. The judge also commented that the creditor had no contact with the debtor, thus discounting any suggestion of improper pressure being placed upon the debtor, another matter which in other situations may be decisive in making the bargain extortionate. The existence of moral pressure may be seen to be a factor in some cases where there is a close relationship between the creditor and the debtor. This was specifically included in the list of factors relating to the creditor discussed above.

The matters above may be seen to be ones which would support the debtor's contention that the bargain was grossly unfair. As for the creditor, it may be argued that the urgent nature of the need for credit is a relevant factor, associated in all probability with a higher degree of risk if it is not possible to carry out a thorough investigation of the debtor's financial and other circumstances. This was one of the relevant factors in *Ketley* v. *Scott*, where the debtor required the loan within hours so as to be able to comply with a notice to complete served on him.

11.10 Onus of proof

If, in proceedings referred to in s.139(1), the debtor or a surety raises an allegation that the credit bargain is extortionate, the onus is then put upon the creditor to prove the contrary (s.171(1)). It does not matter if the agreement is exempt because of the low interest rate exemption, the creditor must discharge the burden of proof. This would appear to be the legal burden, although where the debtor's allegation is based on some factor peculiar to himself, e.g. lack of experience or understanding of the credit bargain, an evidential burden would seem to lie with the debtor to prove such fact or facts, it being insufficient merely to raise the allegation of the extortionate nature of the bargain. If the evidence is evenly balanced, it would seem that the debtor should succeed, the creditor having failed to discharge the ultimate legal burden thrust upon him. Where there is nothing unusual in the credit bargain and the creditor has not departed from ordinary commercial practice in any way, the creditor will have satisfied the burden. This was the outcome in the case of *Coldunell* v. *Gallon*, where the judge made precisely those comments.

11.11 The powers of the court

We remarked earlier that the court has the power under s.139(2) to deal with related agreements. Indeed, this subsection provides the court with a number of wide powers:

> 'In reopening the agreement, the court may, for the purpose of relieving the debtor or a surety from payment of any sum in excess of that fairly due and reasonable, by order —
>
> (*a*) direct accounts to be taken, or (in Scotland) an accounting to be made, between any persons,
>
> (*b*) set aside the whole or part of any obligation imposed on the debtor or a surety by the credit bargain or any related agreement,
>
> (*c*) require the creditor to repay the whole or part of any sum paid under the credit bargain or any related agreement by the debtor or a surety, whether paid to the creditor or any other person,
>
> (*d*) direct the return to the surety of any property provided for the purposes of the security, or
>
> (*e*) alter the terms of the credit agreement or any security instrument.'

The court has the power to order the creditor to reimburse the debtor for amounts which were never paid to the creditor. Section 139(3) makes it clear that an order under s.139(2) may be made even though it may place a burden on the creditor in respect of an advantage unfairly enjoyed by a party to a linked transaction. In the context of a credit-token agreement, therefore, if the supplier reaps an unfair advantage in the contract of supply between himself and the debtor (a linked transaction), the creditor may be forced to reimburse the debtor in respect of that unfair aspect of the bargain, even though there is no benefit at all to the creditor.

An order under s.139(2) is not to alter the effect of any judgment (s.139(4)). Once the creditor has a judgment against the debtor or a surety for the enforcement of the loan or security, an order under s.139(2) cannot be used to circumvent that judgment. This does not mean that completed transactions between the creditor and the debtor cannot be reopened at some later date, as long as no judgment has been entered in respect of that particular transaction. The power to reopen credit agreements came into operation on 16th May 1977 and has retrospective effect, in that it applies to agreements and transactions whenever made (Consumer Credit Act 1974, Sch. 3, para.42).

11.12   Jurisdiction of the courts

Section 139(1) provides that a credit agreement may, if the court thinks just, be reopened on the ground that the credit bargain is extortionate:

'(*a*)   on application for the purpose made by the debtor or any surety to the High Court, county court or sheriff court; or

(*b*)   at the instance of the debtor or a surety in any proceedings to which the debtor and creditor are parties, being proceedings to enforce the credit agreement, any security relating to it, or any linked transaction; or

(*c*)   at the instance of the debtor or a surety in other proceedings in any court where the amount paid or payable under the credit agreement is relevant.'

It is no longer possible to bring proceedings in the High Court under s.139(1)(*a*) following the amendment of s.139(5) and the removal of the financial limits (High Court and County Courts Jurisdiction Order 1991, SI 1991 No.724, art.2(1)(*h*)).

Section 139(1)(*a*) is the appropriate provision to use where there are no current proceedings relating to the credit agreement or the security before the court. In other cases, the High Court and the county courts have concurrent jurisdiction. In only one of the cases discovered by the Office of Fair Trading and mentioned in its 1991 report did the debtor initiate the proceedings under s.139(1)(*a*). In all other cases the creditor had already commenced the action to enforce the agreement and the debtor exercised the right to raise the matter as to the extortionate nature of the bargain in those proceedings. An application to the court is made by originating application where the debtor or surety is relying on s.139(1)(*a*). In other cases, within s.139(1)(*b*) or (*c*), an application is made by notice to the proper officer of the court and to every other party to the proceedings within fourteen days of the service of the originating process on the debtor or surety. The notice is treated as a defence and automatically prevents judgment being entered by default (County Court Rules 1981, Ord.49, r.4(14) and (15)).

11.13   Reopening an agreement on the insolvency of the debtor

The expression 'debtor' as defined in s.189(1) includes the person to whom the debtor's rights have passed by operation of law. Under s.306(1) of the Insolvency Act 1986 the bankrupt's estate vests in the trustee in bankruptcy. It seems to follow from these provisions that the trustee may ask the court to consider whether a credit bargain entered into by the debtor before bankruptcy is extortionate under s.137 of the 1974 Act. It seems that this would be possible under s.139(1)(*b*) or (*c*), where enforcement proceedings were already under way at the instigation of the creditor. Where the trustee wishes to apply to the court to ask for the matter to be considered and no current proceedings are under way in respect of the relevant transaction, it would seem that the provision in s.343 of the Insolvency Act is the correct route.

The section provides that, where a person is or has been a party to a transaction for, or involving, the provision to him of credit, the court may, on the application of his trustee in bankruptcy, make an order in relation to the transaction if it is, or was, extortionate and was entered into not more that three years before the commencement of the bankruptcy. The section states that a transaction is extortionate if by its terms it requires or required grossly exorbitant payments to be made (whether unconditional or contingent) in respect of the provision of credit, or it otherwise grossly contravened ordinary principles of fair dealing. As with the provision in s.137 of the 1974 Act, there is a presumption that the transaction is or was extortionate, thus placing the legal burden of proof on the creditor.

The court may make an order with respect to any transaction containing one or more of the following:

(1)   provision setting aside the whole or part of any obligation created by the transaction;

(2)   provision otherwise varying the terms of the transaction or varying

the terms on which any security for the purposes of the transaction is held;

(3)   provision requiring any person who is or was a party to the transaction to pay to the trustee any sums paid to that person, by virtue of the transaction, by the bankrupt;

(4)   provision requiring any person to surrender to the trustee any property held by him as security for the purposes of the transaction;

(5)   provision directing accounts to be taken between any persons.

These powers are closely modelled on those contained in s.139(2) of the 1974 Act, with minor differences only. Any money or property recovered under these provisions will naturally form part of the bankrupt's estate. Section 343(6) prevents the trustee or the undischarged bankrupt from using the s.139(1)(*a*) procedure in the 1974 Act. Therefore, if the trustee wishes to initiate proceedings to have a transaction declared extortionate, as stated above, he must use the Insolvency Act route, but the 1974 Act is available to the trustee in the other instances.

11.14   Time orders

We have discussed above the court's power to intervene where it is alleged that the credit bargain is extortionate, whether this is done by the debtor or the trustee. We have also previously considered the court's powers to permit enforcement of agreements rendered unenforceable as a result of some failure by the creditor to comply with the many formalities in the Act (Chapter 5). We must now turn to some other powers in the Act which are capable of relating to credit-token agreements. The first and most significant of these is the time order.

Section 129(1) provides that the court may take a time order, if it appears just to do so:

(1)   on an application for an enforcement order; or

(2)   on an application made by a debtor after service on him of either a default notice or a notice under s.76(1) or 98(1); or

(3)   in an action brought by a creditor to enforce a regulated agreement or any security, or recover possession of any goods or land to which a regulated agreement relates.

The power to make a time order depends on one of the trigger events listed in s.129(1). Where the event is an application by the creditor for the court's permission to enforce an otherwise unenforceable agreement, the court may of its own motion make an order. The debtor may apply only when he has received a default notice or a notice under s.76(1) or 98(1). The surety, or a co-debtor not served with a notice of any kind, cannot apply under this provision. These notices will be discussed more fully in the following chapter, but it is useful to note at this stage that the notice served on the debtor must inform him of his right to apply to the court for a time order. This right of the debtor is not frequently used. More often the application for a time order will be made when the creditor has already begun proceedings to enforce the agreement or any security. The evidence tends to suggest that debtors are reactive rather than proactive when applying for time orders. Where the trigger for the making of an order is either the application for an enforcement order or the act of the creditor in suing to enforce the agreement, it appears that the application for the time order may be made by any interested party, i.e. the creditor, debtor or a surety. The court may also do so on its own motion. It should be noted that the power to make a time order arises in nearly every type of situation where some action is taken in relation to the agreement.

Time orders are restricted to regulated agreements, thus ruling out applications in respect of exempt agreements such as American Express or Diner's Club cards. A time order cannot be made in respect of the enforcement of a linked transaction. For example, the debtor may agree to buy an item worth £500 and use the credit-token agreement to pay the deposit of £100. He then refuses to take delivery of the item and to pay the balance of £400. On being sued by the supplier for the £400, the debtor cannot ask the court to make a time order as the supply contact here is only a linked transaction. The position would be different if the token was issued under a two-party agreement, in which case the creditor would also be supplying the goods.

The debtor under a credit-token agreement would wish to apply for a time order only infrequently. This is because of the nature of the agreement, whereby he can settle the account all at once at the end of each accounting period, or exercise the option to take extended credit by paying less than the full amount as long as this is above the agreed minimum figure. In a sense, the debtor has a time factor built into his agreement. However, the need to apply for an order may arise where the debtor has difficulty paying the minimum figure specified in his monthly account, or the creditor is purporting to exercise any contractual right to demand payment in one lump sum because of a breach or otherwise on the part of the debtor.

11.15 Application for time order

As stated above, the application for a time order may be made by an interested party, except that only the debtor may apply following receipt of a default or other notice mentioned earlier. In this latter case, the debtor must apply by originating application. This procedure will normally be used only where there are no current proceedings by the creditor to enforce the agreement. The application must be filed in the court for the district in which the debtor resides or carries on business, and must contain the obvious details about the debtor, the agreement, any sureties, the names and addresses of the parties to be served. More particularly, it must give details of the notice, service of which triggers the debtor's right to apply. The total unpaid balance, any arrears, and the amounts and frequency of repayments, together with the applicant's proposals as to payment of any arrears and future instalments must be specified. Details of the applicant's means are also required. If the breach by the applicant giving rise to the need to apply is non-monetary in nature, the applicant must include proposals for remedying the breach.

In the usual run of things, the creditor will commence proceedings against the debtor. The debtor should make an application for a time order, although this is not strictly necessary, as the court automatically has jurisdiction under s.129. Goode (I[2780]) suggests that the debtor could apply for a time order in proceedings commenced by him against the creditor under s.75 of the 1974 Act, provided he has been served with a default or other appropriate notice. This could also be possible where the creditor made a counterclaim for an enforcement order against the debtor, or to enforce the agreement or any security. In this situation, the court could consider a time order of its own motion.

11.16   Terms and effect of time orders

Section 129(2) states that a time order must provide, as the court considers just, for one or both of:

'(a)   the payment by the debtor or any surety of any sum owed under a regulated agreement or any security by such instalments, payable at such times, as the court, having regard to the means of the debtor and any surety, considers reasonable;

(b)   the remedying by the debtor of any breach of a regulated agreement (other than non-payment of money) within such period as the court may specify.'

Where the order is made under s.129(2)(a), namely, in relation to a money payment, the court must have regard to the debtor's means. However, under s.130(1), where, in accordance with rules of court, an offer to pay any sum by instalments is made by the debtor and accepted by the creditor, the court may in accordance with rules of court make a time order under s.129(2)(*a*) giving effect to the offer without hearing evidence of means.

Normally, the debtor's difficulty will stem from problems with repayment and, consequently, time orders will be made, if at all, under s.129(2)(*a*). Making such an order does not freeze the creditor's rights in other respects under the agreement. This can be important in the context of, e.g., hire-purchase agreements, but is likely to be of only marginal utility in credit-token agreements. In respect of non-monetary breaches and orders made under s.129(2)(*b*), the position is different. By s.130(5), if the agreement is still in force when the time order is made, the creditor's remedies are frozen for the period specified in the time order (as varied or until revoked under s.130(6)). The creditor is thereby prevented from terminating the agreement or attempting to exercise the other rights set out in s.87(1). This prevents action in respect of fresh breaches until such time as the time order is revoked or expires. If the breach is remedied it is treated as never having occurred. If it is not remedied in the time given in the order, or if the time order is revoked, the creditor's rights are unfrozen. It seems that a default notice served before the commencement of the time order continues to run and, once the period specified in the time order has expired, the creditor may take action under the default notice if its time has also expired. If the agreement has terminated prior to the making of the time order, the order cannot affect such termination, but it still freezes any other rights of the creditor for the relevant period. If the breach is remedied, however, it is treated as never having happened.

Where the debtor fails to comply with a time order under s.129(2)(*a*), the creditor is entitled to issue execution for the whole of any unpaid sum.

11.17   Protection orders

The time order is clearly the most important order in relation to all types of regulated agreement. Under s.131 the court may make another type of order, known as a protection order. This can be made on the application of the creditor. If the court thinks it just, it can make an order for the protection of any property of the creditor from damage or depreciation pending the determination of any proceedings under the Act. The section is not limited to hire-purchase and conditional sale agreements. It might be relevant where the credit-token agreement was a two-party agreement and the card had been used to obtain goods from the creditor's store. However, it should be noted that the section applies only where the property belongs to the creditor. Normally, property acquired in this way will be owned (the property will have passed to the debtor) by the debtor at the latest upon delivery of the goods. Only in those rare cases where ownership has not passed under the terms of the contract or the rules in the Sale of Goods Act 1979 could this section be of any value to the creditor. Possibly, if there was a dispute about the quality of the goods and the debtor had purported to reject them, thus effectively transferring ownership back to the creditor, the section would apply, if the goods had, unusually in such circumstances, remained in the possession of the debtor.

11.18 Other powers

In exercising its powers under, in particular, ss.127 and 129 of the 1974 Act, the court may, where it considers it just to do so, in relation to a regulated agreement, include provisions which make the operation of any term of the order conditional on the doing of specified acts by any party to the proceedings, or provisions suspending the operation of any term of the order, either until such time as the court subsequently directs, or until the occurrence of a specified act or omission (s.135(1)). A person affected by such a provision may apply for a variation (s.135(4)). These are supplementary in scope to the provisions in ss.129 to 134 and are very general in their application. It is possible that a court might use them to order a repayment to a debtor by a creditor, but this could be seen as going too far and confusing the powers with the extortionate credit bargain provisions in ss.137 to 140.

A similar comment may be aimed at the provision in s.136 giving the court power to include in any order made under the Act such provision as appears just for amending any agreement or security in consequence of a term of the order. This power must, again, be considered as ancillary only to the other powers contained in ss.127 to 134, so as to avoid any overlap or confusion with the powers in ss.137 to 140.

11.19 Conclusion

We have seen that the courts are given a battery of powers under the 1974 Act to protect the debtor in the main from extortionate credit bargains but also from other hardships which tend to occur. These provisions are potentially extremely wide but evidence of their use in practice is particularly thin. This is especially true in relation to credit-token agreements. This is not to say that these provisions can be forgotten or ignored by creditors, particularly when considering whether to enforce an agreement. Problems concerning extortionate credit bargains should be especially avoided. A finding against a creditor may come to the attention of the Office of Fair Trading and may be a factor to be considered on the grant or renewal of a licence.

CHAPTER 12

Termination of Credit-Token Agreements

12.01 Introduction

The issue of termination of a credit agreement is in many respects no different from the termination of other contracts. The major difference, however, is that the Consumer Credit Act 1974 imposes considerable restrictions on the creditor's right to bring an agreement to an end. It also intervenes in other situations where the creditor seeks to do something under the agreement falling short of termination, e.g. increase the rate of interest on default by the debtor, or make a demand for accelerated payment. In many instances, the contractual terms between the parties are overridden by the provisions of the Act. As a consequence, this is an extremely complex area of the law and demands close attention. It is necessary to have a firm grasp of the applicable common law principles, together with an understanding of how the Act operates to restrict or defer the creditor's common law and contractual rights.

Normally, an agreement comes to an end when it has been fully performed on both sides, or, if for a fixed time, that time has expired. The agreement itself or the common law may provide for the contract to be brought to an end in certain circumstances. A common term in a credit agreement would be to the effect that non-payment of an instalment entitles the creditor to treat the contract as at an end. At common law a serious breach by one party will normally give the innocent party the right to treat the contract as at an end. A contract may be brought to an end, at the election of the innocent party, for misrepresentation, duress, undue influence or fraud, as we have already seen. Furthermore, the common law will declare that a contract is no longer subsisting because an event has occurred which frustrates the object of the contract, or will declare it void for mistake (in very limited circumstances only), illegality or as being contrary to public policy. All these factors may apply equally to credit agreements. A credit-token agreement is likewise affected by such principles, but it is different from many credit agreements in that it

178

is a continuing relationship between the creditor and debtor. It is not possible to say that such a contract has been terminated by performance. In addition, a debtor who no longer wishes to avail himself of the benefit of the token, need merely do nothing. As pointed out earlier, the debtor is under no obligation to use the card. If he chooses not to, the agreement is in practice at an end, although it is capable of being resurrected should the debtor so wish. It might be the case, after a lengthy period without any movement on the account, that the creditor decides to terminate the agreement in accordance with a term to that effect contained in it.

An agreement may provide specifically that either of the parties may terminate the agreement on giving notice to the other. If the requisite notice is given, in normal circumstances the agreement is determined on expiry of the notice. In the case of a regulated consumer credit agreement, the creditor may have to comply with certain provisions before exercising his contractual right in certain circumstances, as we shall see below.

The common law also gives the debtor under a credit agreement the right to pay ahead of time, as well as the right, in the case of a hire-purchase agreement, voluntarily to terminate the agreement. The Consumer Credit Act puts these rights onto a statutory footing, with some modifications. We need consider the voluntary termination right no further as it is restricted to regulated hire-purchase and conditional sale agreements only. The first part of this chapter briefly considers the right to early settlement and the right to a rebate under ss.94 and 95 respectively of the Act. We then consider the creditor's rights of termination or otherwise under the contract or at common law, as affected by the Act. In the first instance, this entails considering the notices to be given under ss.76 and 98 of the Act by the creditor to the debtor in cases of what is known as non-default by the debtor. The Act imposes severe restrictions on the creditor's right to terminate for default and any attempt to increase the interest rate on default. We then consider the restriction imposed on contractual rights of the creditor by the Act on the death of the debtor under a credit agreement. It should be noted that many other restrictions are imposed on the creditor by the Act, but these are relevant in the main to hire-purchase and conditional sale agreements and therefore do not require consideration here.

12.02 Early settlement

In exercising a right of early settlement, the debtor is bringing forward the settlement of his debt to the creditor and is in effect performing his obligation under the contract. Goode states unequivocally (I[1813]) that at common law the debtor is entitled to discharge his indebtedness ahead of time without notice merely by tendering the amount due, provided that the stipulation for payment by instalments was in his favour, so that the creditor would not suffer any prejudice. At common law there was no provision for any rebate on the interest charges in favour of the creditor, consequently there was little chance of any prejudice.

Under s.94(1) of the Act, the debtor under a regulated consumer credit agreement is entitled at any time, by notice to the creditor and the payment to the creditor of all amounts payable by the debtor to him (less any rebate due to him under s.95), to discharge the debtor's indebtedness under the agreement. A notice under s.94(1) may include the exercise by the debtor of any option to purchase goods given to him under the agreement, and deal with any other matter arising on, or in relation to, its termination. The right to early settlement potentially applies to credit-token agreements, as the subsection applies to regulated consumer credit agreements. In practice, however, it is difficult to see in what precise circumstances the right will have any value for the debtor. A credit-token agreement, by its very nature, normally has built into it the right for the debtor to settle early. On receiving the usual monthly account, the debtor may pay all sums outstanding by the due date and incur no interest charges, or pay a lesser sum as long as it is above the specified minimum payment figure. In this latter case, interest charges will usually be added to the account. If the debtor does settle the account in full, this does not bring the agreement to an early end. He has merely settled those sums incurred in the relevant accounting period by use of the credit-token, whereas early settlement in the case of, for example, a hire-purchase agreement truly terminates that particular agreement.

In the unlikely event that a debtor is entitled to exercise the right of early settlement, there are some points to note which apply under the statute by way of contrast with the common law. First, the debtor must give notice in writing of his intention to exercise his right. It seems that the notice need not be in any particular form as long as the debtor's desire to settle early can be ascertained from the wording. There is no mention of a period of time and it seems that the notice may take effect immediately, if that is the wish of the debtor. Second, the right under the subsection is exercisable without any reference to prejudice to the creditor or to whether the stipulation as to payment by instalments was for the benefit of the debtor or not. Third, there is attached to the statutory right a further right, in s.95, to a statutory rebate.

The debtor must tender payment of all amounts payable by him under the agreement to the creditor. Section 173(1) prevents in general terms contracting out of the Act's provisions and this will apply to the right in s.94(1). Any attempt by the creditor to impose terms more stringent than those contained in s.94 will be prohibited. There is nothing, of course, to prevent the creditor from granting more favourable early settlement terms to the debtor. Goode is of the opinion (I[1818]) that the creditor is not entitled to rely on a clause in the relevant agreement precluding the debtor from settling under the agreement without at the same time settling under other agreements that he has with the creditor. Such a clause must be seen as an attempt to subject the debtor's right to a more stringent requirement than is contained in s.94.

The debtor, as observed in para.8.6, has the right under s.97 to a settlement statement on written request. This figure should contain the gross and net settlement figures, after taking account of the rebate for early settlement in calculating the latter. It is worth recalling that the debtor can also ask to be given a termination statement under s.103 (see para.8.7). If the creditor rejects the debtor's offer of tender of the amount due, this does not release the debtor from his obligation to pay the outstanding balance under the agreement. This is despite the fact that s.189(1) specifies that payment includes tender. Goode points (I[1821]) to the opening words of s.189(1), which state that the definitions in the subsection are to apply 'unless the context otherwise requires'. Clearly, tender in this context cannot be interpreted to mean that the debtor is released from liability for the balance under the agreement.

The effect of early settlement under s.94(1) on linked transactions is dealt with in s.96. Section 96(1) provides that, where for any reason the indebtedness of the debtor under a regulated consumer credit agreement is discharged before the time fixed by the agreement, he, and any relative of his, shall at the same time be discharged from any liability under a linked transaction, other than a debt which has already become payable. By s.96(2) this does not apply to a linked transaction which is itself an agreement providing the debtor or a relative of his with credit. Also, regulations may exclude certain linked transactions from the operation of s.96(1). These are the same exemptions as are to be found in the context of cancellation (see para.6.21). It should be noted that the operation of s.96(1) is not restricted to early settlement cases, and may apply in any situation where the agreement is discharged early, apart from breach by the debtor (see Goode, III[97]).

12.03   Rebate for early payment by debtor

The debtor's right to settle early in s.94, discussed immediately above, refers to the debtor paying all outstanding sums due to the creditor, subject to any reduction in the form of a rebate. The rebate is specifically provided for. Section 95(1) states that regulations may be made to provide for the allowance of a rebate of charges for credit to the debtor under a regulated consumer credit agreement where, under s.94, on refinancing, on breach of the agreement, or for any other reason, his indebtedness is discharged or becomes payable before the time fixed by the agreement, or any sum becomes payable by him before the time so fixed. Section 95(2) provides that regulations made under subs.(1) may allow for calculation of the rebate by reference to any sum paid or payable by the debtor or his relative under or in connection with the agreement (whether to the creditor or some other person), including sums under linked transactions and other items in the total charge for credit.

These rules were included in the Act, not necessarily because creditors had in the past not given a rebate, but because any rebates given under the terms of the contract were often derisory. This meant that creditors were receiving their money early with almost the full amount of interest they would have earned if the contract had continued. They were then often in the position to lend the same money again, thus obtaining a second amount of interest covering the same period, or part of it at least, as the original loan.

Regulations have been made (Consumer Credit (Rebate on Early Settlement) Regulations 1983, SI 1983 No.1562), but they do not apply to running-account credit agreements (reg.2(2)(*b*)). The reason for this is that, normally, interest accrues (if at all) only on the balance of the account from time to time outstanding. In this situation, the debtor is not being asked for or asking to be allowed to make early payment, if he chooses to pay the full amount outstanding on his account each month. Jones (pp.166–8) considers the possibility, however, that the debtor would be entitled to a rebate in relation to a credit-token agreement, in circumstances where the agreement had a clause demanding early repayment on the debtor's breach. Section 95(1) specifically applies to breach, but the point is covered by the common law in any event (see *Overstone* v. *Shipway* [1962] 1 All ER 52). Let us assume that on receipt of the monthly account, the debtor chooses to pay the minimum amount specified in it. He continues to pay the appropriate minimum figure each month. He then misses the payment date by a few days. The creditor exercises his right under the agreement to call for payment of the full amount now outstanding. The debtor is being asked to pay ahead of the time fixed for payment under the agreement. There would seem to be no reason why he should not be entitled to a rebate, one which takes account of his breach in its calculation. If the Rebate Regulations themselves do not apply, as appears to be the case, even in this type of situation, the debtor would nonetheless be entitled on breach to rely on the common law if he was obliged to repay the full amount outstanding to the creditor.

It might be argued that the type of clause illustrated in the example above would in any event be subject to the common law rules on penalties and declared to be penal and consequently invalid. However, unless the agreement provides for a sum over and above the full amount due under the agreement to be paid in addition, it is unlikely that the court would consider a clause demanding payment in full as penal.

12.04 Notice before action by creditor

We shall now consider the restrictions on a creditor's action in certain situations. Some of these are often referred to as 'non-default cases' — cases where for a reason not pertaining to any default by the debtor, the creditor wishes to take some action, whether it be to terminate the agreement or restrict the debtor's rights falling short of termination. In the first instance, we shall consider those situations where the creditor wishes to take some action short of bringing the agreement to an end, e.g. demanding earlier payment of a sum of money.

Section 76(1) is the appropriate section. It provides that a creditor is not entitled to enforce a term of a regulated agreement by demanding earlier payment of any sum, or recovering possession of any goods or land, or treating any right conferred on the debtor by the agreement as terminated, restricted or deferred, except by or after giving the debtor not less than seven days' notice of his intention to do so.

The impact of s.76(1) in relation to credit-token agreements is seriously weakened by s.76(2), which provides that subs.(1) applies only where a period for the duration of the agreement is specified in the agreement, and that period has not ended when the creditor does an act mentioned in subs.(1). However, subs.(1) still applies even where a party is entitled to terminate the agreement before its fixed term has expired. Few credit-token agreements are for a fixed term. It should not be assumed that the expiry date on the credit-token itself is an indication that the agreement is for a fixed term, as the document itself needs to be looked at to see if it does contain a fixed time for its duration. Section 76(6) makes it clear that s.76 does not apply to cases involving a breach of the regulated agreement. Section 87 (below) regulates the position as to notices in case of breach.

Section 76 of itself does not give the creditor the right to exercise any of the remedies specified in s.76(1). The creditor can exercise these rights only if he has included them specifically in his standard-form contract. All that s.76 does is to make the creditor give the requisite notice of his intention to invoke one or more of the remedies. The creditor may wish to include clauses accelerating payment, demanding payment in full or granting him the right to terminate the agreement in the event, for example, that the debtor is adjudged bankrupt or has execution levied against his assets or allows judgment to remain outstanding against him for a certain period. Such events are non-breach events, although in many respects they may be considered as serious as a breach event. It seems that the creditor may incorporate his claim for accelerated payment in his s.76 notice rather than waiting for the seven-day period to expire and then serving the accelerated payment demand. As long as the demand takes effect only on expiry of the seven-day period, this seems unobjectionable (Goode, I[2626]).

Where s.76(1) does apply to a credit-token agreement, a notice must be given before the credit card issuer may exercise any contractual rights which fall within the subsection. However, there are three situations where the subsection does not apply. Section 76(4) permits the creditor to take action without notice to treat the debtor's right to draw on any credit as restricted or deferred and enables him to take such steps as may be necessary to make the restriction or deferment effective. If the creditor has by the credit-token agreement reserved this right to himself, he is free to prevent the debtor from using the credit facility immediately. He can without notice terminate the debtor's entitlement to the card and in practice prevent the use by putting the debtor on a stop list circulated to all suppliers who normally accept the card in payment for goods and services. Section 76 will not apply to an overdraft, as this is normally repayable on demand, nor does it apply to non-commercial agreements where no security has been provided (Consumer Credit (Enforcement, Default and Termination Notices) Regulations 1983, SI 1983 No.1561, reg.2(9), made under s.76(5)).

It is clear that the section does not apply in termination cases, where, if the termination is breach-induced, the creditor must employ the procedure in s.87; where it is non-default-based, s.98 is the provision to use. However, there may be circumstances where the creditor wishes to terminate the agreement on the debtor's bankruptcy, for example. He may also wish to bring into force a clause in the contract for accelerated payment. In that event, he may issue one notice under both ss.76 and 98, with the seven-day periods running concurrently.

The debtor served with a notice under s.76 cannot extinguish it as he may do in respect of a default notice. There is no question of compliance with the notice. He has no option except to apply for a time order under s.129, as the service of a s.76(1) notice is one of the triggers for such an application, as we saw in para.11.14.

Service of the notice must be in the prescribed form, and is valid if sent addressed to the debtor by post, or left, at his address last known to the creditor (s.76).

The form prescribed is set out in the 1983 Regulations. It must contain a statement that it is served under s.76(1), together with the information set out in Sch.1 to the Regulations. Briefly, the required information consists of the details of the agreement, the parties, the term to be enforced, the action intended to be taken by the creditor, in particular, and — in clear terms — which one or more of the three actions mentioned in s.76(1) he intends to pursue. If the action relates to a demand for earlier payment, the Regulations require further details: the gross amount due, the amount of any rebate due and the net amount after deducting the rebate. There must also be included a notice in a specific form advising the debtor of his right or that of any surety to apply to the court for a time order. There should be a statement advising the debtor to obtain legal advice from a solicitor, Trading Standards Department or CAB, as well as a prominent warning that the document should be read carefully. The lettering in any notice must be, apart from any signature, easily legible and of a colour readily distinguishable from the colour of the paper. Some of the lettering must be afforded more prominence, particularly the warning and the time order clause. A copy of the notice served on the debtor must also be served on a surety; otherwise the security can be enforced only by order of the court (s.111(2)).

A failure to serve a notice under s.76 has the same implications as the failure to serve a default notice under s.87; this is discussed below. For the majority of credit card issuers, s.76 should not be a problem. It will not apply and the creditor will not have to serve a notice under s.76. He can exercise any rights in the contract immediately and without warning. Of course, he may exercise such rights only if he has taken the trouble to include them in his contract in the first place. If he has not, and he purports to demand earlier payment for non-breach, he himself will be in breach of the credit-token agreement and liable at least to an action in damages by the debtor.

12.05   Notice of termination other than for breach

Section 98 of the Act is the counterpart of s.76 in relation to non-default giving rise to the creditor's right to terminate the agreement. According to s.98(1), the creditor is not entitled to terminate the regulated agreement except by giving the debtor not less than seven days' notice. Like s.76, it applies only to fixed-term contracts, which are still running when the creditor terminates the agreement. Again, if the agreement may be determined by a party before the fixed term elapses, s.98(1) still applies (s.98(2)). Section 98(4) permits the creditor to cut off the credit facility in the same way as was mentioned in the context of s.76 and, as with that section, it does not apply in cases of breach. The section permits the creditor to exercise the right to terminate in the s.98 notice itself, or to wait until the seven-day period has elapsed, and then serve the actual notice of termination. The debtor can do nothing to remedy the situation, except to apply for a time order as in the case of a s.76 notice. The notice must be in the prescribed form, in broadly similar terms to a notice under s.76, but with suitable amendments to reflect the fact that the creditor is either terminating or proposing to terminate the agreement. He must give details of the steps he is taking or proposes to take to effect the termination.

Where the credit-token is outside the scope of the notice requirement in s.98, the creditor has no restriction on his right to terminate the agreement on the basis of a non-default event. It must be emphasised that the creditor may exercise such a right only if he has expressly reserved it to himself by virtue of the credit-token agreement. An unlawful termination by the creditor may entitle the debtor to treat the contract as at an end and sue for damages for any losses incurred as a result of the creditor's breach.

12.06 Termination on default

The provisions discussed immediately above were concerned with the wide range of situations where a creditor may expressly have reserved certain rights in respect of undesirable events falling short of breach. In this section we consider the issue of breach by the debtor, the consequences for the latter and the fetters imposed on the creditor in the likely event that he will wish to take action in respect of that breach. The provisions concerning protected goods and entry on to premises to recover goods in ss.90 to 92 relate only to hire-purchase and conditional sale agreements under the Act. We need not consider these. We are interested in the restriction of the creditor's rights to take action as set out in ss.87 to 89 and the accompanying regulations, namely, the issue and effect of default notices.

12.07 Termination at common law

It is necessary first to consider the effect of a breach by a debtor at common law before going on to see how the Act affects the relative positions of the debtor and creditor. If the creditor includes in the credit-token agreement the right to terminate the agreement for, e.g., late payment of the minimum amount due on the monthly account, and there is delay in payment, naturally the creditor is entitled to treat the contract as at an end. If there is no such clause in the agreement, the failure to pay will still be a breach, but will be regarded as a minor breach only, damages being the only remedy. But the creditor's action will probably be limited to an action in debt for the arrears. However, a 'time of the essence' clause in the agreement elevates the failure to pay into a serious breach entitling the creditor to treat the agreement as at an end and to sue for damages. If time is not of the essence initially, the innocent party is entitled to make it such on giving reasonable notice. If the creditor does not include in the credit-token agreement a clause having this effect, he needs to give notice, after an instalment has been missed, making time of the essence in respect of that payment. If the debtor fails to comply following this, the creditor can treat himself as discharged from the contract. However, as we shall see, where the agreement is regulated his rights are postponed and may even be completely obliterated in certain situations.

12.08   Default notices

By s.87(1), service of a default notice within s.88 is necessary before the creditor can become entitled, by reason of any breach by the debtor of a regulated agreement:
(1)   to terminate the agreement; or
(2)   to demand earlier payment of any sum; or
(3)   to recover possession of any goods or land; or
(4)   to treat any right conferred on the debtor by the agreement as terminated, restricted or deferred; or
(5)   to enforce any security.
A default notice is necessary whatever kind of breach has arisen. It is not restricted to breaches arising from non-payment alone. It is wider than ss.76 and 98 as it covers not only remedies of the creditor expressly provided for in the agreement, but applies also to remedies arising at common law, e.g. a repudiatory breach giving the creditor the right to treat the contract as terminated. According to Goode (I[2635]), s.87 does not apply, however, where the creditor wishes to rescind the contract for misrepresentation or fraud by the debtor, as these remedies arise from matters extraneous to the credit agreement. Likewise, a default notice is not essential if the creditor is suing for arrears, or only for damages arising from the debtor's breach. If the debtor fails to pay the minimum

monthly payment, the creditor need not issue a default notice if he merely claims the amount in arrears. However, if this demand is not complied with and he wishes to exercise the right of termination in the contract, or he has made time of the essence and the debtor has still failed to comply and he wishes to treat the breach as repudiatory, he must issue a default notice. If any action is to be taken against a surety, whether in respect of arrears or otherwise, the creditor must service a notice on the debtor (whether he is to be a party to any proceedings or not) and a copy on the surety. The security is unenforceable without a court order if this is not done (s.111).

One additional significant difference between s.87 on the one hand and s.76 on the other lies in the fact that the creditor cannot include in his default notice a demand for accelerated payment. This can only be done once the default notice has expired and would require a further notice making the demand at that stage.

Section 87 is more likely to apply to credit-token agreements than ss.76 and 98 which, as we have seen, are restricted to agreements for a fixed term. There is no such restriction in s.87, so where there is a default, in the majority of cases, there will be no escape for the creditor from the rigours of ss.87 to 89.

There are three further situations, however, where there is relief from s.87. Section 87(2) allows the creditor to prevent the debtor drawing on the credit facility. This may be done in a fashion similar to that outlined above under the equivalent provisions in ss.76 and 98. This is a very useful provision for the creditor under a credit-token agreement, which at least prevents the debtor from running up even more debts on the account. It should be remembered that the subsection does not give the creditor the right to cut off the supply of credit: it merely allows him to exercise his contractual right without hindrance, if he has been wise enough to include such a matter in the contract with the debtor. Secondly, like ss.76 and 98, s.87 does not apply to non-commercial agreements in relation to which no security is provided. Thirdly, where a breach brings into operation another provision in the agreement, non-compliance by the debtor with that other provision does not mean that the creditor must serve a separate default notice. Section 88(3) provides that it is sufficient if the default notice in respect of the original breach was served. If this notice is not complied with, the creditor is entitled to treat the failure to comply with the other provision as a breach that does not require the service of a s.87(1) notice. An example, would be a clause providing for the payment of the full outstanding balance on non-payment of an instalment.

12.09   Contents of a default notice

The form and contents of a default notice are regulated by s.88 and the 1983 Regulations mentioned earlier in the discussion on ss.76 and 98. In the first instance, s.88(1) states that the default notice must be in the prescribed form and specify:

'(*a*)   the nature of the alleged breach;
 (*b*)   if the breach is capable of remedy, what action is required to remedy it and the date before which that action is to be taken;
 (*c*)   if the breach is not capable of remedy, the sum (if any) required to be paid as compensation for the breach, and the date before which it is to be paid.'

Any date specified under s.88(1) must be not less than seven days after the date of the service of the default notice. The creditor is not to take action as is specified in s.87(1) before the date so specified or (if no requirement is made under s.88(1)) before those seven days have elapsed (s.88(2)).

A breach is considered incapable of remedy unless it can be completely remedied within a reasonable time. Even if it takes longer than the period specified by the creditor in the notice under s.88(1), it may still be remediable. If, however, it is incapable of remedy, the creditor may wish to include a claim for compensation under s.88(1)(*c*), although he is not required to do so. The creditor should still issue a default notice even if he has no desire to claim compensation. Apart from anything else, the debtor needs a warning as to the consequences of non-compliance and information as to his right to ask the court for a time order, as the service of the default notice is another of the triggers for such an application. The court nonetheless has the power to grant a time order, notwithstanding the fact that the breach is incapable of remedy. There may also be jurisdiction in equity to grant relief to a debtor.

It seems that the creditor may include a claim for compensation in circumstances where the breach is capable of remedy. This is not specifically ruled out by s.88(1)(*b*). This may be included in addition to the action required to remedy the breach. No time limit need be specified for the payment of the compensation, unless this happens to be the action required by the creditor to remedy the breach.

The default notice must contain information in the prescribed terms about the consequences of failure to comply with it (s.88(4)). A default notice making a requirement under s.88(1), namely, as to the remedial action under s.88(1)(*b*), or as to payment of compensation under s.88(1)(*c*), may include a provision for the taking of such action as is mentioned in s.87(1) at any time after the restriction in s.88(2) will cease, together with a statement that the provision will be ineffective if the breach is remedied or the compensation paid in accordance with the notice.

Section 89 contains the all-important provision to the effect that if the debtor takes the action specified in the notice, in the specified time, the breach is deemed never to have occurred. Even where the creditor was relying upon a serious breach to justify termination of the agreement, the breach will be treated as cured, irrespective of the creditor's wishes. It also seems that the creditor is not able to rely on that cured breach as evidence that the debtor is a bad payer, or as evidence that the debtor has evinced an intention to repudiate unlawfully his obligations under the contract where there is a subsequent breach. The effect of s.89 is to wipe the slate clean.

12.10   Form of default notice

The discussion above concentrated on the statutory requirements in s.88 in respect of default notices. The Regulations also require a wealth of information to be included. There are similar rules as to legibility and prominence that we have met before in this type of statutory notice. The information to be included is the standard detail of the debtor, the creditor, a description of the agreement, details of the breach, the information as set out in s.88 above, the consequences if the action requested is carried out, the consequences of non-compliance and a clear statement by the creditor of precisely what action he proposes to take. Where the creditor indicates that payment is being brought forward, the notice must include the amount to be paid in gross and net figures after deduction of any stated rebate. The notice must contain the statement about time orders and obtaining advice from appropriate persons or organisations, as discussed in the context of the s.76 notice.

Where the credit-token agreement contains a clause which becomes operative on a breach of another term by the debtor, the consequences in the event of non-compliance with the default notice on the operation of this provision must be spelt out in the notice. As mentioned before, if this is done there is no need to serve an additional notice in respect of that clause.

12.11   Failure to comply with s.87 by the creditor

The failure to comply with the default notice procedure means that the creditor cannot lawfully enforce the agreement in the ways set out in s.87 (or similarly, as appropriate, in the context of ss.76 and 98). Such failure may come about by failing to serve the notice at all, serving an invalid notice, or enforcing the agreement in a prohibited way before the time limit has expired. If the creditor nonetheless proceeds to do the restricted act, the question of the debtor's remedy arises. The Act does not specify any further remedy for this particular provision; according to s.170(1), therefore, there is none. In hire-purchase cases, it has been held that the debtor can recover all payments made under the agreement where the creditor recovered possession of the goods without serving a valid default notice. It would seem that this principle is hardly applicable in relation to a credit-token agreement. It would appear odd if the debtor was without any sanction in such a situation. After all, the purpose of the procedure is to give the debtor an opportunity to set the record straight and get his affairs in order. If he is deprived of the chance to do this, it would be contrary to the statutory purpose. Goode (III[88]) suggests that the debtor might try for an injunction, relying on s.170(3). The injunction might be used to prevent the creditor from enforcing the agreement. On the other hand, if the enforcement has proceeded, the court might grant a mandatory injunction specifically ordering the creditor to comply with the default notice procedure. This may be something of a long shot and it is doubtful whether it would succeed. The debtor would probably be best advised to apply for a time order.

12.12   Death of the debtor

Section 86 of the Act contains provisions which are likely to affect credit-token agreements only on rare occasions. The objective of the section is to impose restrictions on the creditor in relation to any contractual terms which become operational on the death of the debtor and which are designed to introduce more onerous terms. The usual type of clause is one whereby the whole of the outstanding balance becomes due on the death of the debtor.

Where a regulated agreement is fully secured, the creditor is not entitled, by reason of the death of the debtor, to do any of the acts specified in s.87(1). If the regulated agreement at the time of the debtor's death is only partly secured, or not secured at all, the creditor may carry out such acts only on an order of the court. As with ss.76 and 98, the limiting factor is that the section applies only to fixed-term agreements, thus excluding the majority of credit-token agreements from its protection. In any event, should a credit-token agreement be within the section, s.86(4) permits the creditor to stop the use of the card to obtain more credit. This will be relevant where the debtor has asked for an additional card to be provided for a spouse or other member of the family. In addition, s.86(5) provides that the restrictions in the section do not affect the operation of any agreement for payment of sums due under the regulated agreement, or becoming due under it on the death of the debtor, out of the proceeds of an insurance policy. The creditor is entitled to the proceeds of any policy which it was agreed in the credit contract would be paid on the death of the debtor. An act is done by reason of the death of the debtor if it is done under a power in the agreement which is exercisable on the death of the debtor, or exercisable at will and exercised at any time after his death (s.86(6)).

In the few instances where these provisions do make any impact, the creditor needs to provide in the agreement for the right to stop the line of credit. In the majority of cases outside the section, it is still important to remember that the creditor can exercise rights on the death of the debtor only if those rights are expressly included in the credit agreement. One difficulty which may arise after the death relates to authorised users. If such a person uses the card after the death of the debtor but before the creditor manages to put a stop on the use, the creditor may have a problem. Nothing in the credit agreement affects this issue as the user is not a party to the agreement. The creditor will have little option but to pay the supplier. The user cannot be proceeded against as he or she is not a party to the credit agreement. The creditor may not be able to recover from the estate of the debtor, as, at common law, the death will withdraw the card user's authority.

12.13   Default interest

If the debtor fails to make an agreed payment by the due date, the credit-token agreement will normally provide for the creditor to charge interest on the arrears. For example, the debtor may fail to make the minimum payment at the end of one particular month. The creditor may have a clause in the agreement charging interest in respect of those arrears. This is default interest. However, as is his right, the creditor will be entitled under the agreement to charge interest on the remainder of the unpaid balance that the debtor may choose not to pay. This interest charge is not default interest.

Section 93 of the 1974 Act applies only to the default interest under regulated consumer credit agreements. It provides that the debtor is not obliged to pay interest on sums which, in breach of agreement, are unpaid, at a higher rate than the interest rate specified in the agreement. If the credit is interest free, the debtor cannot be charged default interest at all. This is an important section in relation to credit-token agreements. The section restricts the creditor's rights only in respect of default interest. The creditor is free to enforce other rights in the agreement, in particular restricting or deferring a person's ability to draw on the credit facility itself. Any rights falling within s.87 can, of course, be enforced only after service of a valid default notice.

12.14 Conclusion

A number of the matters mentioned above are of only marginal importance in relation to credit-token agreements; for example, statutory rebates and the restrictions in ss.76 and 98 in respect of non-default notices. For the credit card issuer, the main focus of attention must be the default notice procedure in ss.87 to 89. The failure to serve a default notice, or serving an invalid notice, may have serious consequences for the creditor. It is vital, therefore, to have a good grasp of how the restrictions in the provisions operate in relation to the creditor's rights in the contract.

CHAPTER 13

Debit and Cheque Guarantee Cards

13.01 Introduction

In the preceding chapters the discussion has focused almost entirely upon credit card agreements, particularly those which constitute credit-token agreements regulated under the Consumer Credit Act 1974. That focus must now move to other forms of plastic card, namely, debit and cheque guarantee cards. This is not new territory, as there was a discussion in Chapter 1 of the differences between the various types of card. There have also been references throughout the text to debit and cash cards, particularly in Chapter 7, on misuse of credit-tokens. The cash card is considered to be a variant of the usual type of debit card, but is given separate treatment where necessary. It should be mentioned that some credit card agreements, such as the so-called chargecards distributed by American Express and Diner's Club, might be affected by the Code of Banking Practice or decisions of the Banking Ombudsman.

The regulation of debit and cheque guarantee cards has hitherto been left largely to the terms and conditions contained in the issuer's standard-form contract and the vagaries of the common law of contract. We have seen that these types of agreement are left untouched for the most part by the provisions of the 1974 Act which we have discussed. With the introduction of the Banking Ombudsman Scheme several years ago there was a change of approach to the regulation of these kinds of agreement, not just that arising from the less formal procedures involved in such a private ombudsman scheme. The Ombudsman's Terms of Reference (para.14(b)) require him, among other things, to have regard to 'good banking practice' when considering complaints within the scheme. More recently, after a lengthy period of negotiation, the Code of Banking Practice was introduced, designed to regulate the relationship between the bank and the customer in respect of a number of important issues. One of these relates to liability for loss as a result of the misuse of debit and cash cards — a controversial and difficult issue for the Ombudsman, as we saw in Chapter 7. The larger measure of the controversy has been concerned with the problem of 'phantom' withdrawals. We shall consider the way in which these have been handled so far by the Ombudsman and the way in which they are likely to be dealt with in the future following the introduction of the Code.

The discussion starts by considering the legal nature of the debit and cash card agreement, and then that of the cheque guarantee card. This is followed by a detailed look at the provisions of the Code of Banking Practice in so far as it affects card issuers. As the Ombudsman, whether the private scheme of the banks or the statutory one of the building societies, may be seised of the vast majority of complaints made about such cards, we shall consider the Terms of Reference of the banking scheme, and look at some of the information set out in the annual reports. These often give a very useful indication of the way a complaint might go if taken before the Ombudsman for a decision, although it should be emphasised that there is no suggestion that any previous decision is to be taken as binding (see para.14(c) of the Terms of Reference).

13.02 Debit cards

In para.1.6 it was stated that a debit card is a payment device which is in essence a substitute for a cheque. As a result of developments in technology, it is now possible to transfer funds electronically at the point of sale: this is known as EFTPOS. The debit card may be used to pay for goods and services at the premises of those retailers who have agreed with the card issuer to accept payment in that way. The payment by the card issuer will be discounted in accordance with the terms agreed in the contract between the supplier and the card issuer. However, the payment will not involve the supplier in any further paperwork as the money is transferred electronically. There is less paying in at the bank and the money is in the supplier's account in many cases faster than if the customer had paid cash, and appreciably earlier than if the payment had been by cheque or credit card. The customer has the advantage of not having to write out and then record details of the cheque: he or she merely retains the slip handed over at the point of sale and checks his or her bank statement to see that the correct entries have been made. The major disadvantage for the customer is that the money to pay the supplier is normally coming out of a credit balance on his or her current account.

Beyond doubt, the debit card is a useful adjunct to the variety of plastic cards available. The rapid spread in use of these cards has not been matched by any real increase in their regulation. As they are not usually related to the provision of credit, regulation has been left to the parties and the common law as mentioned in the introduction to this chapter. It will no doubt be useful to consider some of the types of terms which may frequently be found in agreements covering the issue of debit cards. In the first instance, however, it will be useful to summarise the impact or, perhaps more aptly, the lack of it, of the Consumer Credit Act 1974 on the debit card.

First, as mentioned before, the debit card does not normally involve the provision of any credit. In Chapter 7, on the other hand, we saw that in some situations the debit card might be considered as a credit-token, at least for the purposes of s.84 of the Act. If the debit card is issued to operate in conjunction with a current account with an agreed overdraft, any use of the debit card which uses up credit will amount to the use of a credit facility within s.83 of the Act, and once a credit-token, the customer gets the significant benefit of the limited liability in s.84. The decision whether the use of the debit card constitutes it a credit-token is less important in many respects because of the Code of Banking Practice. We shall discuss this below as well as any usual contractual terms as to liability for misuse.

Secondly, in Chapter 9 we saw that the debit card, when used to pay for goods and services, is really the same thing as a cheque. The arrangement between retailer and card issuer to accept the card does not amount to pre-existing arrangements within s.187 of the Act. This means that the customer has no comeback against the card issuer under s.75 for the retailer's breach of contract or misrepresentation, even if the debit card was being used in relation to a credit facility, i.e. as a credit-token. Nor, for the same reason, can the customer take advantage of the deemed agency provision in s.56 of the Act (see Chapter 10). Any action for breach of the express or implied terms of the contract, misrepresentation or any other action at common law or under statute must be pursued by the customer against the retailer alone.

Thirdly, precontractual regulation of the debit card agreement consists of the usual common law and statutory rules as to misrepresentation. If the customer has been induced into the agreement by an actionable misrepresentation, the usual remedies are available against the card issuer (see Chapter 4). No formalities are required to enter into a debit card agreement, although written terms and conditions would be normal.

Fourthly, there are, apparently in practice at least, no statutory provisions relating to the cancellation or withdrawal from a debit or cash card agreement. As such an agreement is not normally a regulated agreement, the cancellation provisions in ss.67 to 73 of the 1974 Act do not apply.

Even where the debit card or cash card is issued in conjunction with a current account with an agreed overdraft facility, it should be remembered that nearly all current accounts will in practice be exempt from the Part V provisions, including in particular the cancellation rules. It is theoretically possible for the Consumer Protection (Cancellation of Contracts Concluded Away from Business Premises) Regulations 1987 (see Chapter 6) to apply to an agreement for the supply of a debit or cash card. Goode argues (I[1486]) that 'services' in the context of the Regulations 'evidently includes the provision of loans and overdrafts'. In support of this, he points out that the Regulations specifically exempt contracts for the purchase of land and bridging loans from their scope, leaving us with the assumption that other types of credit facility fall within their range. It would not seem to be extending this too far to suggest that agreements for debit and cash cards are also within the ambit of the Regulations. Two practical points seriously dilute any implications these provisions might have on debit and cash card agreements. First, the supply of the services must take place following an unsolicited visit by a trader to the home of the consumer or of another person or to the consumer's place of work. The obvious way round this is to ensure in every case that a visit of any kind is not made until there is a written request by the customer on file. Second, in practice the discussions relating to the supply of a debit or cash card are normally conducted on the bank or building society premises, or through the post. Conducting them by telephone will not make the Regulations operational either.

As we have seen, there are provisions in the Consumer Credit Act 1974 which specifically apply to withdrawal from a prospective regulated agreement (Chapter 6). The right to withdrawal, however, is left primarily to common law principles and these likewise apply to debit and cash card agreements. By way of contrast with the credit card agreements discussed in Chapter 6, the account-holder under a debit or cash card agreement does not obtain the benefit of the provision in s.57(3) as to whom notice of withdrawal may be given, or the benefit of the cancellation provisions contained in ss.69 to 73 as given by s.57(1). This is so even where the debit or cash card is issued in connection with an overdraft agreement. This is for the same reason as mentioned above, namely, that nearly all overdrafts on current accounts are exempt from the provisions of Part V of the Act.

As a consequence of all this, the customer's right to withdrawal is regulated by common law principles. In practice, of course, if the customer discovers that it is too late to withdraw from an agreement, or that there is no right of cancellation, statutory or otherwise, he or she need merely not use the card. This will effectively cancel the agreement for the use of the card. The only problem which might then arise is the possibility of the card falling into the wrong hands and being liable to misuse. In practice, it would seem better all round if the issuer of a card which was no longer wanted in this way were to accept its surrender or agree to its destruction by the customer, to avoid such difficulties.

Fifthly, as to matters arising during the course of the agreement, the rights of the customer to the provision of information under a debit or cash card contract will depend largely on the terms of the agreement. As we saw in Chapter 8, the 1974 Act provides for the supply of information, in particular relating to the state of the account of the debtor, in some detail. The customer under a debit or cash card agreement is less favoured in this respect, although the Code of Banking Practice has some provisions relating to matters of information.

Judicial control of credit-token agreements has a high profile within the Consumer Credit Act, as we saw in Chapter 11. The extortionate credit bargain provisions and the powers in ss.129 to 136 display, at least in theory, a high degree of willingness to intervene in the relationship between creditor and debtor. Needless to say, the court's powers of intervention in relation to a debit or cash card agreement are much more circumscribed. The customer under such an agreement is left to the vagaries of the common law or principles of equity, should problems arise in relation to the agreement. The Code of Banking Practice does contain some very general statements to the effect that banks, building societies and card issuers will act 'fairly and reasonably in all dealings with their customers'. Any intervention, if at all, is likely to come from a complaint made to the Ombudsman in relation to banks and societies within the relevant schemes.

It is possible that a cash or debit card might come within the scrutiny of the court, if either was associated with a current account with an overdraft facility. The debit or cash card agreement, if separate from the current account agreement, would no doubt be considered to be a related agreement, and even as part of the credit bargain if some charge relating to it was in the total charge for credit. Other than such a rare situation, the two types of agreement are outside the wide powers contained in the 1974 Act.

Finally, the 1974 Act contains no controls or restrictions on the creditor's rights in the agreement or at common law to terminate or do other things short of termination for breach or otherwise. Assuming the creditor has specifically reserved the relevant rights for himself in the agreement, generally he is free to exercise them at will, subject to common law and equitable principles, and occasionally statute, such as the Unfair Contract Terms Act 1977.

13.03   Cheque guarantee cards

The debit card and cash card do have some affinity, at least on the face of it, with a credit-token. However, as we pointed out in para.1.07, the cheque guarantee card is an entirely different thing from the other cards which form the subject matter of this book. Nonetheless, it is sometimes confused with them, and particularly so where the card is a multi-function card combining a debit, cash and guarantee card. Also, in some circumstances a credit card may be used to guarantee a cheque and there seems uncertainty about the legal position of the creditor in such a situation.

The first thing to be noticed about a cheque guarantee card is that, unlike the credit-token, debit or cash card, it is used in conjunction with a cheque. The debit card, it will be recalled, is a substitute for a cheque and, likewise, the other two types of card dispense with the need for a cheque. The cardholder will have a contract with the bank or society issuing the card, permitting the use of the card to guarantee payment of the cheque. The primary liability lies still with the drawer of the cheque, but the guarantee by the bank or society creates a secondary liability in the same way as the normal guarantee. If the card is used in accordance with the instructions, it is regarded as an offer to the world at large that any cheque issued in conjunction with it will be honoured by the guarantor. This will be the case, even where the account of the card-holder has insufficient funds to cover the cheque. This is a breach by the cardholder in the absence of an agreed overdraft, but it does not affect the payee of the cheque. The offer is accepted by the payee when the cheque, supported by the card, is taken in payment. The status in law of a cheque guarantee card was raised in the criminal case of *R* v. *Charles* [1977] AC 112. Lord Diplock took the view (p.182) that the use of the card in connection with the transaction gives the payee a direct contractual right against the card issuer itself to payment on presentation of the cheque, provided the use of the card by the drawer of the cheque to bind the issuer was within the actual or ostensible authority conferred on him by the issuer.

Diamond (p.325) suggests that the issuer will be liable even if the signature on the cheque was forged. The requirement that the signature on the cheque must correspond with the specimen signature on the card 'probably means no more than that the two signatures must look reasonably alike'. Normally, the cheque card will require also that the cheque must be signed in the presence of the payee, the cheque must be drawn on a cheque form bearing the code number shown on the card, the card must still be in force and the card number written on the reverse of the cheque by the payee. In addition, it is practice to insist on production of the cheque book of the drawer for this to be checked and some form of mark made on it to indicate the use of the cheque card. This has the effect of bringing it to the attention of any subsequent payee whether the card is being used frequently. Excessive use of the card within a short time span might raise the suspicion of fraud.

As the card creates a contractual obligation between the issuer and the payee, it is not open to the drawer of the cheque to countermand payment of the cheque. The issuer is bound by his contract to pay. A refusal to pay in such circumstances would jeopardise the whole basis of the arrangements concerning cheque card guarantees.

In Chapter 3 (para.3.02) it was mentioned that Diamond had argued that a cheque guarantee card might be a credit-token where it was used in connection with an overdraft facility at a bank or building society other than that of the customer holding the card. This is not an entirely convincing argument as the card's function is merely to guarantee the payment of the cheque if the person primarily liable, the customer, fails to meet the obligation contained in it. However, Jones (p.101) admits somewhat tentatively, or so it seems, that it might be a credit-token in such circumstances. The agreement for the cheque guarantee card may therefore be a regulated credit-token agreement, having to comply with the appropriate formalities. In any event a cheque guarantee card associated with a current account with an agreed overdraft facility will be part of a regulated agreement.

If the card can be considered a credit-token, it may be that the rules in s.84 on misuse apply to it (see Chapter 7). However, for the most part the cheque guarantee card is likely to be outside the controls of the Consumer Credit Act 1974. Certainly, the provisions of ss.56 and 75 do not apply to transactions in which such a card is used, as it cannot be a DCS agreement so as to attract those sections.

In respect of some of the other controls in the Act discussed in Chapters 3 to 12, the cheque guarantee card will generally fall within the provisions only if it is in some way connected with a regulated agreement. For example, if it is part of the credit bargain for the purposes of s.137, it may be subject to the powers of the court to reopen the credit agreement and deal with any related agreements.

Broadly, the rights of the parties to a cheque card agreement are to be found in the agreement itself, subject to the usual common law rules of contract. Where a credit card, such as Visa or Access, is used to guarantee a cheque, it is being used merely to ensure payment of the cheque as outlined above. It certainly does not invoke in the customer's favour the provisions of s.56 or 75. It is no different in this context from the normal cheque guarantee card.

13.04 Some typical clauses in debit and cheque guarantee card agreements

The most likely clauses to be found in the agreement under which the debit, cash or guarantee card will be issued relate to signing the card on receipt and safeguarding it and — in appropriate cases — the PIN. The customer will be told to sign the card immediately on receipt. There will normally be a clause which states that the card remains the property of the issuer and must be surrendered to the issuer if the agreement is terminated for any reason. The use of the card will normally be liable to suspension or termination by the issuer in its absolute discretion and without notice. The customer may also be given a contractual right to terminate the agreement, but it will normally depend on the surrender or destruction of the card. Some form of exclusion clause is often included. This may seek to exclude all consequential loss howsoever caused, or may be a more limited form of restriction of the issuer's liability. Such a clause, in so far as it seeks to exclude the liability of the issuer for monetary loss arising from the issuer's negligence, is subject to the reasonableness test in s.11 of the Unfair Contract Terms Act 1977 (s.2(2)). Other attempts to exclude other types of contractual liability may be controlled under s.3 of the Act, which similarly subjects any such clause to a reasonableness test (see paras.9.09 and 9.10).

As far as a cheque guarantee card is concerned, it is highly likely that there will be a clause in the agreement or on the cheque book used in conjunction with the card, warning of the danger of keeping card and cheque book together.

The main clause for our purposes will be that relating to safeguarding the PIN in connection with a debit or cash card. The usual clause instructs the customer to memorise the PIN and then to destroy the slip notifying him of the number. Subsequently, the customer is placed under a duty to take 'every' or 'all possible' care to avoid disclosure of the PIN to any other person and to avoid loss of the card. There will also be provisions relating to loss of the card, stating how the loss is to be notified to the issuer and whether confirmation in writing is required. Usually, the agreement will specify that the customer is to be held liable for any loss through misuse until the loss of the card has been notified to the issuer. The Code of Banking Practice also addresses this issue.

13.05 The Code of Banking Practice

The preface to the Code states that the Code sets out the standards of good banking practice to be observed by banks, building societies and card issuers when dealing with personal customers in the UK. The Code became effective on 16th March 1992 and will be reviewed at least once every two years. The Code is voluntary but nearly all banks and building societies subscribe to it.

The governing principles of the Code are the setting of standards of good banking practice, fair and reasonable treatment of customers, enabling customers to understand the operation of their accounts and the provision of banking services in general and the maintenance of security and integrity of banking and card payment systems. Giving information to customers is seen to be an important way of avoiding complaints and difficulties. Part A of the Code is the general part covering banking services in their entirety. Part B concerns us more as it specifically addresses matters relating to the issue of credit and other payment cards. We have considered some of these at appropriate places in the discussion in relation to credit-token agreements. Our main focus will now be the Code's provisions dealing with the security and loss of, and liability for loss of, such cards. Some, as we have seen, are already catered for by the credit-token provisions in ss.83 and 84 of the 1974 Act, including such debit or cash cards as may be considered in the circumstances as credit-tokens (see Chapter 7).

13.06 Issue and security of cards

We have already seen that the Code provides (in para.15.1) that cards should be issued to customers only when they have been requested in writing or to replace or renew existing cards. Because of the massive spread of multi-function cards, para.15.2 provides that card issuers are under a duty to tell customers if a card issued by them has more than one function. It came to light that customers were being issued with PINs contrary to their wishes. Banks were marketing cards with a number of functions but were not prepared to comply with the wishes of a customer who wanted, for example, only a cheque guarantee card for up to £100 and a debit card (such as Switch), but not a cash card. The Code now states that the issuer should comply with the customer's request not to be supplied with a PIN.

There are additional security measures which the issuers are under a duty to undertake. PINs are to be issued separately from the associated card and only the customer is to be notified of the number (Code, para.16.1). Card issuers are to remind customers of their responsibility for the security of their cards and PINs to counter fraud. In particular, the issuer is to lay emphasis on the followings:

(1) customers should not allow anyone else to use their card or PIN;

(2) customers should take all reasonable steps to ensure the card is safe and the PIN kept secret;

(3) customers should never write the PIN on the card or on anything usually kept with it;

(4) customers should never write the PIN down without attempting to disguise it.

These are matters which can easily be, and are usually, contained in the card agreement; it seems, however, that they need to be brought more forcibly to the customer's attention. This can and should be done in the letter sending the card or the PIN. It should be noted that these are not provisions aimed directly at the customer. The duty is placed on the issuer of the card to emphasise these points. No doubt, if these items are included in the contract, they will be considered to be terms of the contract and failure to comply with them will amount to a breach. If the breach results in misuse of the card, however, the loss will normally be dealt with under the relevant provisions of the Code. As we shall see the Code makes the customer liable for sums over £50 only in circumstances where the customer has been fraudulent or possibly guilty of 'gross negligence'. Failure to comply with the terms as to security of the card and/or PIN may not always amount to 'gross negligence', in which case the loss imposed on the customer will be restricted to the limit of £50 set in the Code.

13.07 Loss of card

Card issuers are placed under a duty to inform customers that they must tell their card issuers as soon as reasonably practicable after they discover their card has been lost or stolen, that someone else knows their PIN or that their account includes an apparently incorrect item. Card issuers are to tell customers, and remind them at regular intervals on their statement or by other means, of the place and the telephone number where they can give details of a lost or stolen card at any time of day or night. The number is also to be included in British Telecom directories. Card issuers are obliged to act on telephoned information but may request written confirmation. The issuers are to tell customers, on request, whether they accept notification from card notification organisations. On being advised of loss, possible theft or misuse of the card, the issuers must take steps to prevent further use of the card (Code, para.17). These provisions are normally standard in card agreements. They are very similar to the provisions in s.84 of the Consumer Credit Act discussed in Chapter 7.

13.08   Liability for loss or misuse

This is arguably the most controversial aspect of the Code. Various organisations, including the Banking Ombudsman, had long pressed for a limit on liability, similar to that contained in s.84 of the Act in relation to credit-token agreements, to be imposed in respect of other payment cards such as the debit or cash card. The Ombudsman had resolved some cases, as we have seen, by resorting to the Act where possible. This approach still left the majority of the claims to be dealt with under the terms of the agreement between the parties. As we shall see nearly all these cases went against the customer, particularly where the customer claimed that there had been a 'phantom' withdrawal. The Code, in its final form and after much argument, contains provisions designed to take much of the heat out of the debate.

In the first instance, the Code throws the burden of loss on the card issuer where there is misuse before the card has been received by the customer, a rather watered down version of the 'acceptance' provision in s.66 of the Act (see para.5.11). The issuer is also liable for all transactions not authorised by the customer after notification of the loss or theft of the card or that someone else knows the PIN. This is subject to the proviso that the customer will be liable for all losses if he has been fraudulent or may be liable if grossly negligent. The card issuer is to be responsible if faults have occurred in the machines, or other systems in use, which cause customers to suffer direct loss unless the fault was obvious or advised by a notice or message on display. The card issuer's liability is to be limited to those amounts wrongly charged to the accounts of cus-tomers and any interest on those amounts. The customer's liability is to be limited to the sum of £50 in the event of misuse before the card issuer has been notified of loss or theft of the card or that someone else is aware of the PIN. This is also subject to the fraud and gross negligence provisions mentioned above. In cases of disputed transactions, the burden of proving fraud or gross negligence or that a card has been received by a customer lies with the card issuer, who is entitled to expect co-operation from customers in investigating misuse (Code, para.18). The precise effect of these provisions is discussed below in the light of the Ombudsman's decisions and other recorded views on them.

13.09   Complaints procedures

The Code provides that each card issuer must have its own internal procedures for the proper handling of customers' complaints. This fact must be passed on to customers, who must be informed of how to make their complaint and what further steps are available if they are dissatisfied with its outcome. The Code prescribes that each issuer should belong to one of the further complaint mechanisms, which include the two Ombudsman schemes in this sector. Card issuers are expected to provide customers with literature on the scheme to which they belong.

13.10   Status of the Code

The Code is voluntary and, on the face of it, does not have the force of law. In practice, however, it may well do so. The two Ombudsman schemes are concerned with law and good banking practice when considering complaints, as we shall see. They are likely to see the Code as the absolute minimum expected of members of their scheme. If the card issuer does not subscribe to the Code, a court or the Ombudsman is still likely to consider the Code as indicative of what the reasonable banker would do and apply it almost as if it were a statutory code. Certainly, a card issuer seeking to deny that the Code applies to any given situation will have a considerable burden to bear.

13.11   The Ombudsmen

A plethora of private sector Ombudsman schemes exist these days. Principal among these are the Banking and Building Society Schemes, one (in theory at least) voluntary in nature, the other statutory. The Banking Ombudsman (the voluntary scheme) is the one on which we shall focus attention. The Building Society Scheme has seen such an increase in complaints since its inception that it has been necessary to appoint a second Ombudsman. A large number of the complaints have concerned the use of cards and ATMs. Reference will be made where appropriate to any views of the Ombudsman on the subject of loss arising through misuse. On the face of it, the problem has caused more difficulty for the Banking Ombudsman.

The terms of reference of the Banking Ombudsman are to receive complaints relating to the provision within the UK of banking services by any bank to any individual, to consider and facilitate their satisfaction, settlement or withdrawal whether by agreement, by making recommendations or awards, or by such other means as appears expedient. He is to decide his own procedure, can request information from banks and is not bound by any legal rule of evidence. In certain circumstances, he may make an award of up to £100,000 against a bank, although so far it has not been necessary to resort to this power.

There are a number of limitations on the Ombudsman's powers. The most interesting is that he is not to consider a complaint unless satisfied that the senior management of the bank in question has had the opportunity to consider the matter, but the complainant has not accepted any observations made or the conditions of settlement or satisfaction offered by the bank and deadlock has been reached. Many complaints come to the Ombudsman before this stage has been reached and have to be referred back to the senior management of the bank. The rationale is to ensure that every attempt is made to resolve the dispute internally before the Ombudsman is seised of it.

The role of the Ombudsman is — at one and the same time — to be a mediator, negotiator and, as a final resort, an arbiter of complaints. In making any award or recommendation, he is to have regard to what is, in his opinion, fair in all the circumstances, and is to observe any applicable rule of law or relevant judicial authority. We have already seen that he is to have regard to good banking practice, which will now include the Code. He may deem any maladministration or other inequitable treatment as being in breach of an obligation owed to a complainant by the bank. He is not bound by any previous decision by himself or any predecessor. No doubt, however, the Ombudsman will wish to achieve consistency in his decisions on important issues. This is evident in the way in which individual complaints are selected for inclusion in the annual reports. If a complaint is dealt with in a particular way as reported, this should filter through to the senior management of an institution, who should then seek to deal with similar complaints in accordance with the views of the Ombudsman. This would have the dual effect of reducing the number of complaints that reach the Ombudsman on any particular issue and, at the same time, place a premium on the internal efficiency of the bank.

13.12 Decisions and views of the Ombudsman on payment cards

As mentioned above, the major problem arising from payment cards has concerned liability for misuse. Unlike the position with credit cards, the customer, depending on the terms of his agreement with the issuer, could potentially be liable for all the money abstracted by a thief from the account before notification to the issuer. This seemed unfair on the payment card customer, in view of the credit card user's £50 limit, which in most cases would be insignificant in relation to the overall loss borne by the creditor. The loss of £300 or £400 will be just as devastating to the user of a debit or cash card as to the user of a credit card. There seemed no justification for the distinction. This point was made in the Ombudsman's annual reports for 1988/89 and 1989/90 and elsewhere, and the Code now deals with this issue.

The attitude of both the Banking and Building Society Ombudsmen, although expressing sympathy for the customer, was that there was little that could be done. The issue that particularly made the news was the allegation of 'phantom' withdrawals. The view taken of these was that, provided the bank could produce a satisfactory audit trail in respect of the disputed withdrawal and there was no record of any error within the bank's computer system, any malfunction of the ATM, or any other irregularity at or around the time of the disputed withdrawal, the customer's account could be debited by the bank. The two possibilities were that either the customer was mistaken and had forgotten the transaction, or that the card had been 'borrowed' by a relative, friend or workmate. The latest reports of both Ombudsman schemes, however, refer to the alleged fraud by a bank engineer in Scotland, who obtained access to information while servicing ATMs. It was alleged that this information enabled him to extract money from the accounts of customers. Following this, both Ombudsmen have now accepted perhaps that this is a possibility, whereas before it was dismissed out of hand as implausible. Both have stated that each case must be looked at on its own facts, applying the civil balance of probabilities test to any disputed fact situation. The Banking Ombudsman, in particular, still believes that his earlier analysis is likely to be applicable in all but a minority of 'phantom' withdrawal cases.

It does not seem that the £50 limit established in the Code will have any appreciable effect on this type of case. If the Ombudsman decides, on the balance of probabilities, that the customer did make the withdrawal and has forgotten about it or is otherwise mistaken, there is no misuse for the limitation to work upon. If the customer has been fraudulent, the £50 rule is excluded anyway. If the evidence suggests the card was 'borrowed' by a friend or relative, and misused, the decision may well depend on the circumstances of the unauthorised taking and misuse. If the customer has been guilty of gross negligence, he cannot take advantage of the limitation. If he has permitted the use of the card contrary to the terms of the agreement, he is clearly in breach and liable to the card issuer, at least in damages. On the other hand any misuse by the user of the card will be deemed to be authorised by the customer, who will not be able to prevent the issuer from debiting his account with the full amount attributable to the misuse.

Only in those cases where the customer has been guilty of ordinary negligence — or, indeed, not negligent — in the way in which the other party acquired access to the card and PIN, will the customer be able to shelter behind the £50 limit afforded by the Code. The customer may, however, benefit from the fact that the burden of proving fraud or gross negligence lies, as we have seen, with the card issuer.

13.13   Gross negligence

The final issue requiring discussion concerns the rather difficult concept of 'gross negligence'. The Code provides that a customer will be liable for all losses on the account resulting from his fraud — which is obviously hardly contentious. This provision does not explicitly appear in s.84 of the 1974 Act, but there can be no doubt that the fraudulent credit cardholder cannot take the benefit of the generous £50 limit in such circumstances. In any event, as pointed out above, if the debtor deliberately enabled another to misuse the account, it could be strongly argued that the other person was deemed to be authorised by the debtor, who would not be able to prevent the debiting of the account. However, the Act makes no mention of negligence or the like preventing the customer from taking advantage of s.84. It seems in these circumstances that the Code will operate in the context of s.84 and that the debtor under a credit-token is not to be deprived of the protective umbrella of the £50 limit unless the creditor can establish, at the very least, gross negligence against the customer. To do otherwise would be to perpetuate the difference in treatment between credit and other types of payment card, the very thing the Code is attempting to remove.

The Code does contain a specific reference to gross negligence as possibly defeating a customer claim to rely on the £50 limit. English courts and lawyers are used to the concept of negligence in the ordinary sense, but the concept of 'gross' negligence is alien to the majority, although Scottish lawyers would be able to claim familiarity with it. There is potential for dispute as to where the dividing line between ordinary and gross negligence may lie.

The Banking Ombudsman has indicated that it is gross negligence to record the PIN on the payment card itself, thus depriving the customer of the limitation on loss. He has also indicated that writing the PIN in a diary carried around by the customer, without any attempt to disguise it, is ordinary negligence, in which case the customer may benefit from the limit. To write the PIN down disguised as a telephone or other number is, in the Ombudsman's opinion, not negligence at all.

This perhaps illustrates the potential for dispute on this topic, although it should be emphasised that the burden of proof is placed firmly on the card issuer in these circumstances.

13.14 Conclusion

The problem of liability for loss is one of the most controversial and difficult to resolve aspects of the debit or cash card agreement. The problem is not likely to disappear overnight in view of the increasing numbers of these types of payment card in circulation. At least, on this point, the Code of Banking Practice has brought the rules on liability for loss following misuse into line with those relating to credit-token agreements. It will not do much to resolve the problem of phantom withdrawals, although the customer's assertions in that respect may not be dismissed out of hand so easily in the future in the light of the alleged fraud at the Scottish bank, described in para.13.12.

Index

ATM. *See* Automatic telling
machine (ATM)
Acceptance of credit-token, 75–77
Advertising
advertisement, meaning, 53–54
advertiser, meaning, 54
cash terms, availability of,
57–58
Code of Advertising Standards
and Practice, 52
Consumer Credit Act and,
53–55
content of advertisement, 54–55
control —
Consumer Credit Act and, 53
scope of, 53–54
false advertisement, 58
form of advertisement, 54–55
full credit advertisement, 57
intermediate credit
advertisement, 57
misleading advertisement, 58
regulations —
general points, 56
generally, 55
infringement, 58
scope of, 55–56
simple credit advertisement, 56
Agency of supplier
Consumer Credit Act ss.56 and
75, 156–157
Crowther Committee
proposals, 150

Agency of supplier — *cont.*
deemed agency —
effect of, 152–155
generally, 150–151
duration of negotiations,
151–152
exclusion of agency, 155–156
generally, 149–150, 157
other dealings, 155
Agreement
credit card. *See* Credit card
agreement
credit-token. *See* Credit-token
agreement
running-account credit, analysis
of, 24–25
Allowances
cancellation of agreement, 95
Antecedent negotiations
meaning, 85–86
negotiator, 85–86
oral representations, 87–88
Appropriation of payments,
121–123
Arrangements
meaning, 34–35
Associate
meaning, 17–18
**Association for Payment Clearing
Services**
plastic revolution, effect of, 1
Automatic telling machine (ATM)
credit card, use of, 4